UNDERCOVER POLICING AND THE CORRUPT SECRET SOCIETY WITHIN

'In a room where people unanimously maintain a conspiracy of silence, one word of truth sounds like a pistol shot.'

Czesław Miłosz, Author & Poet

In memory of ex-Detective Chief Superintendent Don Brown who passed away in June 2020.

UNDERCOVER POLICING AND THE CORRUPT SECRET SOCIETY WITHIN

GARRY ROGERS & KEITH POTTER

PEN & SWORD
TRUE CRIME

First published in Great Britain in 2020 by
Pen & Sword True Crime
An imprint of
Pen & Sword Books Ltd
Yorkshire – Philadelphia

Copyright © Garry Rogers & Keith Potter 2020

ISBN 978 1 52677 539 9

The right of Garry Rogers & Keith Potter to be identified as Authors
of this work has been asserted by them in accordance with the
Copyright, Designs and Patents Act 1988.

A CIP catalogue record for this book is
available from the British Library.

Typeset by Mac Style
Printed and bound in the UK by TJ Books Limited,
Padstow, Cornwall.

Pen & Sword Books Limited incorporates the imprints of Atlas,
Archaeology, Aviation, Discovery, Family History, Fiction, History,
Maritime, Military, Military Classics, Politics, Select, Transport,
True Crime, Air World, Frontline Publishing, Leo Cooper, Remember
When, Seaforth Publishing, The Praetorian Press, Wharncliffe
Local History, Wharncliffe Transport, Wharncliffe True Crime
and White Owl.

For a complete list of Pen & Sword titles please contact

PEN & SWORD BOOKS LIMITED
47 Church Street, Barnsley, South Yorkshire, S70 2AS, England
E-mail: enquiries@pen-and-sword.co.uk
Website: www.pen-and-sword.co.uk

Or

PEN AND SWORD BOOKS
1950 Lawrence Rd, Havertown, PA 19083, USA
E-mail: Uspen-and-sword@casematepublishers.com
Website: www.penandswordbooks.com

Contents

Foreword

This book focuses on the life and career of Garry Rogers: a remarkable man, and a former police officer of exemplary public service. It also highlights the discreditable conduct of Greater Manchester Police and a number of that force's senior and chief officers.

I joined Lincolnshire Police as a probationary constable in 1974. Had I known Constable Rogers at the time, I would have looked up to him as a role model. He was the type and character of police officer that I wished to become.

When a person is appointed to the office of constable they become something different to the norm. The role is much more than an occupation; they are not an employee, they are a servant of the Crown, and all police officers hold that office irrespective of rank. Public expectation of police officers is extraordinarily high in terms of honesty, dedication, leadership and that exceptional ability to be all things to all people, depending entirely upon the circumstances pertaining: from crime through public disorder to life and death and so forth. That public expectation is probably higher than for any other role in the UK.

The public reward in real terms for this vocation is to be set aside as a group in society. When police officers say (or admit) what work they do to ordinary people, they are immediately viewed as someone to be regarded with care, somebody different. To know what that is really like, ask the family of a police officer, especially their children. Imagine what it is like to be at school when one (or both) of your parents is a police officer.

All police officers vary in their approach to the policing role. Some are more different than others. A few come to view their role as little more than a job to be endured; they become 'uniform carriers'. Some become disillusioned, often through the attitude of the public, politicians or their bosses, and their performance is affected accordingly. Other officers thrive in the role as if they were born to the vocation. Garry Rogers was one such police officer.

I was a city Shift Inspector in 1986 and my group encompassed the whole spectrum of police officer types. I would have given my eye teeth to have an officer of Garry's calibre working with me. Of the small number of officers who I would describe as excellent, Garry would have stood out as the 'best of the best', an officer who would not be afraid to get 'stuck in', no matter how difficult the situation; an officer who could be relied upon to act not only on his own initiative, but to make the right decisions when required.

I first met Garry on 15 August 1997, when I was a Chief Superintendent seconded to Her Majesty's Inspectorate of Constabulary. By then his role as an undercover officer for Greater Manchester Police was over, and he was suffering badly from the incompetence and wilfulness of senior and chief officers within that force. This was the annual inspection of Greater Manchester Police by HM Inspectorate. All police officers and police employees have the right to ask for an interview during the annual inspection. Garry and I met in the empty force canteen. His was a frank and sincere account of personal strengths and corporate difficulties. Most officers who request an interview have a grumble to make of varying robustness in respect of their force. Garry's position was very different. I quickly grew to respect him, to admire his professionalism, and to like him. He had a fully justified case against Greater Manchester Police. That case, its supporting circumstances and his remarkable police career are fully explained in this book.

It was for his work as an undercover officer that Garry finally received the recognition he richly deserved. On my return to Lincolnshire Police in 2000 I was involved in the recruitment and management of undercover officers in the East Midlands Region. Only the best are accepted, and not all of those selected make the final grade. I cannot emphasize the skills required and the risks involved. Undercover officers seriously risk everything, not only professionally but themselves, their family, their career and, sometimes, life itself.

Foreword

Undercover officers know or come to realize rapidly that theirs is a lonely role. They walk a tightrope. Worst of all, they know that things can go wrong very, very easily: a chance remark, an unfortunate coincidence, a bad turn of events, most of which are well out of their sphere of control. Above all else, undercover officers should be able to trust that their bosses will fully support them in such a dangerous task. Unfortunately, at the back of their minds, undercover officers always suspect that 'when push comes to shove' their senior officers might prove to be unreliable, especially if a career is perceived to be at risk. The same applies to public opinion, always influenced by the press and minority groups, often fickle, slow to congratulate success, and always quick to vilify.

For a fascinating insight into the world of undercover policing and the workings of a major police force, this is the book to read. As you progress through the pages you will soon appreciate how exceptional Garry's police career was. You will also come to understand how badly he was treated by Greater Manchester Police and some of its senior and chief officers. All should have known better. Additionally, as you read the book please be mindful of the considerable impact upon Garry's wife and family. Garry's wellbeing suffered badly as a result of the events but, almost equally, so did theirs. Although it was Garry who rightly received the highest award for his work, in my opinion that honour was awarded not only to him but also to his wife and family. It was fully deserved in each case.

John Tapley
Former Chief Superintendent
and staff officer to Her Majesty's Inspector of Constabulary

Chapter One

From Humble Beginnings

I f I'd been a superstitious man, it could have all been so different... as it was, instead of any concerns about the date, all I had was a burning desire to be a policeman. Which is why, on Tuesday, 1 April 1975 – April Fools' Day – I walked through the front door of Peterloo House, just off St Peter's Square in Manchester City Centre, to begin my career with Greater Manchester Police (GMP), and my first day as a police cadet.

I like a joke as much as anyone, but this was definitely no April Fools' prank. I was exactly 16 years and 6 months old; the youngest I could be to leave school and join the force, so determined was I to become a copper. Joining the cadets was my first step towards achieving that goal, yet to this day I'm still not sure where the desire came from. At that time the police cadet system was a great way of recruiting budding future police officers at an early age. Officers had to be at least 18 years and 6 months old, so the cadet system allowed young men and women to join early, gain two years' experience, and obtain a great insight into the job before becoming a fully-fledged officer.

As a cadet you were attached to the various police departments for six-week placements. Sometimes you were used as the general dogsbody by those who worked there, in which case you were glad when the six weeks were up. I knew it was likely to be difficult at times, but then, thanks mainly to my own indiscretions, my road to joining had already been a pretty bumpy one.

* * *

I was born in Salford's Hope Hospital in 1958, the younger of two children, my brother being two years older. My dad, Bob, was an electrician by trade, and my mum, Jean, did mainly shop work. We lived in Lower Kersal, Salford, not far from the old Cussons soap works. We were initially in a Coronation Street-style, two-up, two-down terraced house with an outside toilet, and then later went up-market into a semi-detached on Littleton Road, backing on to my school, Lower Kersal Primary.

Mum came from a big extended family with everyone living locally, and she really enjoyed the Salford way of life, going to the club every Sunday with her parents. My dad had one obsession: betting on the horses. He was always robbing Peter to pay Paul, and we would regularly keep the front door locked if someone called in case they were after money. He was a good man and his heart was in the right place, but having a bet was his demon. It often caused arguments at home between him and Mum, as it was always she who faced the brunt of it. I think it was this that put me off ever gambling.

Although he was an electrician by trade, Dad had several other jobs, one of which was as a kennel hand for the police, looking after the Alsatians at their Mounted and Dog Section at Swinton Park in Salford. I was about 10 at the time, and whenever I was off school he would take me with him to help with the dogs; once I even sat on a huge police horse. Whether that first sparked my interest or not, I don't know. My brother joined the police cadets ahead of me, so watching and listening as he came home and talked about the job might have been another reason for wanting to join up. However, I can't remember a specific time or incident where I thought, that's it, I'm going to be a policeman. It's not as if my dad or my granddad had been police officers, so it certainly wasn't in the family.

As I say, Dad tried his hand at a number of jobs, and at one point my parents owned a pet shop on Lower Broughton Road in Salford, which was then a thriving shopping area. They had everything in there, including exotic pets such as snakes and Rhesus monkeys. For a while we even had a monkey at home as a pet, until we came home one day and it had escaped from its cage and wrecked the house. We found it under the bed, but every time anyone tried to grab it, it bared its teeth at you! It ended up with the shed as its cage, and then eventually went back to the shop.

The pet shop was a bit of a strange career choice, but I think ultimately Dad wanted to be his own boss and it was an opportunity for him to do that. Once again though, his problem was that he liked a bet. There were no proper books kept for the shop, and when he fancied a horse, he'd take a few pounds out of the till for his betting money. They had the pet shop for two or three years, but in the end it was in financial difficulty so they had to sell up.

However, his career choices may have had a long-lasting impact on his health. After Dad died, we found out that he'd been suffering from a lung disorder, fibrosing alveolitis (Keith Chegwin died of the same disease); towards the end his fingernails started to curl over, which was a symptom of the condition. One of the causes of the disease is thought to be dust, and as an electrician Dad had worked in a lot of old council houses, so that may have been one source. However, you can also get it from birds, and Dad was in the pet shop all the time, so that could also have been the cause. Ultimately we'll never know for sure, but it seems likely that his working life played a significant part in his early death.

* * *

I enjoyed primary school, and having passed the 11+ exam (more by luck than by talent), I earned a place at Salford Grammar School on Eccles Old Road. It was a daunting transition. For starters my primary school was behind our house, whereas Salford Grammar was miles away, and more often than not I had to walk there and back. Going to what many people saw as a posh school also meant I had to wear a uniform that consisted of a green blazer with school badge on the breast pocket (complete with the school motto *Audendum Dextra* ('Daring Right')), a green cap, grey shirt, green and gold striped tie, grey trousers, and carry the obligatory black briefcase. You were seen as a bit of a poncey type if you went from Lower Kersal to Salford Grammar anyway, but walking through some areas of Salford dressed like that meant taking your life in your hands. You were open to ridicule and sometimes even attack by other kids (I always thought it was the briefcase that attracted them like a magnet), so the fight or flight response soon kicked in.

First-year pupils at Salford Grammar were referred to as 'fags' by all the other years, and it was great when you went up into Year Two and could then dish it out to the new 'fags'. The school comprised four 'houses': Lancaster, York, Warwick and the one I was in, Gloucester. My housemaster was Mr Potts, who later gave me a lifeline for which I will always be extremely grateful. There was a well-administered discipline code and some teachers even walked round in full black gowns, especially Mr Poppit. It had the air of a public school education, what with school houses, housemasters, head prefects, caps, gowns and the dreaded school briefcase. The slipper was then still a prolific educational tool for those who misbehaved, and I was on the wrong end of this learning module on several occasions, but I would never go home and tell my parents about it for fear of further admonishment. I suppose it did teach me something.

As there was a mixture of teachers – some who were strict, others who could easily be taken advantage of – so there was a mix of pupils. There were those who came to learn, and others who wanted to be anywhere but school; sadly, I found myself increasingly in the second group. This wasn't helped by some major changes to the school. For the first three years it was the pomp and ceremony of Salford Grammar, but in 1973 the government tried to do away with the grammar school system. When I returned from the summer break into Year 4, Salford Grammar had amalgamated with Pendleton High School for Girls, and as a result became Buille Hill High School. This was a shock to the system; there were no longer boys-only classes, there were girls everywhere you looked, which inevitably affected the learning process even more.

As I said, I was spending more time as part of that group who didn't really want to be in school, and in Year 4 I started to miss – or, as it was better known then, 'wag' – certain lessons. It would be those lessons that I deemed to be of no interest and those teachers who were a bit weaker, and in truth probably preferred for the likes of me not to attend anyway. For example, German lessons were taught by Mr Hunt (or Herr Hunt as we called him), and were top of my list for non-attendance; by contrast I would never have dared to miss maths which, although I hated, was taught by the bearded Mr Ryder. He was a strict, no-nonsense teacher, handy with the slipper and who always scored a direct hit with a piece of chalk or, worse still, the blackboard rubber.

So our aim was to get out of the building and school grounds without being seen, and hide what was now a black school blazer in an electricity substation near to the school, along with my haversack (which had now taken the place of the briefcase) for my school books. Once these were safely stashed, we were free to wander afar until we returned to retrieve them in good time to make the next lesson, all as seamlessly as possible. I may have been ducking out of lessons, but I was getting more of a street education in Salford. We used to have a fair bit of fun in the city centre, doing what kids shouldn't be doing. That included getting caught shoplifting by the staff in a store, although thankfully they just made us put everything back and it didn't go any further. I knocked around with the same group of lads outside of school too. We even went out with sets of keys once, with the idea of taking a car. I could drive by then, and everyone around me was keen for us to get hold of something, although luckily we didn't. That was the way it was though; I think with the lads I was hanging about with and the area we lived in, if you weren't like that you would stand out for all the wrong reasons and you could easily become the victim.

Anyway, the more we got away with wagging school and roaming round Salford, the more we did it. Around this time in 1974, about a year before I left school, we moved house again, this time to Irlams o' th' Height, a more upmarket area of Salford. It was another semi-detached house that required a lot of work, which is probably why my parents could afford it in the first place, although Dad was handy with DIY so it wasn't a problem.

Nearby on New Herbert Street, my Uncle Cliff had a grocer's shop and I would work for him on a Saturday and Sunday to earn some money; before that, the only job I'd had was in Lower Kersal, where I was a paperboy at Chadwick's Newsagents opposite the Racecourse Hotel. Uncle Cliff was kindness personified and would give you his last penny. He often gave it to my dad to get him out of some problem or other (mainly the bookies), and would then have trouble getting it back. He never married and lived with my gran up until his death.

While he was too kind for his own good, he never really thought some things through or saw the potential risks. For example, on Saturdays he would have me doing grocery deliveries to certain elderly customers who lived nearby. I'd learned to drive early on – well before I was 17 – as at the side of our house in Lower Kersal there was a large, open piece of land that was unadopted (handy for when my dad didn't tax his car!). When my brother got an old Austin van to learn to drive in, I used to drive it on the open land and soon became quite proficient. Uncle Cliff had a green 1972 Bedford van, but he didn't like driving; he suffered from bad hands, a legacy of his days working with meat on the cold slabs when he owned a butcher's shop, so he drove with gloves on and he was always hunched over the wheel. He wasn't a good driver either, so he was happy for me to do it. He would just give me the key and ask me to do the deliveries to customers; I don't think it ever crossed his mind that I didn't have a licence…

So here was I at 15, regularly driving his van on the public road (albeit locally) without a licence or insurance. One day I set off from the grocer's shop, and I was sitting at a junction at the end of the road when two officers in a police car drove straight past me. I've got no idea how I reacted, but I know from my own time in the police that most people, if they are guilty of something, will often give it away with their body language. All I can think is that they didn't look at me, because they would have definitely realized I was too young to drive if they had. I was so lucky really; if I'd have had any sort of accident, both Uncle Cliff and I would have been in real trouble. Obviously I never told my dad because he would never have allowed it, but for me at that time it was fantastic and I never gave the consequences a second thought. It was only through sheer good luck that nothing ever happened or that I was never stopped by the police, as with a criminal record the rest of my life would have been a very different story. It's not something I'm proud of, and my poor Uncle Cliff was not a bad guy, just misguided, but it is an example of how my life could have gone one of two ways.

* * *

By Year 5 at Buille Hill High I had decided that I wanted to join the police (maybe because I still couldn't speak German), and was aiming to go into the cadets. I had visited the Police Recruiting Office based at Southmill Street in Manchester with my dad, who spoke with Mr Thomas, the Head of Police Recruiting. I was 16 in October 1974 and wanted to join as soon as possible, but legally the earliest I could leave school was at Easter 1975. Mr Thomas advised me to come back then and take the entrance exam. I was gutted and it made school days even more laborious; my frustration at school was increasing, especially as I felt that I was old enough to leave at 16 but had to wait for a further six months.

I didn't share my policing ambitions with any of my mates though. It wouldn't have gone down well as a kid in Lower Kersal (or Irlams o' th' Height for that matter) as it was one of the tougher areas of Salford to live in. All my mates were from Lower Kersal, and it's not something that they would have been happy about.

All good things must come to an end, and my days of skiving were brought to an abrupt halt thanks to an intervention from my housemaster, Mr Potts. He had spoken with me several times, trying to get me on board and saying I was wasting my abilities and knocking about with the wrong crowd. It went in one ear and out the other. I went through the motions of telling him I would sort things out, but I never did. Unbeknown to me he had written a letter to my parents voicing his concerns about my behaviour and missing lessons, but because of my promises he had not sent it, hoping I would be true to my word.

When nothing changed he wrote a further letter and sent them both to my parents. I can still remember the morning they arrived, and my dad's reaction when he opened it; angry would be an understatement. Looking back now I can understand why. Every parent wants the best for their children, so to be told that your child is wasting their time, their abilities and constantly missing lessons is something you don't want to hear. It caught me by surprise and I had no answers. I was also being threatened with expulsion from school.

In the letter Mr Potts said: 'I am worried about Garry's progress this year and his apparent loss of interest, missing lessons, chemistry in particular, saying that it is unnecessary or uninteresting or both.' He explained that I'd given him assurances that things would improve, and had told him about a possible interview with the police, but that nothing seemed to have changed. He finished: 'I do not like to see talent wasted and I do not particularly like forcing Garry to choose his friends, but I feel that he is wasting his talent at the moment, I do wish to help your son and am experiencing some difficulty in that direction just now.' I've still got those letters, and when I read them back I realize how much of an opportunity I wasted. Going to Salford Grammar and then behaving like I did and coming out without any O-Levels at all was just stupid. It wasn't that I was thick; I just didn't apply myself.

My dad immediately went into school to try to put the wheels back on. He spoke with Mr Potts and he knew by now that I really wanted to join the police. A plan was devised whereby the threat of expulsion would be lifted if I agreed to get my head down for the last six months, attend all classes and work hard. If I did this, they would give me a good write-up for my police application, bearing in mind I would be leaving before taking any O-Levels. This suited me and I duly adhered to it, as much because, not that my dad knew, I didn't want to encounter his wrath again. I still didn't tell anyone at school about my plans to join the police; I just knuckled down, got on with it and went to every lesson.

At home I had a calendar on my bedroom wall and I religiously ticked off each day as I counted down. I became a changed character, and after Christmas I applied to join the cadets. I once again attended Southmill Street and successfully completed the entrance exam. I underwent a medical, had a formal interview, and breathed a huge sigh of relief when I was told I'd been accepted. My acceptance letter duly arrived with a start date of 1 April, just after the Easter bank holiday weekend of 1975. I went to school for the last time on Thursday, 27 March, and after a farewell talk from the headmaster in his office, I walked out, didn't look back and walked all the way home, free at last.

I still hadn't told anyone I was joining the police. No one else who I knocked around with was talking about joining the police; they were all going off into other careers. I knew how they would react – not that

I was scared of them – but it just seemed like the better option to say nothing. Also I'd left school before taking my exams, so that was it.

Since leaving school that day I haven't kept in touch with any of my schoolmates; by my choice of career, I basically exiled myself. My brother went to the secondary modern school, so I suppose it was even more unlikely for him to choose the police as a career, although I've never had that conversation with him and we don't really talk now, so I don't know why he did. Yet that decision to cut myself off is something I've done throughout my life, in and out of the force. I suppose in many ways I'm a bit of a loner, and it's a trait in my character which became even more prominent after my experiences in policing. Looking back, though, it would have been nice to keep in contact with some of those people I was at school with and find out what they are doing now.

I really believe that those experiences I had when I was young and the people I was around ultimately made me a better police officer, particularly for the undercover role I undertook. That might sound crazy to some people – talking about going out and nicking a car, or shoplifting – but I think to have experienced that has made me much more able to go and mingle with people, including criminals, at all levels.

If I hadn't become a copper, I don't know what I would have done. Sometimes I wonder what I would be like, at my age now, if I'd never joined the police – what I would have been doing, and what I would be like as a person – but I really can't answer that, because I've got no idea what I would have done instead. Policing was the only thing on my horizon.

Chapter Two

Time to Grow Up

I had very little time to adjust from being a schoolboy to being a police cadet. On 1 April I was up early, got dressed in my best shirt, tie and jacket, and got a lift into Manchester from my brother who dropped me in St Peter's Square, just outside the Central Library. I took a deep breath, walked the short distance to the main doors at Peterloo House and into the reception area. My heart was pounding and it was now that it hit me. From being in the big-time top of the school in Year 5, here I was at the bottom of the pile in the scary disciplined world of the police. Five days after leaving school I was now in the workplace, and that 'laissez faire' attitude I had at Buille Hill High School wasn't going to cut it here. I'd left with no qualifications, basically because I'd buggered about for a couple of years. I knew straight away that if I buggered about here, I'd be out. Not only that, but because I had no qualifications, if I screwed up here I would end up at the back of the queue when it came to looking for another job.

I was directed to the Cadet Training Department on the fifth floor by reception staff and was met by the uniformed training officers who sat me in a room with several other new starters. It was quite a tense atmosphere, like a doctor's waiting room. As we waited for everyone to arrive, no one was talking, but I'm pretty sure we were all thinking: 'What have I let myself in for?' The head of the department was Chief Inspector Tony Whittle, who called all the girls 'Miss', and the training team consisted of Inspector Dave James (later to become a key figure in my career); Sergeant Roger Roberts, who could do non-stop press-ups; and PCs Don Mackintosh, Harold Bratt and Bob Loftus. In 1994, long after I'd completed my training, Mackintosh was imprisoned for nine years for a series of sex offences against young boys over the previous decade. He eventually committed suicide in 2014 as he was about to face trial over fresh allegations stretching back to the 1970s.

As that first day progressed, the group's inhibitions broke down and we slowly but surely got to know one another. There was a mixture of ages and, at 16 years and 6 months, I was one of the youngest. The attitude was a lot like being in the army: you did as you were told, you did the drills, bulled your boots, uniform dressed, got the right haircut, and whatever the instructors said went. After my initial induction and getting fitted out with my uniform at the clothing stores, the first few months were taken up with attachments to several internal police departments such as the Summons and Warrants Department and the Communications Department, both based at the Crescent Police Station in Salford.

I did a six-week attachment to the Coroner's Office, which at that time was within the old London Road fire station building in the city centre. The office was staffed by two women who were obviously much more experienced than me, in every sense – one of them was always making sexual innuendos, which I suppose today would be called harassment – and the coroner was an old guy called Donald Summerfield who, whenever he moved around, you could hear farting! So to escape the smells and the sexual suggestions, I'd volunteer to go and work down in the basement where all the records were kept. Of course, as an inquisitive teenager, I started looking through some of the old files and cases. I found the pictures and the tape recordings of Lesley Ann Downey taken by Ian Brady and Myra Hindley; that was pretty chilling.

I also worked in the Scenes of Crime Department based at Longsight Police Station and went out on jobs with the Scenes of Crime Officer (SOCO) in his little blue Mini van. We would come in every morning and find out what jobs we needed to go out and do: take fingerprints, photographs, that sort of thing. We came in one morning in July 1975 and had to go to the mortuary in Manchester to photograph the body of Wanda Skala. She'd been murdered, as it turned out later, by serial killer Trevor Joseph Hardy; he had hit her over the head with a brick and then strangled her on a building site off Lightbowne Road in Moston. He had also bitten off one of her nipples; that was part of what he used to do. Hardy murdered three girls, and one of the others – Sharon Mossoph – I knew from a youth club in Salford that I used to go to. Hardy later confessed to seeing her walking along a street

11

on New Year's Eve in 1974; he stabbed her to death, buried her in a shallow grave on a building site in Moston and then returned to the body a couple of times to try to hide it better. When they found her remains, there were teeth marks on her breast.

As a 16-year-old, to see Wanda Skala's body and the damage Hardy had done to her was quite a shock. To be honest I'm not sure what impact it had on me, but you can't see things like that at that age and not be affected somehow. I would hope that nowadays people would be a bit more thoughtful about the process, but no one asked if I was okay seeing that or if I wanted to go outside or anything like that; it was just assumed that you would be fine. I guess I knew I would have to get used to it if I was going to continue in the job.

There were quite a few other placements too: working on a geriatric ward, as they were called then, was another eye-opener. However, the good thing was that we were experiencing a lot of different aspects of life, not just policing roles, as well as understanding the relationship between policing and other institutions, such as hospitals.

To be honest, I was loving it. I loved the job so much when I joined that, to get to work as a cadet, I used to leave the house early and walk into Manchester with my cap and uniform on. It sounds daft now, and if anything had happened I probably wouldn't have had a clue what to do – as a cadet you only have the same powers as a member of the public – but I really wanted people to think I was a copper. I can remember when my brother first joined up and he would come home in his big black police overcoat and his cap. On a Friday we would have fish and chips, and he'd often go to get them from Kidds chip shop in Salford. When he did I'd go with him, then sit in the passenger seat with his coat and cap on and pretend to be a policeman.

I know Mum and Dad were proud of both of us going into the police service. At that time it was viewed – by most law-abiding people at least – as a good career choice. Overall, police officers were respected; we know now that some overstepped the mark, but the vast majority did a good job and had the support of most of the community. No one in the Salford area wanted to be arrested and taken to the Crescent.

* * *

Part and parcel of cadet training was to attend full-time as a student at West Wythenshawe College of Further Education and study O-Levels in Law, Sociology, British Constitution and English Language. So from September 1975 through to July 1976 I was back in my favourite place, the classroom, but this time even further away from home. The police training staff would still attend the college one day a week for physical training sessions to keep us all fit, but apart from that we were basically students on full pay as cadets. Initially I would be up early each day to get the several buses that would take me to Wythenshawe, but I soon had a new focus. I was once again counting down the days, this time to my 17th birthday so that I could take my driving test and get myself a car. In the meantime I used my Uncle Tom's old Honda 90 to get there and back, which I could ride at 16 with a provisional motorcycle licence.

By the time I was 17 in the October I had received my provisional driving licence and booked several lessons with the British School of Motoring in Manchester. My instructor was an ex-policeman who had left the job under a cloud; he never really went into it, so I didn't ask. My driving test was booked for 10 November and, given the experience (legal and otherwise) that I'd already had behind the wheel, I passed first time. Now all I needed was a car.

In my class at the college was a female cadet whose dad was the Chief Superintendent at Salford. She was twelve months older than me and passed her driving test ahead of me. Her dad bought her a brand-new Honda Civic that she used to drive to college, while I was getting soaked on the bike or waiting for buses. My first car was an old D-registered 1966 Vauxhall Viva that my dad had helped me get from Pemberton's car auctions. It cost around £50, so you can imagine what kind of state it was in. I had to carry around a can of Easy Start which I had to spray into the engine air intake to get it started. I always avoided parking anywhere near my colleague for fear of being seen with the bonnet up trying to get the car going! Despite this, I was on the road and that was all that mattered.

Once again, I took my eye off the ball at college and didn't apply myself as much as I should have done. Towards the end, when the exams were on the horizon, I really had to cram the work in. I ended up with passes in English, Law and Sociology, so having left school with no qualifications I now had three O-Levels.

* * *

In July of 1976 I returned to uniform duties and to the six-weekly secondments to police and public departments. These included Traffic at Salford and a stint on a geriatric ward at the old Withington Hospital. One day a week was again classed as a training day; we had to be at the old YMCA building at the side of the Midland Hotel on Peter Street, Manchester, where waiting for us would be Harold Bratt and Bob Loftus, the two PTIs. Around the internal roof space of the YMCA was an indoor running track, and the first job of the morning was for them to run you ragged. After that it was down to the gym for rope-climbing, press-ups and all other manner of keep fit and exercise routines. There were plenty of times when I was sick or thought my heart was about to burst out of my chest, but woe betide anyone who complained; you had to grin and bear it.

This took up all the morning, then after lunch it was back to Peterloo House for law training, and the day finished with drill practice at the old Territorial Army Drill Hall on Cambridge Street. You had to wear your best, ultra-ironed uniform and highly-polished marching boots. Everything was carefully inspected, and if things weren't up to scratch you would end up with a face full of saliva after a close-quarter rollocking by the Drill Sergeant, Tony Judge.

The six-week secondments continued, as did the weekly training days, until eventually I was seconded to my last department, which was always out on the streets. After this I would be off to the Police District Training Centre at Bruche in Warrington for twelve weeks, before being 'sworn in' as a police officer. Being on the streets basically meant being attached to one of the fourteen police divisions which at that time covered the GMP area. You would work either an afternoon or a day shift with uniformed staff on one of those divisions. The fourteen divisions were as follows: A Division – Manchester City Centre;

B Division – Collyhurst; C Division – Grey Mare Lane; D Division – Longsight; E Division – Moss Side; F Division – Salford; G Division – Hyde; J Division – Stockport; K Division – Bolton; L Division – Leigh/Wigan; M Division – Stretford; N Division – Bury; P Division – Rochdale; and Q Division – Oldham.

My street placement was on F Division, at the old Crescent Police Station in Salford. This meant parading with uniformed officers on either days or afternoon shifts, then being paired up with an experienced officer for the rest of the shift to get a proper insight into the job. Whatever came up you would also attend, and Salford was and still is a busy city to cover. Not every officer was happy to have a cadet paired up with them for an eight-hour shift though; you might be cramping their style or, more likely, it forced them to do things properly as they were being observed by a generally unknown pair of eyes.

The streets placement gave me my first experience of making an arrest. It was an afternoon shift (3.00 pm to 11.00 pm) and the male officer I was paired with wasn't in the best physical shape. This is where all the hard work at the YMCA started to pay off. We had a radio message that a group of youths were damaging a public phone box on Robert Hall Street, Ordsall, so we made our way there. As we turned into the street off Trafford Road I could see someone standing in the phone box with a small group outside. They all obviously saw the police sign on the roof of our car and immediately took flight. I kept my eye on the one who had been inside, and I was out of the car and in pursuit through the estate while my colleague was still trying to get out of our Mini.

I eventually gained ground and grabbed hold of the offender, who gave up after a short scuffle. It was at this point that I realized it was a girl, who was apparently well-known in the area for all the wrong reasons. I marched her back to the phone box where the officer was examining the damage to the money collection box under the phone. It was obvious that it was the cash they were after. He wouldn't have had a cat in hell's chance of catching her on his own. She was charged and I had to complete a statement for court, but thankfully she pleaded guilty so that was the end of that. It was a fantastic sense of achievement though, to have made sure we got an arrest while working with someone who didn't really want you there, and whose job I ended up doing for him.

My six weeks on the streets were soon up, and with them my time in the cadets. I'd really enjoyed it, and felt that I'd experienced and learned so much in such a short period of time. I'd certainly grown up a lot since walking into Peterloo House two years earlier. I'd also gained an insight into the job of a police officer which, far from putting me off, just fuelled my enthusiasm to do it for real.

It all finished with a bit of a bang too (quite literally). By this time I was the proud owner of a 1970 Ford Escort estate and, while en route to Peterloo House to see Inspector James for my final report before leaving, a lady drove out of a side street and crashed into the nearside of my pride and joy. No one was injured, but it did make me late for my appointment with Inspector James. I hope it wasn't this that influenced his actions some years later!

Chapter Three

Surviving the Snake Pit

My police career so far seemed to have involved a lot of calendar countdowns and reaching important dates, from leaving school to starting on the police cadet course, being old enough to drive (legally), and completing my two years as a cadet. Now I'd reached another one: 2 April 1977, which meant that I was 18 years and 6 months old and confirmed as a police officer within GMP. I no longer had to have 'Cadet' on the shoulders of my uniform tunic and shirts, but now proudly displayed my four-figure silver collar number, unique to each individual officer and an obvious means of identification. It was called a collar number because originally they were displayed on the collars of the old-style police tunics. My number was '2642', and upon receiving it I walked round as proud as punch; it meant so much to me and I'd worked so hard to get it.

What followed was another two-week induction course, again at Peterloo House, which threw together a mix of former cadets and new recruits from all kinds of backgrounds, and all anxious about what the next twelve weeks at Bruche would hold. Once the induction was done I packed my car, left my mum and dad's on a Sunday night and headed off to Bruche. My home for near enough the next three months would be the infamous Snake Pit, an accommodation block which slept four to a room with no en suite facilities, just one large shared bathroom at the end of each corridor. Although the accommodation blocks were all single-sex, the layout meant that you got no privacy at all, and who you would share with was a lottery. Personalities become even more important when you're living together in such a close environment 24/7. I shared with one other guy from GMP, Dave Russon, and two lads from Cumbria Constabulary; fortunately overall we got on well. In more modern times, before Bruche closed its doors for good, recruits each had their own room with en suite facilities. I can understand why, but I think part of the training process was learning how to get on with so many different characters in such close proximity, something that police officers would inevitably have to do once on shift.

We were placed into classes of around twenty students, with each class designated a letter of the alphabet and allocated two dedicated police trainers. It was their task to impart all the legal knowledge and legislation needed to become an effective police officer. I was in Y class, and our trainers were Sergeant Bob Helm from GMP and a female sergeant from Cumbria whose name unfortunately I can't remember. Y class was 70 per cent male, 30 per cent female, with a broad range of age and experience. I was the only member of the class who was a recent ex-cadet, although one woman had been a cadet at the same time as my brother; she'd then left, and was now coming back to join as a policewoman. Everyone else had come from a civilian background, apart from one ex-soldier. As a class you were required to nominate a leader from the group, who would then be identified by a white lanyard worn on their left shoulder. For some reason – I'm guessing because I had the most recent policing experience – I was nominated as class leader. It was a nice boost, being given that role at 18 and a half, although not all the group were happy, particularly the ex-squaddie.

At the beginning of each week there was an exam based on the previous week's law input, and you had to achieve a pass mark of around 70 per cent (17 out of 25 questions) to continue on the course. If you failed you could be back-classed and ultimately dismissed, so the threat was always hanging over you. To get through you had to remain focused and study hard, and I knew I had to get my head down and really put the hours in to get the pass marks.

Once again there was plenty of physical exertion too, such as running before breakfast and swimming with the infamous Ernie Storr. Every training school has its legendary characters and Ernie was certainly one of the stars at Bruche. This former Royal Marine Commando was renowned as a big socializer who loved to have a drink in the bar. He was hard as nails but a nice guy, and his party piece was to swim a length underwater with a lit cigarette in his mouth. He would smoke it down until it was close to the end, roll it back over into his mouth using his tongue, then swim the length of the pool along the bottom with his mouth shut. When he reached the other end he would come up, open his mouth and blow out a big cloud of smoke before finishing his fag!

While there was obviously time for some rest, relaxation and socializing, overall it was hard work, and discipline played a big part. If you moved around the centre, whether as a class or individually, and you met an inspector or higher rank, you were required to salute them. This took a bit of adjustment for some people, especially those joining from a civilian background. While it was a pain, I understood why it was important: the whole course was quite officious and disciplined as they were trying to turn each individual into an effective and professional police officer.

In Week 10 an Inspector Breen interrupted our lesson to tell everyone what area or division they would be working in when they returned to their force, supposing we successfully completed the course. I was being sent to A Division, Bootle Street Police Station, in Manchester city centre.

Two weeks later I passed my final exams and was preparing for a Training School tradition: the 'dining in' night. In the last week of the course and before the passing-out parade for all successful recruits, all the intake have a 'dining in' night, where the men wear black evening dress and matching bow tie, and the women invest in lovely evening dresses. It's a very formal event with speeches and presentations all geared to marking the end of the intense physical and mental training. Everyone had been looking forward to it – me included – from the moment in Week 1 when a local suit hire company arrived at the Training Centre to measure up all the men for their respective James Bond outfits. The finished suit was then delivered in Week 12.

Of course, when you're training every day, you lose a lot of weight. So when I was measured up in my first week at Bruche, I was carrying a lot more weight than I was by Week 12. Consequently when my evening suit arrived and I tried on the jacket I looked less like Bond and more like Compo from *Last of the Summer Wine*. It was too late to get a new suit, so drastic measures were needed and I had to think on my feet.

Dave Russon, my Snake Pit flatmate, was out and had left his suit, still in the polythene cover, hanging up on the wall in our room. In the blink of an eye, he had my jacket and I had his. When it came to dining in, I duly strolled in looking all 007, while Dave followed on behind, nailing the baggy hand-me-down look. I've never told him that before, so if you're reading this, sorry Dave!

On the Friday morning of Week 12 it was time for our passing-out parade. It's a great occasion, and everyone had put a lot of time, sweat and effort into preparing for this final parade. It was the day that everyone had been dreaming of, the day the exams had been completed and the day we all finally became police officers ready to hit the streets. Everybody's family and friends could attend to watch all the pomp and ceremony as each class and their instructors marched around the drill square for the last time. My dad, mum and brother were standing in the crowd somewhere, although I'm not sure where as I had to keep my eyes forward for fear of putting a foot wrong on the big day. There were police horses, the police band provided the music and the chief constable stood on the dais to take the salute on the final march past, when the whole intake would leave the drill square and form up in front of the main building. Tradition dictated that, after a countdown, all students should then throw their helmets and hats into the air, accompanied by plenty of cheering.

It was at this point that the stark realization hit everyone that everything we had been through together as a class was at an end. Everyone was going to go in whichever direction, and the vast majority of us would never see each other again. What did the job have in store for everyone? Some would go on to complete thirty years, others would not; only time would tell.

I enjoyed the discipline at Bruche, and the training course as a whole; by the end of it I was glad to get out but happy to have gone through it. I do think that discipline within policing has gone too far the other way though, especially today when I see police officers on the streets with their hands in their pockets, chewing gum and covered in tattoos (in the 1970s you could only have a tattoo if it was out of sight). The pendulum on discipline has now swung too far the wrong way; it's been relaxed too much because I think the police came under scrutiny and some criticism for discipline being too harsh in the past and they just don't deal with criticism that well.

That seems to go across the board for policing; they just don't seem to be able to cope with criticism and put the other side of the story. It's a shame, because there are a lot of police officers out there trying hard to do a good job, but you don't hear about that so much. All you hear about is the bad stuff and, as a result, how many people trust the police these days?

Chapter Four

In the Real World:
On the Wrong End of a Rifle

aving left Bruche and completed a two-week Local Procedure
Course back at Peterloo House, I took my first tentative
steps into Bootle Street. I had been instructed to see a Chief
Inspector Poole who was the head of the Divisional Admin Office.
There were three of us who were new recruits for Bootle Street, and
he made us wait well past our time for seeing him, which just added to
the tension. I didn't know it at the time, but keeping you waiting was
an old school leadership tactic just to reinforce who was in charge of
the situation, and one which I was to come across more than once in
my career.

When we did meet him it was obvious that he was full of his own
self-importance and generally talked down to us. He informed me that
I would be joining A Relief at Bootle Street, and would work their shift
pattern. Reliefs actually meant teams and there were five – A, B, C, D
and E – that covered the entire city centre, twenty-four hours a day,
seven days a week. They worked a shift pattern of nights (11.00 pm
to 7.00 am), afternoons (3.00 pm to 11.00 pm), earlies (7.00 am to
3.00 pm) and days (8.00 am to 4.00 pm). I was also told that A Relief
was currently on nights and that I would be joining them the following
evening.

The Chief Superintendent of the division was a man by the name
of Robinson, who looked and walked round like General Patton;
the Superintendent was Eric Gill; and the Chief Inspector was Joe
Diston, who looked like a Japanese rear gunner from the war. It was
quite daunting to be in this environment as a young 18-year-old, as the
police culture at the time gave these bosses a god-like status, whereby
even if they were wrong, they were right. I spent the rest of the day

being shown around the station and the division, getting myself an all-important locker in the basement near to the parade room. When each shift came on duty they had to 'parade on' in the parade room. So, for example, if a particular relief was on afternoons, they would all be standing in the parade room in a line in full uniform, and you were required to produce your appointments for the parade sergeant to check. When I say appointments, I mean your pocket book, truncheon, whistle, handcuffs and – if on nights – your torch. It meant a disciplinary offence for anyone who didn't have them. Once the sergeant was satisfied, the parade would continue and you would be given any relevant information about the area you were covering regarding crimes or observations for particular vehicles or individuals. Finally, you were told which area or beat you were covering for the next eight hours.

I went home that day knowing that the following night I would be meeting my new colleagues at 11.00 pm for an eight-hour night shift. Again, it was a pretty daunting feeling; what would they be like? How would I be received by them? Would I fit into the team? Manchester city centre in the mid-1970s was a pretty lively place to work, and I admit to being filled with dread when I turned up for that first shift but I had nothing to worry about. I couldn't have wished for a better group of men and women to join; they made me really welcome and I quickly settled in.

*　　*　　*

For the next two years I was in my probationary period, where once again, if I didn't come up to scratch I could be dismissed. Initially you worked in the company of an experienced officer before being let loose on the general public. They'd spent three months at Bruche telling us that everything was black and white, and I soon realized that wasn't the case. You're working with officers who have usually got a few years' service, and unless you can do the job you're not going to be accepted by them, so you would end up feeling a bit of an outcast.

I was allocated to PC 4345 Tony Whitehead, who worked each shift in a panda car; the idea was that he would get sent to more jobs being mobile, so it was the perfect learning curve for me. Although I'd been through the cadets and Bruche, I felt like I was now doing it for real. I knew I had four weeks with Tony when if I wasn't sure about something, I could always ask for his advice on what to do next. I also knew I'd got to make the most of those four weeks, because after that the day would come when I had to walk out on my own. I had all that law and training in my head, but I would need to be able to make split-second decisions about how to deal with things. Make the wrong decision, and my job could be on the line.

My first arrest as a fully-fledged police officer was for drunk and incapable; nothing exciting, but something you came across a lot on A Division due to the vast social scene in the city centre. This was my first set of nights and it took place at the back of Victoria Train Station. In the early hours we came across a young guy who was the worse for wear through drink and had fallen asleep in the doorway of an old railway yard. He was so bad he had wet himself, so for his own safety the van was called and he was taken back to Bootle Street to sleep it off in the cells. On nights the cell block always had the distinct smell of three things: vomit, urine and alcohol. Returning to the charge office at the station I had to explain the circumstances of the arrest to the Charge Office Sergeant, whose job it was to either authorize the detention or release the suspect.

The city centre was the smallest of all fourteen divisions in GMP, but one of the busiest. Unlike other divisions, at that time there were very few residents (something that's since changed), and no real community. In the day many people would travel into the city to work or to shop, then go home after work, and later on in the evening, especially at weekends, come out again to socialize. It was madness during the day, quiet around tea-time, and then madness again at night as the social side of the city would get going. People would come to drink and have fun, and many of the problems were due to alcohol or an excess of it.

Officers worked hard but also played hard, and socializing was a big part of the police culture at that time too. For example, after a seven-day afternoon shift which ended on a Tuesday night, the entire shift would invariably go out together after finishing at 11.00 pm, knowing there was no work the following day. This might mean initially going for a curry at a local restaurant, and then on to one of the popular locations at that time, often a nightclub on a boat moored in Pomona Dock at Stretford and imaginatively named 'The Boat'! It had several bars, a dance floor and disco, and was open until 2.00 am so it was an ideal location.

These social events bonded the team together. On other nights we would go en masse to one of many city centre pubs where the landlord or landlady was agreeable to lock the door and let us have a 'lock in'. Betty at the Grenadier on Oldham Street and the Land O' Cakes on Great Ancoats Street were both favourites for this and we spent many happy times there.

I eventually got the okay to go out on patrol on my own, and I'll never forget the feeling as I walked through the main gates at Bootle Street out in the big bad world, in full uniform, thinking that everyone was looking at me and fearful of what I might get sent to or inadvertently come across. This time I wouldn't have anyone from whom I might seek advice and Joe Public wouldn't know I was a newbie. Initially my main foot patrols were Oxford Street and Oldham Street, but not at the same time. Each one of these was a set patrol which you had to walk up and down and be visible for the duration of your shift. You were not officially allowed to enter any premises for a chat – or, God forbid, a brew – with any of the businesses on your patrol, and you would regularly be visited by the patrol sergeant who would have a brief chat, sign your pocket book and then clear off. However, you never knew when he or she would appear.

All patrol sergeants would walk round with a night stick, so–called because before the invention of radios, the sergeant on nights would walk round looking for his officers and would repeatedly bang the stick on the floor. The idea then was that the officer would hear this and make his way to the waiting sergeant. This would obviously be impossible these days what with the constant noise 24/7, but it goes to show how times have changed.

* * *

There were all manner of offences and incidents taking place every day on A Division, and while thefts of motor vehicles weren't particularly uncommon, there was one fairly soon after I started at Bootle Street that I will always remember. We were on nights and in the early hours I was sent to take a report of a stolen car from its owner, just off Albert Square. The car was an old British racing green Mini, and it was a pre-1963 registration number which some would call a personal number plate. The registration had four numbers, for instance 4869 and ended in TJ, so 4869 TJ; at the time, being a fan of Tom Jones, I thought it would have been better placed on his Rolls-Royce or Bentley. I met the owner, took the report with all the relevant details and circulated it as stolen on the Police National Computer (PNC) in the hope that another patrol may come across it and arrest those responsible. Having got all this done, I carried on to the next job.

The night shift finished and at 7.00 am I left Bootle Street to drive home, dreaming of getting into bed. This was a Sunday morning, the roads were pretty quiet and I was on auto-pilot. At the junction of Eccles Old Road and Lancaster Road in Salford I was in the offside lane waiting at traffic lights to turn right. As I sat there I noticed the vehicle in front also waiting to turn right: a racing green Mini, registration number 4869 TJ. My first thought was that the owner must have got their car back, so I tried to see who was driving. All I could see were the eyes of the driver in the rear-view mirror, and it looked like he was on his own.

When the lights turned green and the Mini turned right I followed, then pulled alongside him as we were driving along (so now I was on the wrong side of the road) to get a proper look at the driver. It definitely wasn't the owner. Whoever it was, he stared at me wondering what the hell I was doing on the wrong side of the road! I went into police mode, indicating to him to pull up at the side of the road. To my amazement he did, and I pulled in behind him and got out. I walked to the driver's door, and if he was looking in his wing mirror he could now see the half police uniform I was wearing; it wasn't rocket science to realize what I was.

Just as I got to the driver's door the engine raced and he sped off like Lewis Hamilton, leaving me standing in the road. I ran back to my car and took off after him. He went down Lancaster Road, turned right into Swinton Park Road and up onto Irlam o' th' Heights. I was with him as he drove down onto Broad Street and made his way towards the city centre. It was an early Sunday morning in 1978, there were no mobile phones, and no one really about apart from tired police officers and villains as the morning shifts at the police stations would only just be turning out. I knew I was on my own and the adrenaline started to kick in.

Broad Street is a three-lane carriageway and he was ahead of me in the centre lane. I could see that he was messing with something in between him and the front passenger seat. As I looked closer it seemed to be the butt of a rifle, and he was doing something with it as he drove at speed. The Mini came off ahead of me down a slip road and towards a large roundabout at Pendleton, near to Salford shopping precinct, before it went out of sight. As I came down the slip road and towards the roundabout the car was stopped near the Broughton Road exit; the driver stood facing me with his door wide open, pointing a rifle at my car. Everything went into slow motion, and I had a split second to think about what I should do.

I was a new police officer full of law and legislation about the use of reasonable force, and this was not an everyday occurrence. Would it have been reasonable for me to ram this guy and maybe kill him in the process? Was this a real rifle or an imitation, and would this have made any difference, so long as I believed my life, at that time, was in danger? In the cool light of day and having reflected on this on many occasions, I believe that this argument would have stood up in court, but what I chose to do at the time was carry on driving round the roundabout. This is a large roundabout and as I came back to where he had been, he and the car had gone. He must have driven off down Broughton Road and then disappeared down one of the side roads. I drove down there but it was by then impossible to know which way he had gone. I found a phone box and rang the police control room, which then circulated the details to all patrols for observations. There were no armed response vehicles on the streets of Greater Manchester at that time and, from that day to this, I am none the wiser as to who he was, what he was doing or what he was about to do. The following day saw me viewing photographs of possible suspects at the Criminal Records Office, but none of them came up with any positive results. It remains a mystery, but one I will never forget.

I used this scenario later in my career when I became a law trainer at Bruche. I told students what happened, up to the point where I arrived at the roundabout, and found myself driving towards a guy pointing a rifle at me. In the same situation a lot of them say they would have rammed him, although not all of them are comfortable with that if it was to later turn out that the gun was a fake. I would argue that you would be justified in doing so even if it was an imitation rifle, as at the time I believed it to be the real thing and felt that my life was in danger. Even to this day, I sometimes think to myself, should I have rammed him?

Chapter Five

A Sad Christmas and a Lucky Escape

On Christmas Day 1978, Dad died suddenly in Salford Royal Hospital. He was 42 years old. It was totally unexpected, and a devastating blow.

He'd had a really varied career, and had also worked at Ronsons, the lighter manufacturer, before eventually ending up as a bar fitter for Scottish and Newcastle Breweries. He didn't die following a long illness. Afterwards I found his work diary for the brewery, which had his jobs in for the next few days, but he also wrote on those pages about the little things that had happened each day, or maybe just about the weather. In the few weeks leading up to his death, he'd put in the diary a few entries about struggling to get his breath. Two weeks before he died he'd been to the doctors where they did a blood pressure check, which was all okay, and tested his lungs by blowing – I think what they would now call a 'peak flow test' – and that was all okay as well. However, his comment in the diary was simply: 'I can't understand why I can't breathe properly.' Two weeks later he was gone.

Reading those comments now with the benefit of hindsight, they all make sense. You can see he was putting down his innermost thoughts and fears, but he wasn't telling anyone else, other than the doctor. That December, Dad had been coming in from work in the cold weather, and just lying in front of the gas fire because he couldn't get warm. On 18 December I got a call at work to say he'd been taken to hospital; he'd lain down to warm up again, then got up after a while to close the curtains and collapsed. They took him to Salford Royal, and I went straight there to see him. They admitted him for the week, so we knew he would be in for Christmas Day.

We went up each day during the week. Mum had gone to see him the day before Christmas Eve, so the next day I told her I'd go. If Dad had been at home they were going to spend the evening with friends, so I said to Mum that I'd go to the hospital while she got ready, and then I'd come back and drop her round to their friends. There was no big concern about Dad's health; when I got up there on Christmas Eve, he told me not to stay the whole hour but to get off and get Mum to their friends. So I left after half an hour, walked down the ward and turned to wave back, although he wasn't looking.

Next morning, Mum came and woke me up about 7.00 am; the hospital had been on the phone, saying we needed to go up because Dad wasn't too good. I think I already knew then that he was dead. As we were driving towards the hospital I could see through a window where his bed was, and the curtains were drawn around the bed. When we got there we were taken to the matron's office, and at this stage I still don't think Mum had a clue. They told us straight away that Dad had died. Just 42 years old. Even though I'd worked out what was going on, it was still a hell of a shock. I pushed past the nurses, went to his bed and opened the curtains; he was still lying there.

I'm not sure if anyone else can really imagine what it was like. Mum and I had gone to see him as my brother was staying at his girlfriend's, and we got to the hospital to be told Dad had died. We then went home, with Dad's belongings in a bag. We were driving home on Christmas morning, and in everybody else's house they were opening presents, celebrating the fact that Santa had been. We just sat in the living room, looking at each other. What do you do? We were just in shock, I think.

It's always been at the back of my mind that the night before, when I left, there was only a skeleton staff on duty for Christmas Eve and those who were working were getting ready to have a bit of a do. I don't blame them for that – it was Christmas after all – but I wonder whether, if Dad had taken ill, anyone would have noticed if there was a bit of a party going on? I couldn't understand how he could go from sitting up talking and looking okay one minute to being dead the next; maybe he had an idea of what was coming and that's why he sent me off early. We'll never know the answer to that.

I have many things for which to thank him, but none more so than stepping in and sorting me out when my schooling was going pear-shaped. Without both the kick up the arse I needed and the support he gave me, things would have been very different. Thank you Dad.

* * *

At the time Dad died, my brother and I were both working at Bootle Street. We got summoned in to see Chief Inspector Joe Diston who, after the usual polite condolences, went on to tell us that only one of us could have compassionate leave to help sort out the funeral. My brother, being the eldest, had the time off and I went back to work. It was the last place I wanted to be, particularly as the funeral was going to be delayed until well into January 1979 due to the number of deaths over the Christmas period.

When I look back now, I think the way the police handled it was pretty diabolical. How did they expect you to function? I was only 20, and to have to carry on working through that personal loss was tough. If I'm honest, it probably did have an effect on me and my personality. If I had been doing a 'normal' job then I think my employer's reaction would have been different, but I was basically told to get on with it. I don't think they would get away with that these days, but that was the culture then; you did as you were told and you didn't ask questions.

Within a week of Dad dying and with me back on full shift, I got called to the sudden death of a man in his 40s in the NCP car park. I was just expected to deal with it, which I did. Yet again, looking back, it's maybe no surprise that I went off the rails for a while. I was smoking and drinking too much, finishing work, going straight out afterwards and not getting home until the early hours. I would normally be out and about with one of the lads on my team, PC 2230 Anthony (Tony) Walter Quinn, who was from Ordsall in Salford. Like me, joining the police was going against the grain for someone from his background – some in his community probably even viewed it as disloyal – but overall he was respected for his decision and he still lived in the heart of Ordsall.

That may have been one of the reasons we got on so well: we were like best mates, and we'd go out all over the place. We were both single and we would make the most of our free time which, in some ways, helped me to deal with losing Dad.

Despite everything, I somehow managed to successfully complete the Police Standard Car course, which authorized me to drive police panda cars and the police vans. The cycle of city centre patrols and rotating shifts continued as normal, until one day – Tuesday, 8 May 1979 – I found myself standing on the corner of Oldham Street and Piccadilly as part of my day shift patrol. Nothing untoward was happening and everyone was getting on with their day. I checked my watch, and it was nearing the time for my tea break back at Bootle Street. I started to walk the steady, in-built police walk back to the station. No sooner had I got back than messages were being transmitted over the radio about a fire at Woolworths store on the corner of Oldham Street and Piccadilly, exactly where I had just come from.

I got back there as quickly as I could, and the scene was now one of total devastation as flames engulfed the building. It was completely at odds with the normality of just a few minutes earlier. Along with other officers I was deployed at the scene, helping with traffic diversions while the fire brigade attempted to extinguish the fire. They were struggling, and as the blaze grew worse more crews were sent for.

Ten people died that day; 90 per cent of the second floor was seriously damaged by the fire, which spread rapidly and took numerous crews to eventually get under control. Several firemen were also injured. Woolworths was a six-storey building and it was believed that 500 customers and staff were inside at the time of the fire. The store had no fire sprinkler system fitted. Only the first floor was untouched by the flames, although all the stock was water-damaged.

Later I ventured into the building, up the stairwell on the Oldham Street side, and went into the restaurant area on the upper floor, which took the brunt of the fire. It was a scene of total carnage; everything was charred and blackened, people's belongings were strewn everywhere. There were shoes and handbags still sitting underneath what remained of tables and chairs.

I also remember this distinctly for another reason. When I got to the top of the stairs I heard someone shout from the bottom, and as I looked round there was a face I'll never forget. I nearly jumped out of my skin, bearing in mind where I was and what had taken place. This gentleman appeared out of the darkness. While one side of his face was completely normal, he had lost all the muscle on the other side, which meant that the skin sagged down almost to his chest. You can imagine him shouting to me, me turning round and in the dark seeing this image. He looked like he'd been a victim of the fire himself. Apparently he was a local councillor in Manchester and was asking about the fire; he was a really nice guy, but I don't think he realized what a fright he gave me.

*　*　*

I've always believed that small choices and sometimes little bits of luck – good or bad – can be life-changing. There have been plenty of examples in my own life and career: from not being seen by the police while driving Uncle Cliff's van and so escaping a criminal record, to deciding not to ram the roundabout gunman, which could have seen me lose my job or even be shot. Yet for whatever reason I was smart, quick or lucky enough to make the right choice. Another incident that took place while I was still pretty new to the job and could have changed my career and life forever happened on a reasonably quiet afternoon shift (3.00 to 11.00 pm). Working on the van was one of the jobs that everyone in uniform wanted to do; if you had a good team on the van you were always busy, and when other officers had someone that they needed help with or who had to be taken to the station and locked up, they wanted to know they could rely on you to get to them quickly. Because of that, it was usually the officers with most service who worked on them.

However, on this particular day I had some time off booked from 7.00 to 11.00 pm, so I was only working half a shift, and I was given the honour of working on the van for four hours with an officer who had many more years' service than me. He was a real action man, a big guy who used to walk around like he had a roll of carpet tucked under each arm. To this day I don't know how I ended up being paired up with him for those four hours – I can only think his normal partner was otherwise engaged – and while he looked quite intimidating, he wasn't much of a talker. Those four hours dragged and felt more like eight, but eventually my 7.00 pm early finish came round and I was off.

After I'd left, an intruder alarm went off at the old Pauldens department store near Piccadilly Gardens, which meant someone might be breaking in, and all available patrols were sent to the store, including 'action man' in the van. Once the officers were all there they began searching each floor of the store, and my van partner was on one of the upper floors. While he was searching the floor he took a shine to a belt that was on one of the displays and slid it into his pocket. This was the 1970s, and CCTV wasn't as common as it is today, but it was in Pauldens. Security staff monitoring the cameras and looking for the possible thief who had triggered the alarms saw him steal the belt; he was later detained, the belt was recovered and all the afternoon shift were kept on at work while the incident was dealt with.

I knew nothing about any of this until I came into work the next day, but I soon realized that if I hadn't finished early that day, I would have been on the van with him and would have attended the alarm call at Pauldens. I know it's all ifs, buts and maybes, but it's more than feasible that I could have been on the same floor as 'action man' and seen him take the belt. So as a police officer still young in service, the question is, what would I have done?

I would have had the dilemma of turning a blind eye or arresting him myself. To be completely honest, I don't know the answer. I'd like to think that I would have argued with him, but I just can't see myself turning to an officer with so much more service and experience than me and saying: 'You're under arrest.' If I had done so, that would have been me finished in the police anyway, given the culture at the time. I would definitely have been 'persona non grata' to a certain element within the job; remember, this was the 1970s and anyone who has watched a TV programme like *Life on Mars* would know that arresting a colleague for doing something like that just wouldn't happen.

So I might have pretended I didn't see it, but with CCTV there, I would have been as guilty as him if I hadn't arrested him or reported it.

He might even have offered me one, in which case I really would have been in a lose-lose situation. I would have turned it down, but unless I'd arrested him (and effectively ruined my career anyway), I would have been disciplined and sacked. Or he might not have done it in front of me.

Fortunately, I'll never know the answer. I'm just lucky I wasn't put in that position. 'Action man' was charged with theft, convicted and quite rightly sacked from the police. There was a lot of pressure on young officers to be accepted within the job, and you sometimes felt you had to acquiesce and say nothing regarding certain behaviour or aspects of the culture at that time, particularly if a senior or more experienced officer was involved. To a certain extent, this was still the case years later when I took the force to task over what happened to me further down the line.

Chapter Six

Another Shock

We finished a run of afternoons on Tuesday, 3 July 1979 and as was the norm, we'd arranged to go out as a group after the shift was over at 11.00 pm. A few weeks earlier Tony Quinn had been transferred from uniformed foot patrol duties to work the same shift pattern as us, but at the Central Detention Centre (CDC) above the old Magistrates' Court building in Manchester, where prisoners were held awaiting transfers or to attend court. It was something that everyone on A Division had to do at some point, and at least during the winter you were out of the cold.

Tony still hadn't passed his driving test, so on some shifts I'd pick him up on the way into work, but it got to the point when he needed his own transport and I had both a bike and a car so he bought my Honda 175cc to use; you could drive a bike that size then as a learner. We went to one of the GMP police clubs so that Tony could learn to ride it, and although he was a bit wobbly to start with, he soon got the hang of it. That was it: he was off with his own transport.

That evening I was on the van; the van crew worked from 4.00 pm to 12.00 midnight rather than 3.00 to 11.00 pm to allow for the overlap at 11.00 pm and ensure there were still police patrols out and about while the night crew paraded on. We drove into the yard at Bootle Street not long after 11.00 pm and all my relief were there, suited and booted and ready to go out. Tony had made his way over from the CDC and was standing there with them. I stopped and had a quick chat with him through the passenger window, and he explained that they were all going to The Boat and wanted to know if I would be going when I finished. I said I'd wait and see if we got involved in any jobs and, if not, I may come across later.

I can remember thinking at the time that when I got off shift, I'd go and have a drink with them. It just never happened. For whatever reason, and maybe because I was still getting over my dad's death, I decided at finishing time to go straight home and go to bed. The next thing I remember is someone knocking on my front door at 5.00 am on the Wednesday. When I looked out through the bedroom window I could see two colleagues from my relief standing in front of the door. I went down and opened it, and it was clear they were both in a state of shock. They told me that Tony had been killed in an accident while riding his motorbike – the one he'd recently bought from me – along Deansgate in Manchester, near to Knott Mill. He hit a lamppost on the corner and was killed at the scene. I closed the front door and tried to take in what I had just been told, bearing in mind I had been speaking to him just a few hours earlier. It was devastating. I'd now lost my dad and my best mate in the space of six months.

It transpired that Tony had left his bike parked up at Bootle Street, and when everyone had finished at The Boat and decided to go on to someone's house for a few more drinks, he'd got a lift back to the nick to pick up his bike. The lad who gave him a lift followed him along Deansgate and, as they were approaching a bend in the road by Knott Mill Station, Tony seemed to look behind him just for a second. When he looked back, he just didn't make the bend but carried straight on and hit the lamppost. Apparently he broke his jaw, which was pushed up and into his brain, so he died instantly.

I'm sure Tony would have had a drink, although I've no idea how much, but when you put that together with the fact that he wasn't the most experienced of motorcyclists, then it wouldn't take a lot to affect his balance on two wheels. Also at the back of my mind, there's always the question of what would have happened if I had gone for a drink with them? Would he still have gone back to get his bike? Would we have jumped in someone else's car together? Would he still be alive? You just don't know.

What I do know is that Tony Quinn was a mate in a million, and if he was alive today I'm sure we would still have been good friends. His death had a massive impact; not just on me, but on the whole shift. When you work as a team you become very close-knit, a tight unit, and Tony was well thought of and well liked. To have someone die in that way, at that age – he was only 21 – was horrendous. Yet we had to carry on, come back after our two days off and work as a shift again. We were lucky that we had a good inspector on that shift, so at that level it was good, although there was nothing like the counselling or support people receive nowadays.

Tony had a full ceremonial funeral, with uniformed colleagues lining the service roads in the cemetery at Agecroft in Salford; I was a pallbearer, along with several other close colleagues. He was a loyal and trusted friend, and a great policeman.

I still go to his grave now. He's buried in the same cemetery as my dad. I go there every year on Christmas Day, the day Dad died, to see the Book of Remembrance for my mum and dad – I've not missed a day since Dad passed away – and then I go and visit Tony's grave. I often wonder if Tony had still been around whether I would have found it different, maybe easier, having to deal with the crap that's gone on since.

Chapter Seven

On Two and Four Wheels

Shortly before Tony died I had successfully completed my two-year probation period and was now confirmed as a police officer, which basically meant that they could no longer get rid of me unless I did something either drastically wrong or criminal. I was getting itchy feet at Bootle Street – after nearly two and half years in the city centre I was bored, I wanted to move on – and when I was transferred to the CDC for my stint there a few months after Tony's death it made me realize that I needed a change. I've always enjoyed driving, especially having learned so young, and when an opportunity arose to apply for an Advanced Driving Course, I went for it.

The pre-requisite for this was that anyone who applied, was accepted and then successfully completed the course would have to transfer to the T Department or Traffic section. I was interviewed, accepted and, after only three months at the CDC, I transferred to Salford Traffic Unit at the Crescent on the F Division. Actually it was all done the wrong way round: I transferred before going on the course, and for all they knew I could have been the worst driver in the world. I was just glad to get away and start afresh somewhere else, and I knew if I could get this driving qualification it could help to open other doors for me.

Anyway, I then went on the course which was held at the Force Driving School at Longsight, where every morning you would have to parade on and be inspected by the driving school staff. Some of them really loved their position of power. One particular short-arse sergeant by the name of Taylor strutted around with the peak on his cap pulled down like an SS officer; he would get right into the face of certain students in an intimidating manner. People who knew him said he'd never seen an angry man and was in the Driving School to hide away from the so-called sharp end. The only good thing about him was that, due to his height, he couldn't look down on you.

My instructor was a guy called Brian Rigby, who was quite laid back and coming towards the end of his service. My co-student on the course was Barry Howarth, also from Salford. After the parade, all students had to do a vehicle inspection of the car they were going out in that day, checking that things such as oil, petrol and water were all okay and that the vehicle was safe for the long drive ahead as on the course you would often go to the Lake District or Wales and cover a good few miles.

One particular morning the three of us set off in a 3.5-litre Rover, Barry and I having done the checks and told Brian that everything was okay. A short time later there was a strange rattling noise coming from the front, so he told us to pull up while he checked it out. Brian had a red face at the best of times, but looking at him through the windscreen I realized that this colour red was not the norm...on checking the front nearside tyre he found that the wheel nuts were all loose. Had we got going at speed on the motorway this could have been fatal. It brought it home that the vehicle checks are there for a reason and I never failed to do them properly after that. This aside, the course went well; I really enjoyed it, and at the end both Barry and I passed. I now had my Advanced Car Driving authority which would allow me to drive with 'blues and twos' – blue lights and sirens – to any job requiring them.

*　*　*

The Traffic Department was responsible for patrolling the major road systems throughout Greater Manchester and the main traffic cars at the time were lightning-fast, 3-litre Ford Capris. It was once again a shift pattern of days, nights, afternoons and earlies, and you usually worked solo in the cars so that they could put more vehicles out. The red and white livery (referred to as jam butty cars) was a great deterrent when seen on the roads, and a much more frequent sight than today. I enjoyed the change from walking a single beat like Oldham Street in the city centre to now having a high-powered car and a vast area to cover, and I never ceased to get a buzz from using the blues and twos when responding to emergencies.

Inevitably on traffic you would have a police vehicle accident (PVA) at some point, probably more than one, although my first was quite bizarre as I was stationary at the time. I was on nights on Eccles New Road when a motorcycle flew past me at speed and immediately grabbed my attention. As I caught up with it I put the blue lights on and indicated to the rider to pull over to the side of the road. He had other ideas, and accelerated away. Setting off after him, I informed the Control Room that I was in pursuit and gave them the registration number. My first thoughts were that it was nicked, but it came back over the radio as not having been reported stolen, with an address for the owner in Salford. I continued the pursuit, giving a commentary over the radio so that other nearby patrols could assist. The bike eventually went down Wilton Road off Eccles Old Road, and the rider stopped outside a house on the corner of one of the side avenues. I was still on my own as I pulled up alongside the bike with the blues and twos in full flow. The rider was trying to get off the bike, and as I opened the driver's door I heard an almighty crash. He had jumped off the bike and then let it go rather than putting it on its stand; it fell sideways onto the front wing of the Capri, damaging it as it did so, which made me even more annoyed!

The rider ran off up the garden path of the house and straight in through the open front door. It was only at this point that I realized the house was full of people, with a party of some kind going on. I managed to keep my eye on the mystery biker, even though he'd been wearing a helmet, and when I got in the house and through all the bodies in the hallway I grabbed hold of him. After a short struggle I marched him outside. This was one of the downsides of being in these fancy, high-powered cars; once you got out and left it you had no means of communication. I needed to get back out and hope someone had got to the last location I'd given out and if not, to get to the radio to get assistance there. If anyone in the house had tried to help him I could have been in trouble, and these days, if I ran into a house on my own like that they would have had me. Thankfully someone had made it on scene, and our biker was soon arrested and on his way to the Crescent.

His reason, it turned out, for shooting off was that it was not his bike; it belonged to his mate who was at the party and who had allowed him to go and have a ride on it. The problem was that he had no insurance, so when I tried to stop him he panicked and off he went. Both he and the owner were reported for offences and later pleaded guilty. For my troubles, the circumstances of what happened and the damage to the car meant that it was reported as a PVA, despite both vehicles being at a standstill and him deliberately letting go of the bike so it crashed against the car. No matter how many times I explained this back in the office, there were some who jokingly refused to believe me, claiming that I must have rammed the bike and catapulted the rider into the hallway of the house.

Being left in the lurch with no radio contact was an occupational hazard for a single-crewed traffic officer, and it wasn't long before I once again found myself with my hands full and struggling to call for back-up. It was another night shift on Eccles New Road, and I sat completing some reports in the patrol car, visible to passing traffic. A double-decker bus pulled up in front of me and the driver opened the doors and came to speak to me. It was about 2.30 am, and he said there were three drunken lads on the top deck, causing trouble and refusing to get off.

I got out of the car and went up to the top deck, as the driver stayed downstairs. These three were the only people up there, so I told them what he'd said, reinforcing the point that he wanted them off. There were some general moans, groans and expletives, but eventually they all got up and slowly made their way downstairs and off the bus, giving the driver a mouthful as they passed. I followed them off and we were now all standing on the footpath near to my parked police car. The moans and groans continued, particularly from one of them who was far from happy. At this point I heard the doors of the bus shut behind me and turned to see it move off, leaving me with the problem of Curly, Larry and Moe.

Once the bus had left, the mouthiest one of the group started to shout to the others that, seeing as there was only one copper, they could sort me out. Before getting out of the car I hadn't told the Control Room where I was or what I was doing as I thought I would have been on and off the bus in no time. I was on and off, but now with a whole new problem.

By now the trio was getting increasingly agitated and braver by the second, and I knew I had to do something and do it quickly. I grabbed the mouthy one round the neck and pulled him into the road while shouting at the other two to keep back or they would be arrested too. As we stood in the road I could see the lights of a vehicle approaching us, so I flagged it down as best I could. As it got closer I was relieved to see it was an ambulance. It stopped, the crew got out and I asked them to get in my car and shout up on my radio that I needed assistance and to give my location. They apparently started shouting 'Mayday' down the police radio as they didn't know my call sign or any of the police protocols, but whatever they shouted, it worked. In no time back-up arrived and the main protagonist was taken to the Crescent and charged, while his two mates were allowed to go. This could have gone the other way and, if it had, I could have been there for some time before anyone located me, so this was another lesson learned.

I definitely didn't think about it this way at the time, but looking back, both the situation with the biker and the bus drunks were examples of me being able to think on my feet, take decisions and act quickly when I needed to. Even if those actions left me somewhat exposed to risk, if they were the right thing to do to get the job done, then I was comfortable doing that. That was another trait which, in due course, would come in handy when I moved into undercover work. Not everyone reacts in the same way, and I think some people, if things start going off script, will just back away and say: 'No, I'm not doing that, that's not how it was meant to go.'

* * *

While I was in the Traffic Department the opportunity arose to apply for an Advanced Motorcycle Course, and I was keen to have a go as I'd had bikes of my own and already had my full rider's licence. I'd been on traffic for about fifteen months and was ready for a move. I got on to the course, and after several weeks at Longsight Driving School going out daily to parts of Wales and the Lake District, I got my Advanced Motorcycle ticket. Before I knew it, I was transferred to

Number 3 Motorcycle Wing of GMP based at Plant Hill police station in Blackley, from where we covered the A, B, C and F Divisions; quite a large area with plenty to go at. The great thing about the bikes was that they were not allowed to work nights for safety reasons, so we were finished by 10.00 pm.

I preferred riding the bikes to driving the traffic cars, and I already knew that I enjoyed working alone. I didn't get off to the best start on the bikes though. On my very first day I went out with an experienced colleague, who was showing me the area and the hospitals we went to when they required ambulance escorts. We went to the front of St Mary's Hospital in Manchester, and I was tentatively following him as we pulled up on the ramp. I went to put my right foot down to keep the bike upright, but as I waited to feel the concrete base on my boot, it seemed that someone had taken the floor away.... The bike continued to go sideways until it was past the point of no return, and due to its weight I had to let it go. It ended up on its side at the main doors, in full view of everyone there. Thank God there were no mobile phones with cameras in those days.

I hadn't fully realized the extent of the ramp as it sloped downwards, which was why I couldn't feel the floor until it was too late. It's amazing in situations like that how you find some extra strength, and I jumped down and lifted the bike up. Thankfully, due to the side crash bars, there was very little damage, although I had to endure the jokes and innuendoes later back at the office. Like everything else, it was a learning curve and I never did it again.

Working these inner city divisions meant that there was all manner of crime and offences to deal with, and the great thing was that you worked on a different division each day; variety, as they say, is the spice of life. It wasn't without its risks though. On one shift I was riding along Queen's Road towards Rochdale Road. As I crossed Oldham Road, passing the old Playhouse Theatre, there were three lanes: two carrying on towards Rochdale Road and the offside lane turning back to Oldham Road. I was riding in the middle lane intending to go to Rochdale Road; slightly ahead of me in the nearside lane was a saloon car. As we got to the point of no return for using the third lane, the car driver must have looked again at the signs, realized he was going the wrong way, and – without any warning – drove from the left-hand lane across to the third lane, just missing the front of my bike. I swerved and then fell off into the road with the bike on my right leg.

I was stuck in this position, and as I looked up from the tarmac I just saw the car and its driver disappear round the bend back to Oldham Road without stopping. I was fortunate that there were no other vehicles behind me, and also that there was a man standing at the bus stop who witnessed the whole incident. He ran across to help me and help lift the bike away so I could get up. He was also quick-thinking enough to take down the registration number of the car, which was later stopped in Oldham.

I went to hospital and had treatment on a large swelling on my right elbow, which I must have hit on the ground as I tried to save myself, and bruising and grazing to my right leg. The story was that the driver was an out-of-town salesman who was lost: seeing the sign for Oldham at the last minute, he manoeuvred without looking and drove off, knocking me down as he went. He was reported for several driving offences and pleaded not guilty. It went to court where I gave evidence, as did the guy from the bus stop, and the salesman was later found guilty and fined. After the trial he came to me and apologized for pleading not guilty but said he 'had to try'! I was gobsmacked, although I suppose I shouldn't have been; it meant he knew he had done wrong but still attempted to proclaim his innocence just in case.

I was left needing regular physiotherapy on my arm, and was given a percentage of disability as to its use because I couldn't straighten it fully. I was also restricted to the office for a while as I couldn't ride the bike. It was at this same location some eighteen years later (31 August 1999) that PC Raja Ahmed was killed when an offender in a stolen car rammed his police bike into the traffic on Oldham Road and into the path of an articulated lorry.

One of the duties of a motorcycle patrol officer was to escort other vehicles, such as ambulances to hospitals in some emergency situations, and wide or abnormal loads. In the run-up to Christmas in 1982 I was tasked with escorting an abnormal load through Manchester City

Centre during the busy daytime period. Such loads have their route dictated to them, and they have to adhere to that route to avoid hazards such as low bridges or junctions that are too tight for them to navigate. The driver would be given a copy of his route, and on this occasion I met up with him where he was parked up to check his copy with the one I'd been given by the Control Room. They matched, and we duly set off with me at the front clearing the way so that this monster of a vehicle could command the centre of the road.

We went around Piccadilly Gardens and the next section of the route was Oldham Street, which would have taken us up to Great Ancoats Street and away from the city centre. Oldham Street was already busy with Christmas shoppers, and the council had duly installed the annual Christmas lights, stretching across from one lamppost to the next, all the way down the road.

Everything seemed to be going well until I heard what I thought were bombs going off. When I looked back I could see that the height of the abnormal load hadn't been taken into account by whoever planned the route and it became ensnared in the dangling lights, ripping them from the lampposts; the bulbs were then smashing on the road in explosive style. We immediately stopped, and had to call out the council to get the lorry free and back on its way. I'm glad to say that it wasn't my fault as I was only following the instructions both the driver and I had been given. Thankfully no one was injured, but someone in Traffic Management, who was responsible for this fiasco, must have had their ears bent behind closed doors. Apparently my new nickname that year was 'The Grinch': the man who ruined Christmas.

My time on the bike wing soon came and went, and there was a common theme appearing. It was clear that I couldn't stay in one place too long as I grew bored too easily. By now I had also secured a Class 1 Heavy Goods Vehicle licence; the question was, where could I put all of these skills to good use?

Chapter Eight

Going Undercover

Some police officers join up and never move from the division they start in, completing their thirty years in the same place. There's nothing wrong with that, but it was never going to suit me. I think it broadens your horizons and gives you a better perspective if you move around the force and experience different aspects of it.

With this in mind, when an advert came up for the job of surveillance motorcyclist with Number 1 Regional Crime Squad, I decided to apply for it. The Regional Crime Squad (RCS) – which later became the National Crime Squad (NCS) – was funded by all the police forces across England and Wales, and dealt with crime and criminality that transcended force boundaries. In reality this meant that the RCS dealt with the criminal activity that local forces didn't have the time or resources to tackle.

I didn't really know what the job would entail as the RCS was still pretty hush-hush, but what I did know sounded fantastic and something totally different from what I had experienced in policing so far. To become a member of the RCS you were seconded from your home force for a period of three years. The chance to move from day-to-day uniform policing to this was one I didn't think I'd get, but I put in for it anyway.

I went for the interview at the RCS HQ based at Salford Central Police Station on The Crescent, and I was one of two officers interested in the job; the other being one of my colleagues from the bike wing, Bob Littlewood. It was hard to prepare for the interview because so much of what the whole department did was on a need-to-know basis.

What I did know was that the job would entail being part of a plain clothes surveillance team, riding an unmarked police motorcycle. The idea was to follow suspected criminals and catch them at it, or gather intelligence on what they were up to without being seen. One interview question was how I would feel about being asked to ride the bike the wrong way around a roundabout and whether I would do it. I was told there would be occasions – and later there were many – when to keep up with targets who were up to no good and who didn't give a damn about red lights and traffic regulations, I would need to ride in an unconventional way. It was pretty clear that if you weren't up for this, the job wasn't for you. I said I would do it, as long as it was safe.

I knew these things went on, and sometimes for an operation to succeed you have to fight fire with fire, but you can never forget that you are a police officer and the safety of yourself and the public must be paramount. A good analogy is a villain who takes a loaded gun on a job. He probably won't think twice about firing it when in trouble and would shoot at anyone and everyone in his way. However, a police firearms officer can't do that: he or she has to take extra time before firing to assess the situation and be sure that it is safe to do so or risk finding themselves charged with offences.

I was successful at the interview and must have said the right things (which was something Bob never let me forget). So on the morning of Monday, 31 October 1983 I swapped my police uniform for plain clothes and stepped into the fascinating world of the Regional Crime Squad. As it turned out, I wouldn't see that uniform again for quite some time. I was based at the old Lancashire County Police Station in Castle Street, Bolton. The office was on the top floor, next to an old, imposing, dark-wood-panelled court room, which had long since seen any trials. The office consisted of a chief inspector, two detective inspectors, seven detective sergeants and eight detective constables, including me, and the team was a mix of GMP and Lancashire officers.

Everyone had to be trained in both mobile and foot surveillance, so it wasn't long before I was on my residential course at Hutton Hall in Preston. My advanced driving abilities had worked in my favour when applying for the job, and were put to good use on this course, although my unfortunate run with stationary PVAs continued when we were out on a training exercise in Southport. Our plain surveillance vehicle was parked in a side street in a line of vehicles. I was inside with the instructor and two other students, one of whom had been driving. We were listening to the ongoing radio commentary and waiting for a signal to move off again. While there was this lull in proceedings, the instructor decided it was time for a change of driver and asked me to take over. I duly moved from the back seat into the driver's seat and we continued to wait.

A short time later a flat-back truck that was parked immediately in front of us started up, reversed, and went straight into the front of our car, damaging the bonnet and lights. So even though I hadn't actually started the car or turned the wheel, I was now officially the driver and the PVA report was recorded against me. For the next few hours we were off the course, making statements at the local police station.

That aside, the skills I learned on traffic stood me in good stead for the surveillance course, where I was picked out for my driving ability. It's an important part of the skills you need on surveillance; for example, to make ground in an unmarked car, you might have to go through red lights or break speed limits, and as far as members of the public are concerned you're just another idiot driving badly. The bottom line is that if you have an accident, or cause one, you can be charged with driving without due care and attention.

* * *

The main work of the RCS revolved around the use of informants and surveillance. An informant would pass on information to their handler (a police officer) about some organized ongoing criminal activity. If appropriate, an operation would then be set up to follow the suspects at a discreet distance. The aim was either to gather enough evidence to form a strong case at a later date in court, or to catch them in the act of committing the crime.

A surveillance team would usually consist of at least five cars and a motorbike. Surveillance isn't as glamorous as it might sound: there's a lot of waiting around and trying to anticipate what's going to happen, which doesn't suit everyone but it didn't bother me. I think it's fair to say you need to have a certain skill set or particular personality traits to do surveillance or undercover work. You do have to be able to put up with a certain amount of boredom, although if you're on an operation and watching someone's property, it's because you know at some point that someone is going to come out. You also need to be prepared to work unusual hours. You need to be out and ready to go early in the morning, happy to wait until things start moving, and then ready to stay moving with them, however long and however far that may take you, because criminals, by and large, don't have the same routine as you or me. They don't get up at a set time and go off to work; their lives are often more chaotic, less structured. Even when you're working undercover, they may arrange to meet you the next day at a certain time and then just not turn up because they've been out on the beer the night before. Villains aren't going to worry about that – they'll just rearrange – so you have to be able to work with that and adapt to it.

It was the same with targets we were following: they could emerge or move around at any time. We had a really good team in the office and we worked well together. When we had an operation on we would have our target, we'd turn out early in the morning so that we were plotted up – in place and ready – to pick up the target, and then we would wait. I was on the bike, which was a bit of a nightmare in winter. If we knew we were going to be in for a bit of a wait, we'd get to where we needed to be, I'd park the bike up near one of our cars and then jump in the back. I'd be moving around quite a lot between the different teams in the cars, and chatting away about the job or whatever else was happening.

Once we got the message to stand by and it looked like there was going to be some movement, I was back out on the bike, getting everything plugged in and ready to go, and then we would be off. The buzz you get from that standby message, and when you get going, following a target and able to see what they are doing without them knowing you're there: for me, that was brilliant.

There could be some long days involved. When the target moves, you have to be prepared, and everyone in the office would always have an overnight bag because you would never know where you might end up. We once followed a team of burglars from Manchester who eventually attempted to break into an old stately home just outside London; they were all arrested and because of the surveillance evidence they all pleaded guilty; a lot better outcome than having to run a lengthy trial.

It was certainly work hard, play hard; once the job was done, it was everyone into the pub. To be honest, I didn't really like that side of things. I know it was the RCS, so it was a bit like the old Sweeney image – Jack Regan and his mates in the pub – and when they went for a drink it was always in the same pubs, so they were known as police. However, quite often officers would be talking about the job and I always thought that was unprofessional. You could never be sure who else was in there and who might be listening. Once a few beers had gone down, people's guard dropped and their tongues became looser, and they could be talking about things that you really wouldn't want the wrong people to hear.

*   *   *

One particular operation that got the blood pumping – and ended up with a successful result – was against a pair of criminals from Salford suspected of committing robberies on cash-in-transit vans across the north-west. With the usual early morning start, we had information that they were at one of two addresses several miles apart and were about to commit a further offence. The surveillance team split into two, with one at each address to keep a lookout for any sign of the targets. Both teams were in radio contact with each other, and if there were any sightings or movement of the targets, the team furthest away would have to move quickly to get back as a full team to follow them.

The inevitable happened and the pair set off from one of the addresses in a car. This was relayed to the other team who were then listening to the surveillance commentary while heading towards the target location to try to get back in the game. I was with the team at the address from which the suspects moved off, and because there were fewer of us the surveillance had to be a bit more discreet. Whenever anyone is about to commit any kind of major crime, they are looking for one thing: the police.

They made their way into Trafford Park and when they reached Trafford Park Road there was a cash-in-transit van just about to make a delivery to a bank. The target car slowed down as it went past the bank and the van, and they had a good look at it. They drove a bit further and turned left into a side street. The second half of the team had still not arrived, so there was just me on the motorbike and a car with two colleagues, one of whom was now out on foot with an 'eyeball' on the car. It had driven up the side street, turned round and was now parked facing Trafford Park Road, at the side of a pub on the corner of the junction. It came across the radio that the passenger was out of the car and was walking across some wasteland at the back of the pub towards the bank. The driver had remained in the car with the engine running.

My heart was pumping ten to the dozen as I listened to this, but I couldn't see anything so I was totally reliant on the officer on foot to keep us informed of what was happening. It looked like something was going to take place and we were still several team members down. Suddenly the passenger ran at the security guard, grabbed one of the money bags he had just taken from the van and began hot-footing it back to the waiting car. The officer on foot sprang into action and, after a short chase, rugby-tackled the passenger in the middle of the road. The bag dropped and money was all over the road, but his pal round the corner was totally oblivious as he was unable to see what was going on.

My other colleague went to help the rugby-tackling hero subdue his prey, as this robber was now doing his best to escape. There was now the car driver to sort out and only me left. The bike is normally well protected and kept out of the way from prying eyes, but on this occasion needs must. I rode round into the side street and stopped the bike just in front of the car but not close enough to arouse his suspicions, and I made no attempt to look at him. I got off and was looking up and down as if to look for an address, so that to all intents and purposes I could have been a motorcycle courier. As I walked alongside the driver's door I noticed that the window was open so I made my move and asked the driver if he knew what the time was. As he went to answer I grabbed the ignition key, switched the engine off and pulled them out all in one movement.

He suddenly realized what was happening and the old fight-or-flight instinct kicked in; he wanted to do both, but he had to get out of the car first. He pushed the door open and as he got out I grabbed him, identified myself as a police officer and told him he was under arrest for attempted robbery. This made matters worse, and he was even more intent on getting away. I wrestled with him until I eventually got him to the floor, where I basically lay on top of him to keep hold of him. I was sweating like the proverbial pig, dressed in motorcycle leathers and a crash helmet. After what felt like an eternity the rest of the team arrived and normality resumed. These two were later charged and convicted of numerous offences of robbery similar to the one we observed, and received custodial sentences. We were all commended for our actions.

*　*　*

While most of our surveillance operations involved a bit of planning time, the RCS team could also respond to incidents pretty quickly when necessary. I was making my way back to the office on the surveillance bike through Salford one day when I spotted a lad on Lancaster Road who I knew from my days in Lower Kersal and who was a prolific criminal. He caught my attention as he was walking along the road quite naturally and then, all of a sudden, he would disappear up the garden path of a private house, reappearing a short time later. He would then do the same thing again further along the road.

I guessed he didn't have many friends on this road and it soon became apparent that he was looking for an opportunity to break in or steal something. I kept a discreet distance and radioed in to the office to see if anyone was available to turn out and follow him. Within twenty minutes a full surveillance team was there, and we continued to watch his suspicious behaviour which continued unabated as he was totally oblivious to the fact that he was being observed. He eventually made his way to Hope Hospital on Eccles Old Road and went into the nurses' accommodation block. It was impossible for anyone to follow him in on foot as they would have stood out like a sore thumb, so we surrounded the area and exits and waited for him to come out. When he did, he jumped straight onto a passing bus.

While part of the team followed the bus, others went into the nurses' block and soon discovered that he had broken into several private rooms. This was all we needed; we brought the bus to a standstill and he was arrested. In his possession were numerous items taken from the nurses' block. He was charged, convicted and locked up for burglary. I received a commendation for my professionalism and diligent observations.

Chapter Nine

Supergrasses, CID and Exam Successes

It was clear that the RCS could commit time and staff to watch criminals in a way that individual forces couldn't. It's also fair to say that to carry out that surveillance you regularly took your life into your own hands, trying to keep up safely and discreetly with villains. Alongside well-trained surveillance teams, informants were crucial to the work of the RCS. The best cultivator of informants – and the best undercover officer I've ever worked with – was Harry,* who at this time was a detective sergeant in the Bolton office. He later rose to become detective chief inspector and was my boss in the Covert Operations Department. I learned a lot from the man, and have much for which to be grateful to him.

I got on well with Harry from the start. He was a superb guy to work for, very clever and incredibly shrewd in his approach. His jobs were always 'quality', well-planned and meticulously coordinated. As always, the proof of the pudding was in the eating: you only need to look at the success he had and the way he was able to handle informants. One such job that started in the office in 1983 was Operation Belgium. While leads on new jobs were coming into the office all the time, Operation Belgium was rumbling on behind the scenes, run by Harry and strictly on a need-to-know basis. His aim was to get two known armed robbers, Fred Scott and Lenny Pilot, to turn supergrass, inform against each other as well as everyone else, and then take out a whole team of armed robbers across Manchester and the north-west who had been active for years. As a result of his success in doing so, in January 1984, 150 detectives raided 10 homes across the region.

---

* This name has been changed, as Harry continues to work in criminal justice but has given his support to the writing of this book.

Everything about Operation Belgium was kept in-house for fear of the information reaching the wrong ears. It was great for me and a massive learning curve at my stage of service to be able to see at first-hand an operation like this progress from its infancy up to its conclusion on the arrest day, and then the subsequent trials at Lancaster Crown Court. I worked closely with the interview teams who had been selected to get all the information written down in statement form from Scott and Pilot. While this process took place, Scott was housed in the full cell block at Littleborough police station and I used to go for a run with him around Hollingworth Lake on his exercise break (always closely supervised).

When Pilot was giving his statements prior to the arrest day he was in Lancaster prison, and the fact that he had been granted 'supergrass' status was not in the public domain. It was at this point that I got my first taste of being an undercover officer, but in an easy way. I had to drive to Lancaster prison early each morning posing as a private hire taxi driver – complete with all the badges and plates – in order to collect Pilot and a prison officer escort, take him to give his statements and then bring him back at night. Very few at the prison were in on this, and most thought he was being brought out to be interviewed by police for other offences he had committed. This pretence was kept up and worked well, and no one was any the wiser.

Later I travelled in the prison van with Scott on the daily journey to Lancaster Crown Court and then sat in the court while he faced his former criminal partners and gave evidence against them. Some of them thought he would never do it, but when it comes to survival of the fittest, self-preservation kicks in, and when the time came he faced the rest of the gang across the courtroom – no screens or anything – and gave evidence about what they had all been doing. As a result of their actions they both received lesser sentences, new identities and served their time in the special informants' wing of a prison down south.

The operation proved to be very successful, and many of the inner core of the gang received long-term custodial sentences, the longest being fourteen years. To be part of that, being involved in the operation to get as much information as possible out of these two supergrasses, and to be in the inner sanctum, spending time with them on a daily basis and talking to them, was quite something. They say that as an undercover officer you can sometimes develop a form of Stockholm syndrome in which you lose track of reality and of who you are. I've never lost track of who I was, what I was doing or the job I was there to complete. However, I can honestly say that some of the people I met while working as an undercover officer would have been better friends in real life than some police officers because of the type of characters they were. I can see that if I had been a villain, they would have been a good mate. They are human beings, at the end of the day, and while they've chosen a way of life that involves stealing or dealing in whatever they do, they've still got certain traits that can make them a nice person or a person easy to get on with. That's what also adds insult to injury for them when they find out you're not who they think you are, and that sense of hatred is even more intense.

* * *

I became quite adept at surveillance work, and regularly went to Hutton Hall to work on courses as a motorcycle surveillance instructor. This would be on the last week of the course when all the students were being assessed on their ability to do this type of work 'live' out on the road. I loved all aspects of being on the RCS, including the work and the colleagues. I also got the chance while on the squad to attend courses I might not otherwise have had the opportunity to take. These included a pivot peripheral surveillance course, which was all to do with hostage and kidnap situations, and a basic firearms course held at Diggle near Oldham which authorized me to use police handguns.

By 1986 I was again looking ahead, knowing that my three-year secondment was coming up for review. In the January I attended a ten-week CID course held at Wakefield in West Yorkshire. I travelled there each Sunday night and returned home the following Friday evening, and at that time of the year the weather was pretty grim going up the M62 to Yorkshire. The course was for all officers who planned a career in CID, and it went into much more detail on all the main crime offences

– theft, burglary, robbery, deception, murder and manslaughter – to give officers a better working knowledge of them. There were weekly exams which you had to pass, and definitions of offences that you had to learn, some parrot-fashion. They were broken down into 'must knows' and 'need to knows'. I was never one for being stuck inside and would much rather be out and about, but I knew I had to get my head down once again, especially for the big 'shit or bust' exam in Week 10. I was glad when it was over; I passed and went back to the RCS and back to surveillance work.

Later that year it was announced that they were going to form three dedicated drugs units (DDUs) within the north-west: one at Salford, one at Preston and the other at Bebbington on Merseyside. I applied, was interviewed and got the job at the Preston branch, so just as my initial three years were up I got an extra three-year secondment to the DDU in October 1986. From Preston we covered the Lancashire and Cumbria areas, and in the office there were four of us from GMP, two from Cumbria and another four from Lancashire. The offices were set up to counter the growing problem with drug-related offences, from producing to dealing. However, the unit was never as slick or well-organized as the RCS office in Bolton. There seemed to be a lack of quality jobs coming through, and I felt the people in it just weren't as professional as the RCS team. To my mind they were playing at it.

Outside work, my wife and I already had our first child and our second was on the way, so I just wanted to get home after work every day; Preston was a fair way from where we lived. As a result I wasn't one for going to the pub: I had a home life, and I wasn't prepared to run the gauntlet of having a few drinks and then driving home. That means I wasn't a team player when it came to socializing. I had no problem with that, but I'm not sure if others did as I've got no idea what they said about me in the bar. I soon realized the move had been a mistake and I became disillusioned, so whenever I got the chance I would be off to Blackpool or Manchester to work on jobs with the RCS.

It also prompted me, especially after the intense recent CID course, to continue studying. In October 1987 I took and passed the sergeants' promotion exam. At that time the rules were that if you passed the sergeants' exam and you had more than five years' service, you were automatically entered into the inspectors' exam the following April. So, being on a roll, I continued and in April 1988 passed the inspectors' exam too. Once you passed the promotion exams, the next hurdle before you could be promoted was to attend and be successful at a promotion board. This would consist of an Assistant Chief Constable (ACC) and two chief superintendents. On 25 July 1988 I attended a board consisting of ACC G. James, Chief Superintendent Easton and Chief Superintendent Burton. The Regional Coordinator of the RCS had prepared the following report on me:

Constable Rogers is an extremely mature, competent officer with 11 years' service. During his secondment to the No 1 Regional Crime Squad he displayed outstanding enthusiasm in the discharge of his day-to-day duties. In my opinion, Constable Rogers is a natural leader, always keen to accept responsibility. He adopted a professional approach to his duties from the outset and also displayed to his supervisory officers an in-depth knowledge of 'practical policing'.

He found no difficulties in exercising sound judgement in several complicated operational situations. I have no hesitation whatsoever in recommending this officer for immediate promotion. He was a credit to his Force and an officer who I consider, if given the opportunity, will advance rapidly in the service.

D.W. Olsen, Det Chief Superintendent,

Regional Co-Ordinator.

Chapter Ten

A Familiar Face Brings Another Move

By now I had completed two years on the DDU, but having passed the exams and being disillusioned, I asked to return to force early in search of promotion. I went to Farnworth in Bolton to complete a six-month CID course. This is something any officer wishing to go into CID full-time had to successfully complete to see if they had the required skills for this position. Officers normally completed the course in the division or area where they worked in uniform, so you would know all your colleagues and all the local villains. By now I had been away from the force for five years, and being at Farnworth where overall I was unknown made the job that much harder. I didn't enjoy it as the office felt like a bit of a closed shop, and they didn't particularly like outsiders coming in; they didn't know you, so they didn't trust you. Once again I was counting off the days and I was glad when the six months were up. I passed and could move on, but to where?

While working one particular Saturday at Farnworth I bumped into Harry in the canteen. I hadn't seen or spoken to him since leaving the RCS for the DDU in 1986. He was obviously there for other reasons than having something to eat – he was running around like a ferret, with a phone and a radio, and he didn't have time to talk – so it was clear that he was involved in some kind of hush-hush operation. Straight away I was intrigued. I discovered that he was now a detective inspector, and that he was in charge of an undercover unit referred to as Omega. It had been set up to tackle football hooliganism, which was a rapidly escalating problem in the 1980s, and on that Saturday they were heavily involved in Operation Gamma, which was the infiltration of the hooligan element of Bolton Wanderers FC. That operation went on to be a great success, with the arrest and conviction of many so-called fans.

I went home that day knowing this was something I'd like to get involved in. I'd always been interested in undercover policing since working with Harry on the RCS and seeing first-hand the undercover jobs he was involved in. It all seemed more exciting, more challenging and potentially more rewarding than the normal day-to-day policing. Yet how could you apply for something that was once again shrouded in secrecy and operated on a strictly need-to-know basis?

After completing my CID course I was made acting sergeant on the motorcycle wing, this time based at Castle Street in Bolton where I had earlier worked on the RCS. The motorcycle wing was based on the bottom floor of the building and there were still some old RCS colleagues from when I was there. As acting sergeant I was in charge of eight PCs, and we mainly covered Bolton and Bury. One particular day I had been to an accident in Prestwich and had to call in at the old Prestwich police station on Bury New Road. While I was standing in the rear office I bumped into DC Andy*, someone with whom I had worked at Bootle Street, who told me that he now worked on the Omega Unit as one of their technical officers. The Omega 'secret office' was on the entire top floor of this old police station, and you could only go up if invited; but as I was with Andy, who knew I'd worked with Harry on the RCS, he asked me if I wanted to go up and see the team. I could see by the looks on some of the faces up there that they were not best pleased to have me entering their sacred domain, although no one said anything.

I decided to strike while the iron was hot and knocked on Harry's office door. He invited me in and was surprised to see me dressed in uniform, bearing in mind where we had last spoken a few weeks earlier. I had always got on well with him and I believe that he always saw me as someone he could trust to get the job done properly. By this time he had been awarded the Queen's Police Medal (QPM) for his services to policing and undercover work in particular. At that stage it was quite an achievement for someone of his rank to receive the QPM as it was normally only given to senior officers. I admit I was in awe of his award.

---

* We have opted to only use this individual's first name to help conceal their identity.

We chatted and, wearing my heart on my sleeve, I told him I was really interested in undercover work and would love an opportunity to get involved. He said he would put in to see if I could go on the course; everyone who worked on the unit had to complete the deep infiltration course. This wasn't the sort of job that went around on police orders (the usual way that vacancies within forces were advertised), so I knew I would be lucky to get a shot at it. Harry also made it clear that there were no guarantees and that I would have to pass the course; if I failed that, working on the unit wasn't an option.

At this stage I hadn't said anything about a change of career direction to my wife. I don't think she would have fully understood what I was letting myself in for and at that point, I'm not sure I did either. Maybe I was being a bit selfish, but I knew policing was going to be my career and I wanted to enjoy my time in the job and better myself as much as I could. Working as an undercover officer seemed to be one way to do that.

A few months later I was notified that I had a place on the course, and in November 1989 I spent two weeks at Sedgeley Park Training School in Prestwich. The course was residential and was very intensive; you were tested to the hilt, both physically and mentally, to see if you could cope with the demands of undercover police work. I knew I had the right credentials and background to do the job and do it successfully. I passed, and returned to acting sergeant duties but my heart wasn't in it and I couldn't wait to move to Omega.

By February 1990 I had been told I would be transferring to the Omega Unit. The motorcycle wing was now also aware of this, and the powers that be were keen to keep me working on the bikes. They asked me if I thought I was doing the right thing, and offered me a position of acting sergeant at Longsight with the chance of being made up to full sergeant. I had to make the choice between moving up in rank and staying on the bikes, or going to work undercover. I knew I didn't want to follow the norm: I wanted to do something that was different, exciting, challenging, and that not a lot of other officers would or could do. So I suppose it was no surprise that Omega won and I said goodbye to the stripes.

A Familiar Face Brings Another Move

It must seem like I was transferring from one place to another with apparent ease. As I said before, I was never happy to stay in one place: I always had to be on the move, doing something different. I've no regrets about that. Up to the point of me getting all the aggravation that followed, these changes were something I thrived on. I did transfer many times, but those moves were all achieved by applying for positions and courses like everyone else. I sat interviews and exams, and I like to think that I got through totally on merit rather than employing any 'old pals act'. The only occasion on which I had to seek advice was how to get into Omega as those vacancies were never advertised, so I made my approach to Harry. However, he wouldn't have let me in the office purely on any old affiliation to the RCS; I had to work hard and prove I had what it took. If anyone knew whether someone was up to it or not, it was Harry.

Chapter Eleven

Omega and the Not-so-beautiful Game

Having successfully completed the course and the interview process, at the beginning of February 1990 I joined the Omega team as one of only six full-time undercover officers in the force. The office consisted of Harry as detective inspector, an admin sergeant, a covert sergeant, the six covert officers and two technical officers. So groundbreaking was this new police department that Harry's chain of command took him straight up to Assistant Chief Constable Malcolm George, with no one in between.

At the time, hooliganism was a serious problem and GMP knew they had to do something about it. You don't just set up an elite undercover unit, taking officers out of other teams to work on it, with all the funding, man hours and equipment they need, without good reason. Manchester was one of the first forces in the country to invest heavily in undercover officers infiltrating football gangs. The Met Police had been running a similar operation, and when I started having problems a few years later I had the chance to go and work with Merseyside Police to help them set up their own unit, which used GMP as a template. However, it certainly wasn't commonplace, and the Omega approach was pretty cutting-edge at the time.

The fact that we were a full-time undercover unit with officers who concentrated only on undercover work was one of the things that set us apart. The Met's SO10 department – its Covert Operations Group – was responsible for undercover policing across London and further afield, but while they had full-time staff at the group's offices, those working undercover were usually drafted in from other roles, or were volunteers, and only worked on specific cases. So they came in and out of undercover work as they were needed. By comparison, we worked undercover full-time – we were trained to take on that role to the highest level – and we didn't combine it with other policing roles. While we were part of Omega, we only worked on undercover policing. That approach was in large part down to Harry saying 'This is how it's got to be done', rather than him being told how to set it up.

It's fair to say that I was really looking forward to being part of the squad, excited about the prospect of working with Harry again, and relishing the idea of getting involved in some serious cases, but the first operation soon brought me back down to earth.

At this stage the Omega Unit was still focused solely on football hooligans, and by the time I started, the operation targeting the violent element among the Bolton Wanderers fans had come to an end. The team had now moved on to Operation Mars, which concentrated on tackling Manchester United's sizeable and seemingly well-organized hooligan faction. One other officer joined the team on the same day as me, and it was expected that we would both get involved covertly in Operation Mars. However, before any new job, officers going undercover had to go through all the intelligence on the targets of the operation, including every one of their associates, to make sure that we would not be known to any of them. Being recognized – not just as a copper but as someone who clearly isn't the person you're claiming to be – is a risk that you try to mitigate as far as possible (although you can never eliminate it completely). It not only threatens your own personal safety, but potentially jeopardizes the cover of everyone else you are working with on that job, as well as the operation as a whole.

So we sat and went through all the information and pictures that had been gathered so far. As we did, I recognized an associate of one of the main targets as someone I used to go to school with. There was always the possibility that if I happened to bump into him he would recognize me, remember who I was or, even worse, remember that I had joined the police after leaving school. As I said before, there weren't many lads from our area who joined the police, so it could easily have been the sort of detail that would stick in someone's memory.

Straight away, this ruled me out of being deployed covertly on this job. I felt like I'd fallen at the very first hurdle. I had to be utilized on the overt side, which was better than nothing I suppose. So I got stuck into the technical side of the job, filming the hooligans on match days from various observation points. When Manchester United played at home, we used these vantage points to monitor hooligans and gain evidence about their activities, as well as keeping track of our own officers. One position we regularly used gave us a great view across the area surrounding the Grey Parrot, one of the pubs where United fans and hooligans would meet up and drink before the game.

On one particular match day we had two covert officers deployed among the troublemakers. They seemed to be well integrated in the hooligan element, known as the Red Army (along with some of the separate groups within that, such as the Men in Black), and they were drinking with them as usual in the pub and getting ready to head down to the ground. Suddenly the shout went up – 'we're off' – and the thugs started pouring out of the pub. At the front was a bloke called Tony O'Neill, who was known as 'the general'. I'm not sure if that's a name he came up with himself or if it's what they called him, but he's since written a couple of books about his time as a football hooligan. Anyway, he led them off down the road and they kept on coming out of the pub, including our two undercover guys; it was incredible to see the number of people who had actually squeezed in there!

They made their way through the estates towards the ground, and we were following them on camera. Suddenly they all came to a standstill. It was soon clear that they had pointed out our two officers, whose hearts must have dropped. No one ever worked out whether they knew the two guys were police or just suspected it, or if it was something they had said, or they simply didn't trust them. Whatever the reason, they weren't happy, and both men got a real hiding. It was pretty calculated: they didn't do it in the pub; instead they took them out into the middle of an estate, stopped, and then gave them a kicking. Once they'd gathered round them we couldn't see who was doing what, and by the time anyone was able to reach them, everyone pulled away and these two lads were on the floor, having taken a bad beating. Obviously, as well as being a painful and nasty experience, their cover was then completely blown for football jobs.

Having seen something like that happen made me even more alert: I understood exactly what these people were capable of and I knew I should never take them for granted. It also made me realize that I could never be 100 per cent sure that someone wouldn't recognize me, especially with a team like Manchester United. They are one of the biggest and therefore most followed teams in the world, so you had to accept that you could go into a pub anywhere in the country – or abroad – on a match day, and walk into someone who knew you.

* * *

As I started on that February morning, Harry had secured a major new contract from the Football Association (FA): the covert policing of all of England's home and away football matches, including the fast-approaching Italia 90 World Cup tournament, which started in June. This work was normally the domain of the Met, but they had lost the contract with the FA due to 'anomalies' and a fair few raised eyebrows in relation to the credibility of their historical evidence logs. Our successes at club level, combined with the Met's cock-ups, meant that the Omega Unit would now be running the undercover policing of England's football hooligans on the international stage. It also meant that, on my first day in the team, I was told that I would be going to Italy in June for the duration of the tournament, or at least for as long as the England team was still in it.

I spent the next few months working on the overt side and being used on match days to film covertly from obs points. The aim was to get as much video evidence as possible of criminal activity by fans, whether that was fighting each other, attacking the police, smashing windows and damaging property, or generally going on the rampage. June came around quickly, and in the early hours of 9 June I flew out to Sardinia for Italia 90 and the start of Operation Atlas. The date is ingrained in my memory for another reason. It was also the day my mum remarried, following the death of my dad in 1978. I couldn't be in two places at once, and this was not only my first big covert role but also a unique opportunity that I knew I couldn't pass up. The job came first, and I had to tell Mum I couldn't be there in person, but I would be thinking of her. Fortunately, she understood.

The night before I went to Italy I made the decision to shave my head completely and get into the role properly. I had the full Kojak, and one of the bars in Sardinia where we used to go with the England fans gave me a round metal drinks tray with Telly Savalas on it because of my head. It felt strange going through Manchester Airport, but it was a look that I kept for most of my undercover career and it would always attract attention from the authorities. Given that I was either pretending to be a football hooligan or a criminal of some sort, that was no bad thing, but it meant I got my bags checked and was frisked down more than any businessman in a pinstripe suit. It was obvious stereotyping, and in a way I always found it pretty amusing.

There was a lot of focus on football hooliganism generally in the build-up to Italia 90. English fans had a long-established reputation for causing trouble, and at this stage club sides were still banned from playing in Europe. The ban followed on from the Heysel Stadium disaster in Brussels in May 1985 when thirty-nine fans – mostly Italian Juventus supporters – were killed when a wall collapsed as they tried to escape a charge by Liverpool hooligans. The club ban was due to be lifted after the World Cup, so there was plenty of focus on how the English fans would behave and a lot of people were expecting the worst. Previous problems in Stockholm the year before Italia 90 had even prompted the then Prime Minister Margaret Thatcher to urge the FA to consider withdrawing England from the finals. However, when it came to hooliganism, England fans weren't the only concern: the Dutch and West Germans already had a notorious reputation, and others weren't far behind.

In the UK the people involved in football hooliganism came from all walks of life. It's something that's been written about and discussed in depth in the past; particularly the fact that people who, during the week, hold down a normal, respectable job and who wouldn't come across as violent or a thug, then become a totally different animal on match day or around a tournament. It's an accepted fact now, as court cases, documentaries and other coverage have exposed the double lives that some of these hooligans lead, but at the time it was still quite an eye-opener for me.

There's also been plenty of debate about whether the people involved in football violence are actually fans of the team or just fans of fighting. From my experience I think it does start with a love for the club. However, once you're part of that family of supporters and you're going drinking and watching matches with people who feel as passionately about the club as you do, it's very easy to become part of another, more hard-core group and an element of belonging to that group is to go fighting with them. So if you choose to be part of that second, hard-core group, you're choosing the fighting and the violence that comes with it. As a genuine football fan – United, City or any other team – you can stay clear of that violence if you want to.

Having said that, it's not always so simple at international level, partly because of England's reputation for football violence on the global stage. There have been times when I've been abroad with England, and the team I've been with weren't causing trouble but we still ended up on the receiving end.

So it was against this backdrop that I and four other covert officers arrived on Sardinia, England's base for the pool games. Our job was to live and breathe every day with the massed contingent of travelling England fans. A control room was set up on the island, and we had a number to ring with a code name. While we were out and about with genuine fans and hooligans in the bars, every now and then we would check in with the team, update them as to where we were, and give them any information about plans the hooligans might be making or potential targets, which could then help the local police to frustrate or prevent any planned trouble. The team could also pass back any intelligence that might be relevant to what we were doing. The idea was to keep in fairly regular contact; if the team hadn't heard from you for a while they would then start checking around using the name under which you were working to see if anyone had been brought in. In Sardinia, there were only a handful of places they could take you if you were part of a group of arrested fans.

It wasn't too hard to check in without arousing suspicion. You're out and about, particularly if it's a nice sunny day, and you're moving from group to group and bar to bar, so if you're not around for a while, no one has any reason to suspect anything. During the day, in that sort of situation, people are just having a good time – they're on a 'jolly' – and the violence tends to happen on match days.

However, you do have to find a way of drinking, or appearing to drink, without getting drunk. There are always loads of glasses around, so whether you put down a full pint glass and pick up an almost empty one or pour yours away or mix up your drink, whatever you do, you need to keep up with them while staying sober. That's not a problem they have; there were plenty of people who missed matches because, having been drinking all day, they were too bladdered to go anywhere by the time it got to the game. That would suggest again that they were not proper football fans, they were just getting their buzz from the violence. I think anyone who was a real fan, having spent all that time and money following a team abroad, would make sure that they at least made it to the game.

The authorities in Italy went to great lengths to accommodate the travelling fans and actually set up large camp sites complete with bathing facilities. The English fans were top of the league for spending each and every day drinking in the many bars on the sea front and in the back streets of Sardinia. Also one thing that always amazed me was the mentality of football fans at international level. For example, on normal match days at home you might have Manchester United playing Manchester City: before, during and after the game the opposing fans would be at each other's throats. When it came to England, there would be a mix of fans from all over the country that would come together as one, be friends and wage war on whoever the England team was playing.

There were many occasions when trouble flared instantaneously and we had no chance to send any sort of warning to the control room. Equally, there were many times when plans were being made in advance about where they would all meet, what they would all do and what the signal would be to start the trouble. We were able to pass that information on, and help to prevent some of the major disorder that had been seen in other tournaments and at other games.

There were still significant flashpoints involving English fans in Sardinia, although on at least one occasion it was the local Sardinian thugs who were behind the problems. However, some of the most serious World Cup violence involving English fans happened at the resort of Rimini on the Adriatic coast following England's progress from the group stages, when fixtures moved back onto the Italian mainland. One major clash left more than 20 people injured (mostly Italians), as running battles involving up to 400 British hooligans broke out. Local police eventually quelled the outbreak with riot tactics and the use of tear gas, and the following day 246 English supporters were deported.

We were caught up in the middle of those clashes, and when you're in that situation with someone firing tear gas at you, you run just like everyone else. As the rioting took hold, I focused on protecting myself. You instinctively look for a safe position, and I stood still with my back against the wall of a building, alongside a couple of other fans. I thought the danger was coming from behind, but it was difficult to see much in any direction because of all the tear gas. There were rocks and rubble flying through the air, both towards us and back again towards the police. Suddenly the lad next to me went down with blood pouring from his head; he'd been hit by a rock lobbed from somewhere, although it was impossible to work out where.

As the police moved in, we ran again. Eventually they caught us in a pincer movement and made us all lay flat on our backs on a garage forecourt. By now the police had had enough – which was understandable, although some of their tactics and the violent approach they had employed had done little to calm or defuse the situation – and woe betide anyone who tried to get up from the floor. If they saw you trying to stand up, you were in for a battering. If they spotted anyone with a camera or trying to take pictures, they would come round and smash the camera to bits with their baton or the butt of a rifle, but I managed to discreetly keep hold of my camera and take some pictures, which I still have today. It was a terrifying scenario, and all the while I was thinking: 'The team are going to have no idea where we are, so how are they going to get us out of this one?'

I've got no idea what happened to the lad who was hit by a rock, but it underlined once again that however much you plan an operation, you have to be able to adjust to the unexpected and it isn't a game. This was the reality of undercover work, and of football violence. If that rock had hit me, it could have been the end of my career: I could have been blinded or badly hurt. It was much the same when, on a later operation, as part of a raid set up on drug dealers we were targeting, I had my cheek broken while being arrested (more of that later!); again, that could have been much worse. The point is, much as you can take reasonable safety steps, you can't cater for every eventuality.

You have to have complete faith in your welfare unit, and the fact that they are going to get you out okay. We were such a tight unit that I never had any doubts they would always eventually get us out, although what happened with the two lads that match day at Old Trafford brought it home that things can go wrong. I did worry in Rimini though, because when it kicked off and we were being chased through the streets, no welfare or technical officers would have known where we were. They couldn't have kept up with us, so for a while we were on our own, but it didn't take long for them to track us down and get us away from there without arousing suspicion.

I spent a total of four weeks in Italy, up until the England team was knocked out in the semi-finals of Italia 90 by West Germany, leading to those famous scenes of a young Paul Gascoigne in tears. During that time I witnessed and experienced some of the worst outbreaks of premeditated violence I had ever seen. Despite those major but relatively isolated scenes, the operation was deemed to be a significant success, and on my return to the UK, I was commended by GMP Chief Constable James Anderton.

The achievements of the Omega Unit were even attracting media attention. A report in the *Manchester Evening News* from Wednesday, 11 July under the headline 'Secret Soccer Cops Win The Big Match', stated the following:

A team of Manchester undercover soccer cops risked their lives to help defeat English hooligans intent on ruining the World Cup. Posing as yobs, they infiltrated the military-style higher ranks of the thugs in Italy as they made plans to attack rival fans. Several acts of mayhem were averted because the Omega squad men tipped off Italian police. The remarkable success of the small dedicated squad has helped take English soccer back into Europe next season.

* * *

The first six months on the squad had certainly been eventful and, fair to say, a baptism of fire. As well as working on the overt side of Operation Mars, I'd run the gauntlet with the England hooligans, helping to successfully avert more serious violence. I'd also been arrested and mistreated by the Italian police for simply being with the English fan group in the wrong place at the wrong time. They didn't know that we were police officers, so we were treated the same as those causing the trouble because of how we looked: guilty by association. Operation Atlas continued, and over the coming years I travelled to all of England's home games as well as most of the away matches including Spain, Poland, Holland, Turkey, Berlin, Russia and Sweden. We were constantly developing new contacts with fans all over the country, who we would meet up with when travelling with the England team. We also understood how England's reputation for violence – well deserved, historically – could lead to fans who hadn't caused trouble still being arrested and locked up.

One example was a trip to Izmir, Turkey for an England game in May 1991. Once again we were in a bar with the English faithful the night before the match. It was crowded, but it was all good-natured and there was no trouble or fighting of any sort. Next minute, there was a huge crash and glass was going everywhere. Chairs from outside started flying through the windows. Everyone began spilling out onto the street; for me and many others, this was just out of self-preservation and wanting to get away from the trouble, but I know there were others who wanted to fight with whoever had attacked the pub. Just as we came out of the pub and stood there in the street, so the police turned up in very large numbers. Most of the English fans, including me and others from the undercover team, were arrested and carted off to a local Turkish prison.

It soon became clear that it was the Turkish contingent outside who had brought trouble to the bar. They knew that English fans were in there; what they didn't know, and clearly didn't care about, was whether these were just average, everyday fans here for the game or hooligans here for a fight. They simply started throwing tables and chairs in through the windows, and then stood outside drawing their fingers across their throats as the fans started piling out. The police then arrived and made up their own minds about what had gone on. So in this instance it was the Turkish fans who had started trouble and the Turkish fans who had caused all the damage, but it was still the English fans who were arrested. As usual, the newspapers the following day (especially back in the UK) carried stories about English fans rioting and the appalling behaviour of hooligans abroad.

Most people will have their own idea of what a Turkish jail is like; well, the reality is probably worse. The other officers and I in the undercover team, along with most of the England fans from the bar, spent the night in the Turkish jail, which really wasn't part of the plan. It was certainly very different to being arrested and held in this country. About forty of us were crammed into a wrought-iron holding cell; in one corner there was a hole in the ground, which comprised the 'facilities'. It was stifling hot and it stank; a really horrible stench.

It was a long night and pretty horrendous. By this stage we were well integrated into what we were doing, and we were able to adapt to whatever situation arose, but it was still a tough night. We knew there was nothing we could do, except wait it out with all the other fans. In fact, although we knew the welfare team would eventually catch up with us and would have been able to get us out, it was important that we didn't get released earlier or quicker than anyone else, because then people would begin to ask questions. So it was the following morning before fans started being taken out in little groups to go to court.

People were taken in no particular order, so when we were eventually removed from the cell, everyone just assumed it was our turn to go to court and take whatever punishment was coming our way. By this stage the welfare team had spoken to our Turkish counterparts, and we never made it into the courtroom. We were back out with the English fans later in the day, moaning about how much we'd been fined for the damage, just like everyone else.

In the end it worked in our favour, because it gave us more credibility with the fans and the hooligans alike. It became a shared experience, something we could talk about with other people – even targets – when we were at other games. 'Remember what happened to us in Turkey that night?' gives you a lot of cachet with them, and a certain amount of respect. You couldn't talk about it unless you were there, and this lot knew we were there. So despite the genuine fear when the windows started smashing in the bar, the threats from the Turkish fans and the heat and stench of that overcrowded holding cell, there were still positives to be found in such situations.

* * *

The Omega Unit's operations against hooligans from Bolton Wanderers, Manchester United and Manchester City were seen as very successful. Partly on the strength of that, but also because of the mistakes made by the Met, we got the job to do at all the England games, home and away, and that operation was deemed a success too. Nevertheless, the reality is that you are never going to stamp out the problem of football hooliganism; it will never completely go away. If you take one generation out, another one will come up in its place, and when you look at what happened at Euro 2016 in Marseille, it's clear that hooligans from other countries have taken things to a whole new level. There were mixed martial arts guys, athletic blokes with what looked like some military training, and half of them didn't even drink. They seemed ready to kill people.

That's a long way from an organized punch-up at a Saturday afternoon league match.

Chapter Twelve

Expanding Omega: From Achilles to Miracle

Working as an undercover officer in the Omega Unit – as in any other undercover role – had some very specific challenges. For a start, you had to be 'de-policed'. It's no surprise that, having worked for several years as a copper, you pick up ways of speaking, of standing, of walking – in fact, a complete way of behaving – that hooligans or criminals can sniff out pretty quickly as a police background. I can remember one of the guys on a training course who had met someone in a pub and who he genuinely believed was a villain. What he didn't know was that it was a set-up and all part of the training process. Anyway, as the conversation moved on, this 'villain' was offering him some obviously stolen goods at a knockdown price, and the guy was keen to keep the potential target interested so he said: 'Okay, I'll go away and make some enquiries and get back to you.' We all sat there, including the officer, listening back to a recording of this conversation in the pub, and we were all thinking the same thing: that's just not the language a villain would use. What villain would say: 'I'm going to go away and make some enquiries'?

The same guy also had a habit of rocking on his feet a bit. What with the choice of words and the body language, all he was short of to give him away was a uniform! These non-verbal communications (NVCs) might just be small giveaways, but if they are things you've done for a long time, they become habitual; if they're instinctive things, they may show that you're feeling under pressure in a situation that you should be regarding as normal. However, the habits, the NVCs and the language, all put together, are a giveaway, so you need to be 'de-policed'. That becomes even harder if you're spending time socializing with other coppers, or working alongside them between other jobs.

So once you were on the unit, you were effectively taken out of normal policing; we were no longer allowed to go to police stations, we didn't go on police training courses and we couldn't openly socialize with other police officers. For me, that wasn't really a hardship. All you had to do was think about the fact that when you were trying to infiltrate a criminal conspiracy or gang, the last thing you wanted to do was come out with something that spooked them; at best it could make them slightly suspicious of you and the job would never get anywhere, but at worst – depending on the people around you – it could be a potentially fatal mistake. As far as I was concerned the whole de-policing process was a safeguard for myself and the unit, and as an undercover officer I had to stick to these principles to have any chance of succeeding.

We definitely were succeeding. In fact, the football successes prompted the force to rethink its approach to undercover work in general and realize that this particular police tool could be used to much greater advantage. The Omega Unit was originally under the control of uniform operations, but with the decision to expand its remit to take in more serious aspects of crime, Omega became known as the Covert Operations Department and was attached to the force's V Department: CID. As part of that move, Harry also came under a bit more scrutiny. Having previously reported directly to the ACC in charge of uniform operations, he now reported to Detective Chief Superintendent Dave James, my former Inspector in the Cadets and now the head of CID. When it came to undercover work the ACC operations had been guided by Harry; he had no undercover experience himself and didn't need to get involved in the fine detail, so Harry was effectively given carte blanche over undercover operations. While as far as I knew, Detective Chief Superintendent James also had no undercover experience, I got the impression that he was very much in charge of the Covert Operations Department and that Harry would be more closely led by the head of CID.

It was not just the chain of command that would change, though. Working on football hooliganism operations is a totally different thing to going undercover on other crime jobs. The main reason is that most of the time as a football hooligan you're part of a group, a mob;

when you're working on a criminal operation it's much more likely to be on a one-to-one basis. So as part of the Omega Unit, there were five of us working as undercover officers and we were seen as a group of five lads following England, home and away. As a group we made other contacts and 'friendships', people who would travel abroad with us and introduce us to their mates. Also we then built on the shared experiences – like the Turkish prison – so we constantly had things to talk to other fans about. Before long the five of us were part of a much bigger group, all with a bond.

Criminal operations are very different. You usually have details coming in from an informant, who can set up an introduction but the job will then stand or fall on that first contact and how it goes down. Anyone who says they aren't concerned when they're going in to do that is a liar, because you don't know this person, and you don't really know how they're going to act or react. While you may have read quite a bit about them from intelligence reports, that's not always a good thing: there's a danger, when you need things to talk about as you try to build a relationship with a target, that you mention something or draw on some information that you wouldn't normally know.

How you put yourself across on that first meeting can also set the tone for how things will go. As I said earlier, I'm a big believer in NVCs as the signs that give information away, and not just when it comes to being de-policed. For example, if I'm meeting a target and we're about to go off and do something illegal or potentially dangerous, there's a natural tendency to look away from a person rather than maintaining eye contact when talking about things that you feel are instinctively wrong. You need to be aware of that and fight that tendency, keep that eye contact and make them feel at ease with you, or risk giving away NVC clues that would suggest you're not the criminal you're pretending to be. You can't control all NVCs though. The vein pumping in the neck is one. You just have to hope that it's taken for enthusiasm or positive nervous energy rather than any indicator of fear.

* * *

While it was a very different type of undercover work, infiltrating the football gangs had given me a good grounding and I was chosen by Harry to do the first job in the office under our new name. The job was Operation Achilles and was based in the Bolton, Crumpsall and Salford areas. We had information that a team from Bolton was dealing large amounts of the Class B drug amphetamine. I infiltrated a specific area of Bolton where the targets were known to frequent, mainly using a particular pub and gym, and over several months I was able to build up a good rapport and friendship with two of the main targets. I was socializing with them at weekends, and met their friends in Manchester and Liverpool.

Once we had built up a strong enough relationship, I bought 9oz of amphetamine from them and then ordered a further 2 kilos with the promise of buying even more. We had the potential to continue this operation longer and recover even greater amounts of the drug, but the powers that be decided to arrest them with the 2 kilos. On the morning of the deal I met the two targets in Bolton, where they appeared carrying a black bin liner with soil on it; the 2 kilos of amphetamine were inside. They had buried the drugs somewhere safe, just in case the police raided. They then followed me to an office block in Stretford where they believed I was meeting a friend of mine who was a record producer and who was having a party at the weekend, which is why the amphetamine was required. What they didn't know was that there was no record producer, and instead the office block was well stocked with burly police officers who, at a given signal, were going to move in and arrest them with the gear. Like most drug dealers, they were renowned for being a bit unpredictable and it was highly likely they would try anything to escape if cornered.

We arrived in two separate cars, with them following me, and I parked in the office block car park; being ever vigilant, they parked in the service road outside. From the moment they pulled up, they were being discreetly observed from one of the upper floors. As I left my car I indicated to them that I would be back shortly as they didn't want to come in, they just wanted the money. The decision was taken to move in and arrest them at that stage, and when the signal was given the arrest team were quick off the mark, but it still didn't stop the targets attempting to drive off. Drastic action was needed: the windscreen and side windows of their car were smashed, and they were quickly dragged out and arrested. They were later charged, pleaded guilty in court and were given jail sentences.

I was over the moon with the result, and I had enjoyed meeting and outwitting the targets so much that I couldn't wait for the next job. It's an unbelievable feeling. You've been putting all this hard work into it, playing a part, trying to move everything along to a point where it all comes together so that you can strike and get good arrests out of it. You have plenty of ups and downs along the way; you're dealing with villains, so they're not reliable 9-to-5 people. You get meetings arranged where people never show up, often because they've just had a skinful the night before or they're on the ale that day and can't be bothered. That's just how they live their lives; it can be pretty chaotic, and you have to roll with that.

That can be tough though, because while your contact or target just doesn't show up because of a hangover, you've been planning all the details of the meeting, working out all the possible scenarios and trying to ensure you get the sort of evidence that's going to give you the best chance of a conviction. You'll have worked out where you need to place the cameras, what you're going to do about recording the conversation (e.g. whether you're going to wear anything), and what are the contingency plans if something unexpected happens: he might turn up with a different story or say he needs to take you to see someone else.

So with all that going on, when it does come together it's a real adrenaline buzz, maybe as a good as a drug in itself, and I didn't have to wait too long for the next buzz to come along.

*   *   *

A short time later I was given another job, code-named Operation Boulder. The information we had was that the owner of a record stall on the indoor market at Moss Side was supplying large amounts of heroin across Manchester. I was introduced to the first target, a Jamaican guy, at his record stall. The area had been plotted up by police back-up teams and I was only supposed to be going into the market to meet him, and then make arrangements to meet up again. However, things rarely go according to plan, and as an undercover officer you can't be too inflexible or they will see right through you.

We had a chat in the market hall, and it was clear he felt safe about supplying me with a kilo of heroin. He was thinking on his feet; he looked at me, decided I was okay, and just said: 'Come with me.' If I had said no at that point, there was a good chance I would blow the whole job, so I followed him. I assumed we were going to the back of the market, but as we got there he walked out of the rear door and onto Denhill Road, where there were no surveillance teams plotted up and no cameras about. There was a line of cabs parked up, and he clicked his fingers and waved one over: an old Volvo driven by another Caribbean guy. He pulled up and I was told to get in the back.

This wasn't part of the plan. Despite people at various vantage points in and around the front of the market, no one knew what was happening and there were no mobile surveillance teams about as we didn't think we'd need them.

We drove off and headed towards Withington, where it turned out I was about to meet the man with the gear. We pulled up outside a house; a guy came out, got in the car and just said: 'Drive.' This was the dealer, nicknamed 'the Lizard', and if you saw his face you would understand why. Not long after we'd pulled away the Lizard spotted a marked police car behind us, which spooked him slightly and he was into my ribs about who I knew and how I'd got to know them. In my head I started to wonder if he thought the car had something to do with me; after all, I know I'm a copper! While I could think about that for a split second, I couldn't show it. In truth he probably drove around seeing cop cars all day long, and I'm guessing he hated the police, so it was no surprise that he reacted that way when he saw one. However, the reality was, throughout all of this, he was pretty much cool as a cucumber.

We drove around Withington discussing the deal, and agreed that I would buy 19oz of heroin later that day from an address in the Bradford area of Manchester. There were certainly times while we were driving round when, at the back of my mind, I was thinking if it all goes wrong, or they work out I'm a copper, how am I going to get out of here? Yet you have to keep that under control and make sure you don't give away any of those NVCs. Remember, the Lizard is nice and calm. This is his regular environment, so if I was genuinely sorting out a deal with him, why would I be getting stressed? Anyway, he must have been okay with me because we did the deal, dropped the Lizard back at his house, and then the stall owner took me back to the market.

I left him at his stall, walked out the front of the market, made sure I wasn't being followed, then headed back to the car and back to the office for the debrief. It was an interesting session. There were a few people who weren't too keen that I'd disappeared off with the stall holder, but I explained that I couldn't have said no; if we wanted to move the job on, I had to go with him. It was the right result, but I also knew that, if I'd been taken away from the market, given a good hiding and dumped somewhere, the response would have been different. It would have been my mistake for taking that risk, and I would have been seen as a bit of a loose cannon, going off on my own like that.

A lot of people assume that in crime operations, undercover officers are always in contact with back-up, either by wearing a wire or always being watched but, just as with the football work, there are times when you are out on your own. You have to think quickly and adapt to what's going on without blowing your cover. It takes training and perfecting the right skills to do that, but I think it's also down to the type of person you are and your own character traits.

Your team isn't always there to hold your hand, so you have to be comfortable calling the shots and making decisions about the job which balance your own safety with the success of the operation. I was always happy to do that because I knew that for every operation, I'd put as much preparation in as I could, I'd be as professional as I could and I knew what I was doing. Eventually I was to discover that not all senior officers were willing to operate at that level.

Later that day when I got to the address to pick up the heroin – which was the home of the main target's girlfriend – there was a bit of an argument as he wanted to see the money first and I wanted to see the heroin. I was allowed to test a sample of it, which was kept in a pepper pot in a kitchen cupboard. When I say test it I don't mean use it; I put a small sample in a piece of silver foil and then heated it from underneath with a lighter. If it's 'good gear' it will begin to bubble and then run down the foil, but if it's crap it will just burn, go black and stick to the foil.

This was good gear. Another argument then started because I wanted to see all 19oz and he wanted to see the money, which I told him was outside in the car. It was a classic example of how nobody trusts anyone in this game and eventually his girlfriend stepped in. He then made a phone call, and a short time later a woman (who it later transpired was his neighbour and the wife of a Nigerian diplomat) came into the house with a plastic carrier bag. We went into the kitchen and nineteen plastic sachets were emptied onto the kitchen work surface with an ounce of heroin in each one. Satisfied that he had the goods, I went outside, in theory to get the money, but I gave a pre-arranged signal and the strike was on. The target, his girlfriend and the neighbour were all arrested with the gear still on the worktops. Another 3oz were later found at the neighbour's house, which was obviously the target's safe house for his stash.

The two females pleaded guilty and were given three years' imprisonment. The main target pleaded not guilty, so I had to give evidence from behind screens (to protect my identity) at Bolton Crown Court; he was found guilty and sentenced to eight years.

With the conclusion of the operation I received a commendation from the new Chief Constable, David Wilmot:

Constable 'V'2642 Garry Rogers is commended for outstanding Police service in connection with 'His professionalism, bravery and great personal courage shown in infiltrating with criminals involved in serious drug offences, thereby obtaining evidence and intelligence which resulted in three persons being arrested and convicted.'

* * *

By this stage the drugs trade in Moss Side was a major problem and the focus of several individual and team operations for the unit. Operation China was running in the area while I was involved in another solo job. There was an old derelict house in the centre of Moss Side, near Gooch Close, the cul-de-sac that was later redeveloped but had become synonymous with the infamous 'Gooch Close Gang' or 'the Gooch', a criminal gang responsible for drug-dealing and a number of shootings. It was clearly a pretty tough area. The unit had managed to fit a covert camera into the attic of this house, which looked down onto what was known as 'the market square', although this wasn't your usual market. The whole area was controlled by drug dealers, most of whom were of Caribbean heritage. As a member of the public, you wouldn't be able to get in there (and you wouldn't want to) unless you were known, because the nearby roads and alleys were patrolled by young blokes on bikes who were the eyes, ears and security for the dealers. The square was where all the dealing went on.

The operation was able to get a couple of undercover officers into the square as regular buyers, buying heroin and cocaine. Eventually there was enough evidence for a series of arrests, and more than fifty people were charged and convicted of drug-related offences.

However, things moved on again after that success, and dealers started making much greater use of pay-as-you-go mobile phones. So the department launched Operation Miracle, which again used undercover officers playing the part of users who would walk into the Moss Side estates, find a phone box and ring the mobile numbers of drug dealers that had been gathered by intelligence. Sometimes you would get a knock-back; dealers weren't always keen to sell to people who they didn't already know, and they also changed their phones like some people change their socks, so the numbers could be out of date pretty quickly, but the hope was that you would hit on a right number and they would choose to deal to you. They would ask you where you were; the phone box you were using would be covered by a surveillance camera, as would the surrounding area, and the idea was to get the dealer to come themselves or send someone either to the phone box or somewhere nearby and deliver the gear, either heroin or crack cocaine.

That deal would then be filmed and you would try to get another deal, or possibly two, from the same dealer on the same number, all on camera. Later down the line there would be a strike day, all the dealers would be arrested, and the aim was to have enough video footage of each dealer, together with evidence from the undercover officers about each deal, to get them convicted.

It was a dangerous operation, being right in the heart of Moss Side, and it was the first time any force (as far as we knew) had tried anything like this. However, given the level of violence, numbers of shootings and gang fights that were going on in the area, nearly all related to the drugs trade, the potential benefits were seen to outweigh the risks.

One day I was in a phone box on the corner of Great Western Street in Moss Side, just off Princess Road, and there was a camera in a nearby building looking down on the phone box. I tried the numbers but got a knock-back, and as I came out of the phone box a black guy coming past asked me what I was after. I told him I needed some crack, and he said 'Come with me.'

The brief was to get someone to come there, but again, it was another situation where unless you were willing to be flexible, you were going to miss an opportunity to move the job on, so I went with him. We crossed over Princess Road into the heart of the estate opposite. We came across several young lads on pushbikes who were basically the security for the estate, but because I was with this guy I was fine to get past them. We eventually arrived at what looked like a derelict house, and my new mate banged on the door. The fella who answered the door looked like Mr T: big, pumped up and covered in gold chains. It was all very efficient, very quick and I ended up buying crack from him, which meant that I had an 'in' so I could go back there again.

As we were walking away, the guy who had taken me to the dealer asked for some of the crack; that was his payment for getting me in there and for sorting me out with a dealer, but it immediately left me with a dilemma. If I said no, there was no guarantee I was going to get off the estate without a beating or worse. He could have just called some mates over and taken the whole lot off me. Even if I had got away with it, I was likely to be coming back in here as part of an ongoing operation, and the chances of bumping into him again were pretty good, so I might get a less-than-friendly reception in the future. Yet if I gave him some, then technically I would have been dealing a Class A drug as a police officer, and that was one of those lines we were not meant to cross.

I didn't take too long in weighing up my options though, and let him have some of the crack. When I got back to the unit, it wasn't a problem; I knew I could explain it by saying it was the only way to guarantee my own safety and that if I hadn't done it I would have been in much greater danger. I never bumped into the first guy again, but I did go back to the property and score again off Mr T. When it was time to carry out the strikes I was able to identify both the property and the individual, who was well-known as a drug dealer and was convicted along with many others as part of the operation.

Miracle was as dangerous as any other operation – in fact, more dangerous than some others I'd been involved in – and certainly more dangerous than others that had been taken on by the department. Moss Side at the time was an intimidating place to be. Plenty of people had been the victims of shootings: during a five-year period, 27 people had died and 250 people were injured in shootings on the estate, including a lot of innocent bystanders, and that didn't take into account the violent attacks carried out by gangs from the estate in other areas of the city. If this area was tough for the mainly Afro-Caribbean local community, then a white, unknown, undercover cop was potentially an easy target and one mistake away from becoming the latest shooting statistic. So once again it was no surprise when we were put in for an award. As it turned out though, the recognition of the whole team's efforts in this particular job was to become a bone of contention.

Chapter Thirteen

A New Partner, and Rough Justice

I felt like I was now on a bit of a roll. The football work continued to rumble on in the background, and I had a 'legend' – a name and a false CV – which had been my hooligan persona from the start. It didn't usually interfere with our other operations; in fact, later on our undercover characters proved to be a useful background story for our hooligan work. People often think that undercover officers work on one operation at a time, but that's not always the way. For each new job in which I got involved, I'd receive a new legend, a new name and a new CV, which I had to make sure was imprinted on my memory to avoid contradicting myself and arousing any suspicion.

The big rule was that no full name was to be used on more than one operation. It was a rule that was usually strictly adhered to, and when that rule was broken further down the line it became a major problem. However, while you had a different surname and CV, your first name usually stayed the same, so I was always 'Garry' something. I usually had a nickname too; some were taken from kids I'd been at school with, others from people I knew, such as Tony Quinn. For one job I was Quinny, short for Garry Quinn. It's a lot easier to remember one first name (especially if it's your own!) and no one would ever say in the street 'Hello Garry Quinn'; it would always be 'Hello Garry' or 'Hello Quinny', or whatever nickname they knew you by. You did as much as you could to make sure that you never ran into the targets or contacts from one operation while you were in the company of those from another job. Yet you can't control everything, so if you bumped into someone in the street and got a quick hello, if it was the first name that's fine, and if it was a nickname, it's not too hard to explain why different people would know you by different nicknames.

When it comes to managing your identities, everyone has to do what works best for them. I had to go down to London a few times, and I did a job with a contact of Harry's in SO10. He picked me up and we were driving to a pub to meet one of his criminal contacts when he just pulled over at the side of the road. I wasn't sure what was happening, but I was conscious that this was one of the main guys in SO10, so I didn't say anything. He was a big fella, but he put the driver's seat down flat and lay horizontal in the car, without saying a word. He just lay there, for five minutes at least, in silence. Then he sat up, brought the chair back up and said: 'Right, I'm ready now.'

I realized he was just getting his mindset right, making the mental change to become the person he was going to be on this job. I laughed at that at the time – not to him, but to myself – thinking what the hell is that all about? Why would you need to do that? Yet afterwards, looking back, I understood it more. It was what he needed to do to prepare, and it was going to be quite a high-pressure meeting: he was introducing me to his contacts as a villain from Manchester, so there was quite a lot at stake. It's horses for courses: however you deal with it, whatever works for you, that's what you've got to do.

By mid-1991 another freshly-trained undercover officer by the name of Reg* was recruited to the office. He had come from the Drugs Squad and was a natural for this type of work. He settled in well, we became good friends both in and out of the office, and almost immediately we started to work together on jobs. The cover story was that Reg and I were brothers, and it couldn't have been put together better. We looked like we could be related – we both had shaved heads for a start – and we worked together really well. It was also good to be working with a partner, which took the pressure off me as an individual a bit more.

On any undercover job there always has to be someone who 'goes in' first to try to get the job off the ground; only then do they introduce other officers if they're not working on their own. On all but one of the undercover jobs Reg and I completed together, I was the first man in.

---

* This name has been changed to protect the identity of the officer.

That wasn't by choice. If it was decided I was right for the job, I would be given all the information to read and make sure I didn't know anyone involved in the job before a welfare officer would set up a meeting with the informant. However, if I hadn't been the right person for the job – or someone else would be the best to go in first – it would be given to them. That first meeting with an informant was a crucial one, because they were risking a lot; they had to be happy that if they were going to take you into a particular situation or environment, you weren't going to do or say anything that could drop them in it. They needed to know that you were the right person for them to be introducing into that scenario.

If that first meeting went well, I would then sit down with the informant and between us we would work out the best cover story for how we knew each other. We needed to work out how we could have met in the past, where our paths could have crossed, and then why we'd arrived at the point we had at the time. Apart from that, as an undercover officer you wouldn't know anything else about the informant. They would have been an operational contact that was passed on to the unit from other officers, but those officers wouldn't know who I was. So to a large extent you had to take the informant at face value: he (or she) was likely to be a criminal, so their behaviour could be unpredictable, and there was always the risk that they might drop the ball. However, they also had a lot to lose, so you needed to have a bit of faith that they wouldn't lose the plot, and that once you had your back story sorted, things would go smoothly.

If we got on okay, we could then work out a way for him to introduce me to the target and we would take it from there. Once I was established, I could introduce Reg as my brother, and in all but one of the jobs we did, that was the process.

*   *   *

Just before Reg started in the office, we began Operation Forth, which focused on two targets from Manchester who had only recently been released from prison, having been sentenced to eight years for importing drugs. Now they were actively supplying once again in the Greater Manchester area. We had an informant who was well in with them, and who I had met and got on well with. The job needed time spent on it, but I was eventually introduced to and became friends with the two targets. I went out socially with them, met their families and managed to build up a level of trust. Up till this point I had been working the job on my own, but when Reg started it was decided to introduce him as my brother.

We were using premises in the city centre, one of a series of units along the railway arches, just around the corner from the Hacienda club. The cover was that Reg and I had a 'business', and we wanted to turn the unit into a wine bar which we could then use as a front for dealing drugs. I initially bought a kilo of amphetamine from them for £2,500, which they supplied to me at an address in Blackley. Normally they would have been arrested at this point, but the force had agreed – for the first time – to let this money go so that we could place a bigger order, and then arrest them while taking more drugs off the streets. With this in mind I placed another order for 6 kilos, and a large quantity of 'white dove' ecstasy tablets.

The pair had already accepted me without seeing the planned wine bar set up, but when they did visit you could see the greed take over. They were obviously thinking: 'What a place this is, just down the road from the Hacienda, and the guy seems okay; we're going to make a killing!' They met Reg too, and we had a good drink together and got on well. Now they were seeing the potential of this as a regular deal, they really wanted to please us, so they started giving me suggestions about how we could lay out the unit to make the best use of the space as a wine bar, and they were chuffed when I played along and said their ideas were great and were better than what we had been planning.

All of this just underlined how important it was to have a good legend and a solid back story. I could have told them that I was looking to set up a bar in town and I wanted them to supply me, and they may have been in two minds; was I genuine or not? Was I really going to set up a bar, or could I be a time-waster, or worse, a copper…but showing them the unit helped to convince them that I was the real deal. I could have taken them to the pub I was drinking in, where I was known as Garry McAlinden, a villain who liked to dabble in a bit of dealing. Or I could have taken them back to the house I had set up as part of my story, where everything was addressed to Garry McAlinden and as far as the neighbours were concerned, I WAS Garry McAlinden.

That entire back story has to work and fit together, because successful villains might not always be the sharpest and they may sometimes get greedy, but they still won't trust anyone whose story doesn't add up. Putting all that in place doesn't happen overnight as there's a lot to it, but the pay-off – convincing a dealer that you're someone they want to do business with, getting the evidence, then having them nicked and convicted – makes it worth all the effort.

We were on track for that pay-off, although there was still work to be done and plenty of opportunity for things to go wrong, right up to the last minute. Our targets wanted to do the deal in 2-kilo batches, but the force wouldn't allow for any more money to be handed over, so it was decided that they would be arrested on the delivery of the first 2 kilos to our wine bar unit. I said we'd built up a level of trust, but no one in the drug business trusts anyone completely and they were still cautious, even when talking on the phone. I have recordings of conversations between us, which refer to how they were getting on with sorting out 'the big tins and the little tins', as if we were talking about paint we'd ordered for refurbishing the bar. The little tins were actually the ecstasy, while the big tins were the kilos of amphetamine; as far as they were concerned, you never knew who might be listening.

On the morning of the deal, the Drug Squad and arrest teams were all supposedly briefed on what was about to take place, the layout of where it was happening, and just who was involved. The plan was that the targets would arrive with the first 2 kilos and bring it into the bar. When I was satisfied it was all okay I would tell them that I was going to get Reg to bring the money in from the car outside, and once they'd been paid, they would then leave to bring the next batch. They were fine with it being done this way as no one with any sense would have the money on the premises just in case someone tried to rip them off; as I said earlier, no one trusts anyone in this business.

So the targets were totally relaxed in the bar as I casually walked to the front door to bring Reg in. Instead, as I stepped outside I gave the pre-arranged signal for the arrest teams to strike. As soon as I saw them coming I was off up the road, leaving the targets in the premises with the gear and a lot of explaining to do. I should have escaped, disappeared and notched up another successful job, but the plan was about to go a bit awry.

As I ran off, the initial arrest team pulled up in a truck outside the bar and stormed in. I was now well up the road, but there was a back-up arrest team coming towards me, who grabbed me and started a scuffle. I thought they were trying to make it look good so I carried on struggling, thinking they would let me go shortly. Instead, they clearly thought I was one of the targets escaping. What actually happened was that they up-ended me and my face hit the footpath; a searing pain shot through my left cheekbone and I felt a tooth crack on the upper left side of my jaw.

I had steam coming out of my ears as I had tried in vain to escape as planned, but I soon realized what had happened and kept quiet as I was picked up off the floor, handcuffed, told I was under arrest and then placed in the back of a police car. The two main targets were being brought out at the same time and saw me being arrested; fortunately, Reg had no involvement at this stage and was well out of the way as all of this unfolded. I was taken to Bootle Street Police Station in Manchester, booked in, searched, then placed in a cell with the targets further up the cell block, with them shouting to me to 'keep quiet and say nothing'.

My left eye was sore, and I didn't know it at the time but my cheekbone was broken. I was more concerned about the situation I was in and how I was going to get out of there. I knew everything that happened had been observed from a distance by the welfare team as there was an observation point set up to watch the unit, and it was they who had given the arrest call after seeing my signal. I knew it would be just a matter of time before they arrived to get me out. Sure enough, a member of the custody staff came to my cell and I was told I was going for interview, which was mainly for the benefit of the two targets who again shouted out to me as I walked off. Once I was out of sight and earshot of them I was met by a member of my welfare team and left the station.

Because of the concerns over my eye I went straight to Hope Hospital in Salford, where they diagnosed the fracture to my cheekbone. As the hours passed my eye began to swell and was extremely tender, and I reported sick as a result. What had happened was a major embarrassment to the force but in particular to the Drugs Squad whose job this was and who had overall control of the arrest plan. It later transpired that nobody on the briefing that morning had been made aware of what the undercover officers involved actually looked like. After this cock-up it was set in stone that on all future undercover operations such as this, a photograph of the undercover officer or officers would be taken on the morning of the arrest and shown to all officers at any subsequent briefing so that there could be no doubt and to prevent this happening again. Superintendent Broxton of the Drugs Squad was so embarrassed that he visited me at home and gave me a bottle of whisky as a gesture of goodwill.

I was asked if I wanted the matter taken any further, but I just wanted the incident recorded on my personal file in case at some point in the future I had a problem with my eye or my sight and as a result had to leave the job. I was assured this would be done and that was the end of it. I knew the officers concerned were just doing their job and, as they saw it, I was a drugs dealer trying to escape. I was meeting force with force when they grabbed hold of me; the only questionable action on their part was whether the force they used was reasonable in the circumstances, considering there was only one of me and at least four of them.

The two targets were interviewed and both denied any knowledge of the 2 kilos, stating that they were only visiting and that it must belong to the owner of the bar (bearing in mind at this point they didn't know I was a policeman). After committing themselves to this story, they were then told that I was in fact an undercover police officer, which must have been like being hit with a sledgehammer. It completely scuppered their story, and put a totally different emphasis on what they had been doing and just what their involvement had been.

As a result they were both charged with supply; both later pleaded guilty at Manchester Crown Court as the evidence against them was overwhelming. They each received four and a half years' imprisonment. It was a great result and a lot of hard work had gone into it. Not every case runs perfectly; now and again things go wrong as in this case, but everything you do is a massive learning curve and each time I was involved in an operation I would take what I had learned on to the next job.

Chapter Fourteen

The Home Front

It's fair to say that, with the success we were having in both the football hooligan operations and in infiltrating some pretty hardened criminal gangs, the job was going very well. Also I'm the first to admit that I loved doing it: the challenges, having to think on your feet, the difference we could make, even the level of risk. I couldn't think of anything else I'd rather be doing.

There were, however, inevitable down sides, the most obvious of which (although not always apparent to me at the time) was the impact on my family and my personal life. It was not just about being away from home for long periods of time or working unsociable hours, although that was a strain in itself. There were other issues too. For example, there was the way I looked. By now I was 17 stone, had a shaved head and had both ears pierced. I couldn't change that appearance – that was who I needed to be for work – and anyway, the last thing I wanted people to think was that I was a policeman.

Yet everyone is guilty to a certain extent of judging people on their appearance. I'm guilty of it now, when I go and pick my grandchildren up from school. You look around at one or two parents and think blimey, what's happening there, and I suppose that was what was going through people's heads whenever I turned up at my kids' school.

For example, when I went to one of my children's parents' evenings I could see people looking at me warily, and sense that some of the other parents were thinking, 'Don't let our Tommy play with their kids', purely based on the way I looked. I probably didn't help the situation; the vast majority of them wouldn't have known I was a policeman, and I made sure that I cut off from people as much as I could. I didn't want to get into general conversation with anyone who might ask what I did for a living, because then I would have to lie to them. So although my appearance obviously led to assumptions about the sort of person I was, the fact that I looked like a wrong 'un meant that it was also easier to avoid getting into difficult conversations.

It was the same with holidays, and again, my appearance didn't help. Some people just blend into a crowd, but not a 17-stone shaven-headed man with earrings. As Detective Chief Inspector Ken Seddon (remember the name) was to put in a confidential report that I shouldn't have seen: 'Garry is basically once seen, never forgotten.'

My private life, and sometimes wider family life, became very compact, squeezed more and more into a box as I had to be careful where I went or who I was seen with when not at work. There were family weddings locally that I didn't go to because I didn't know if there would be anyone there who was associated with the targets on any of our jobs. Without knowing that for sure, I just couldn't risk going, so I would have to rule myself out. My wife would go with the three kids. Inevitably, people wanted to know why I wasn't there, and then it started to look like I was either rude or just not interested.

She also knew that if we were out together and I suddenly walked off on my own, she was not to follow me as it meant I had probably seen someone from my 'other life' and so couldn't be seen with her. That happened a few times. My background was that I was supposed to be divorced, so why would I be out with someone who seemed to be my wife? However, it meant that I could never really relax; I was always looking around, looking ahead, just in case anyone was about. The jobs in which I was involved would stand or fall with me; if I did something stupid or made a mistake or just got unlucky, I could close down a whole operation.

So in the end it became easier to not do the normal family things, but of course, that took its toll too. I know my wife thought I was just being miserable, and I can't blame her for that as she didn't know the whole story, and I didn't want to tell her the whole story. It was much easier for both of us if she didn't know all the details. Again, it was a difficult situation. I didn't always realize how much it was affecting my family at the time as I was focused on what I was doing in order to stay safe.

It's also amazing what kids hear and see that you don't know they've taken in. When my son was quite young, still at primary school, we could see he wasn't himself, that things weren't right. Eventually we got to see a specialist at the hospital, and they identified that he was worried about someone at home. It was me he was worried about; it turned out that he was getting grief at school from another boy, whose mum had told him that I was an undercover policeman. I've got no idea how she knew, but my son was being questioned about it at school, so my wife had to go round to see the other mum and sort things out.

To this day, my son has never spoken to me about it, but it made me realize the impact my work had on my children. I was a dad who looked the way I did, who would be going out to work or coming home from work at all sorts of hours, who would rarely go to family functions, and who would never talk about what I did at work. They knew I was a policeman, but that they shouldn't tell anyone else I was policeman, and they knew I certainly didn't look like a policeman! Looking back now, I think it put a lot of pressure on them and I know that it was wrong. It was necessary and I don't know how else I could have handled it, but it was wrong. Maybe people who take on that sort of undercover job shouldn't be married with kids...

There was also the issue of having to be in character, with certain behavioural traits, for so much of the time that some of those traits seep into your own personality. It's one thing trying to juggle those various identities at work. Trying to leave them all behind when you come away from work is a different thing altogether. I'm not sure how you do that. I'm not even sure if it's possible, because you can't just switch off from it.

If you're not careful, it's easy for some of the character traits and behaviours of the person you are in a particular operation to start coming out in your personal life. I know my wife felt that happened sometimes with me, and she would soon tell me. It could be that those traits are in you anyway; maybe that's the reason I had a measure of success in playing certain types of characters, because deep down there was a bit of them in me, particularly when I look back to how I was as a kid, and think about how things could have gone very differently.

There were also occasions when I reacted way too aggressively to people; verbally, not physically. I can remember one trip we took to Blackpool as a family and we'd been looking for somewhere to park. We finally found a space on the end of a line of parked cars. We parked up and got out, and as we did this old guy came out and said we shouldn't be parking there. I just flipped. I completely lost it, no one spoke to me, and my wife was disgusted at the way I'd spoken to the old guy. I don't know whether that reaction was just as a result of the pressure of work or because some of the behavioural traits I had to adopt at work were cropping up in my private life. Whatever the reason, it was like someone had just touched a raw nerve.

I know she really struggled to understand that. She felt that I was behaving like a monster, and that was said later: that the force had created a monster and didn't know what to do with it.

Chapter Fifteen

No Stripes, but a Superstitious Killer

By mid-1991 I had been made acting sergeant in charge of the covert officers, so I decided to try getting the rank permanently by attending a further promotion board. Although I'd already passed a board in 1988, I'd knocked back the chance to take up a sergeant's post when the opportunity came to join the undercover unit, and since then they'd moved the goal posts. As I hadn't been promoted yet, my previous successful board counted for nothing and I would have to do it all again. It was the same for all officers who wanted to get promoted, and while I would have to re-sit the promotion board, the passes I achieved in 1987 and 1988 still counted.

I have no idea how much the three senior officers sitting on the board this time around had been told about the type of work I was doing, but probably very little. So I can imagine they were rather surprised to see a 17-stone, shaven-headed, stereotypical Manchester villain (in appearance at least) walk through the door.

The whole system had changed from the board I had attended three years earlier. This time you completed group work with your peers, sorting out an in-tray of paperwork and prioritizing it in order of importance. Then you all sat in a circle and debated a particular policing scenario, all the while being observed for your input and whether you cut across anyone else while they were speaking. I felt like a fish out of water, and wanted to be anywhere other than there. Maybe, through my NVCs, that feeling showed.

I thought I'd done well: I answered everything they threw at me, and I felt I was thoroughly prepared. Yet despite having been good enough to become a sergeant three years earlier, I failed. I felt at the time – and still do today – that the decision of the promotion board was partly down to senior officers judging me on the way I looked. I knew people outside the job were going to make that kind of judgement – and in certain situations, that was exactly what I wanted them to do – but I hadn't expected people inside the job to do the same. I looked the way I did so that I could do the job they asked me to do, and I was doing it as well as I could and as well as anyone else was doing theirs.

To some senior officers though, the whole concept of undercover policing was completely alien. They'd never seen an undercover officer, never met one, and had no idea of how we worked. I could have talked to officers of all ranks then about what we did as part of the unit, the work in which we were involved, and there would have been a look of disbelief on their faces. I think it would be much the same today. There are many officers who go through their service largely doing just one type of policing such as uniform patrol or traffic or CID. I'm not knocking them; what they do is vital, but some of them have a very blinkered view about what policing is and little understanding of how other officers have to do their jobs.

*   *   *

In August 1991 the office was asked to consider the feasibility of infiltrating a gang of travellers in the Ancoats and Cheetham Hill areas of Manchester to try to discover whether one of them had been responsible for the murder of a 63-year-old man. The unit accepted the job, which was the only one where Reg went in first. It was a really difficult job: trying to get accepted by that community is tough, and Reg spent nearly two months working his way into their company, gaining their trust. That meant spending many hours with a particularly vicious group of men. They were involved in some serious violent disturbances in rough pubs around the area, as well as robberies and attempted robberies of innocent people; also the regular threat of violence against anyone they didn't know, for almost any reason.

Reg eventually met the main target, who he found to be a violent, abusive person, particularly after a few drinks. We'd had information that this traveller had killed the man on Princess Road, Moss Side early on New Year's Day 1991. Although Reg had got to know the target, he was struggling to take things further. Harry decided that I would come into the job too; it wasn't about me riding in on a white charger to save the day or anything like that, but sometimes jobs need a fresh impetus. It could easily have been the other way round: I could have gone in first, and then needed Reg to come in and move the job on.

Anyway, I was introduced once again as Reg's brother, and we were going down the same route of being armed robbers. However, this time there was a twist. There had been something on *Crimewatch* about an armed robbery in which the victim had been shot dead. The photofit of the suspects looked quite a bit like us, and the target had got it into his head that we were responsible. When it came up in conversation, we carried that on and let him think that it was me.

That gave him an instant bond with us; when we were out and about in the pubs, he was drawn to us because he believed that, like him, we had killed someone. He started talking to me about the 'angel of death'. 'Every night, when I go to bed, I see the angel of death coming for me,' he explained. 'But when I look at you, I see the angel of death standing beside you too. Me and you are like brothers.' He really believed that as murderers, we were kindred spirits, and as it went on, he clearly thought there was an understanding, a bond of trust between us.

One day he took us to a derelict house and showed me where he had burned all his clothes after he had killed the man. Eventually, he explained how it had happened. His version was that it was New Year's Day morning, he had been out drinking all night, and he was on his way home. He asked a man for a light; the guy, who had also been drinking, told him to 'fuck off' and then – according to our target – went to push him. So he punched the guy in the side of the head; except he had a Phillips screwdriver in his hand at the time. His claim was that it was self-defence and an accident.

Part of the description certainly rang true. We knew that the man had been found collapsed on Princess Road and it was believed that he had suffered a heart attack. It was only at the post-mortem that they found the hole through his ear, into his brain.

I got on really well with the target's girlfriend – nothing more than friendship, but I seemed to be someone she'd talk to – and obviously it helped having someone else onside, as well as relaxing him a bit too. I was in their house once: it was a complete hole, they were living in really rough conditions, and while we were downstairs I could hear the kids crying and screaming in an upstairs bedroom, apparently unfed and in a pretty poor condition. Things like that make the job really hard to do, because you wouldn't be human if you didn't worry about their welfare. However, the priority was getting the evidence we needed to put this man away for murder before he did it again.

The target was eventually arrested, made a full admission, and later at Liverpool Crown Court pleaded guilty to manslaughter and was sentenced to eight years' imprisonment. The fact that he pleaded guilty was a big relief, because the rules around the disclosure of evidence from informants had changed while the operation had been under way and we would have had to risk exposing our informant if we had gone to a full trial.

Both Reg and I were commended by the Chief Constable, Mr Wilmot, for this operation. The commendation read as follows:

Commended for outstanding Police service in connection with his tenacity, determination and courage shown in infiltrating a gang of violent criminals thereby identifying and arresting a man subsequently convicted of manslaughter.

1975 and proud as punch in my new police cadet uniform.

1977 and the newly-appointed police constable at Bruche on my passing-out parade. (Note the white lanyard; this indicated class leader.)

1980. I passed the Advanced Motorcycle Course and transferred to road patrol duties.

My best friend and colleague Tony Quinn's gravestone, which I still visit every year.

1983. Covert surveillance motorcyclist with the elite Regional Crime Squad transcending force boundaries.

Sardinia 1990 World Cup. Living and breathing with the English fans. This team were from Manchester and Mansfield. Note the Manchester banner with 'Beer Monsters' on it. The daily diet and an apt description.

Italia 1990, Sardinia. This was a message daubed on a wall which is what the locals truly felt about the travelling so-called English football fans.

I secretly took this photo while lying on the floor of a garage forecourt after English fans had gone on a rampage and were eventually shut down by tear gas-shooting Carabinieri. If they had seen me they would have smashed my camera to pieces.

The main road prior to the English rampage with the Carabinieri vehicles blocking the road. This is where the fan who was standing next to me during the rampage was hit in the face with a brick.

Euro Championships 1992 Sweden. Living and breathing with some friendly foreign fans in the main square in Malmo.

1992, Operation Forth. My facial injury (broken cheekbone) immediately after my over-zealous arrest by the Drugs Squad when they believed me to be an escaping drug dealer.

Another view of my injury after a trip to hospital and getting cleaned up.

Operation Bluebell: based in Newquay with a flat and car, awaiting importation from Spain.

Merseyside Police — CUSTODY RECORD — STATION COPY

POLICE STATION Admiral St.

Reason for Arrest Susp Possession of a Controlled Drug.

PRISONERS RIGHTS
A notice setting out my rights has been read to me and I have also been provided with a written notice setting out my entitlements while in custody.
Signature Y.
Time 18·20. Date 03·04·92.
Appropriate adult/Interpreter

Time ____ Date ____

Notification of named person
Requested ✓
Not requested ☐
Details of nominated person ____
Time ____ Date ____

I want a Solicitor as soon as practicable.
Signature ____
Time ____ Date ____
Appropriate adult/Interpreter

Time ____ Date ____

I do not want a Solicitor at this time
Signature ____
Time ____ Date ____
Appropriate adult/Interpreter

PROPERTY

Cash		
£50 notes		
£20 notes		
£10 notes	10	00
£5 notes		
£1 notes or coins	4	00
Silver	4	45
Bronze	0	57
Total £	19	02

1. 1 x Belt.
2. 1 x Watch.
3. 1 x Comb.
4. 1 x Bro Necklace
5. 1 x Y.M. card
6. Pair of ...
7. Telecom ...
8. 6 x key's.
9. D/Licence.
10. Brown Leather ...
11. 1 x Pen.
12. 1 x car card
13. P/Papers
14.
15.
16.

Searched by No.
Time 18·10.
Seal No. 001292.
Signature of Detained Person Y.
Signature of Custody Officer Sgt 5903f.

Items retained by Detained Person

UNIQUE NUMBER
YEAR DV SUB — CONSEC. NO
2 12 - - 9 4 8 6

SURNAME Quinn
Mr/Mrs/Miss/Ms
MAIDEN NAME Gary.
FIRST NAMES Gary.

ADDRESS 25a ...
GrumpSall
TEL
Occ/Sch Self Employed
Age D.O.B. 02
Place of Birth
Height Sex M/F

PLACE OF ARREST Lawrence
ARRESTED BY
NAME Clarke
Rank/No. Sgt 6599 STATION

TIME

Arrested at
Arrived at Station 18.03

My detention sheet after being arrested/detained with the main targets of Operation Dorothy and taken to Admiral Street police station on suspicion of possession of a controlled drug.

An indication of my drastic weight loss after the rot set in, tests for cancer and admission to heart care unit at hospital.

Well, try to stop for a moment
And just allow yourself to be
For, it's when the mind is calm
That from troubles we break free.
You'll come to know the strength
That is waiting there for you -
The point of inner wisdom
That will always see you through.
For, you'll realise that times
Come along to everyone
When they think that the clouds
Will never vanish and be gone. *THEY DO*

Yet, by simply being calm
And just by letting go,
You'll allow this inner wisdom
To let the answers flow.
So, may these words that you've read
Help and encourage you
To never think of quitting -
No matter what you do! *IT ALL*

MY CARD SAYS
IT ALL
I ALWAYS PRAY TO YOUR DAD FOR HELP X
HELLO GARRY. AS YOU SEE I AM ALWAYS
THINKING OFF YOU. & THIS CARD JUST
STOOD OUT IN THE SHOP. I WAS DRAWN
TO IT. I THOUGHT MY GARRY COULD DO WITH
THIS. IT HURTS ME TO THINK THE SCUM BAGS
OUT THER. AFTER YOU WORKED SO HARD
BUT NEVER MIND). YOU HAVE A FAMILY WHO
LOVE YOU LOTS, & LOTS I AM HAPPY TO THINK
YOU & STEPHEN ARE OUT OFF IT. BUGGER THEM.
SO PLEASE LOOK AFTER YOURSELF ALWAYS. ★
FAMILY ARE THE BEST LOVE YOU MUM. XXXXX
XXXXX

A card sent to me by my late mum during my troubles with certain senior officers within GMP which clearly shows her anguish and upset for me as she witnessed my deterioration.

D Wilmot Esq QPM DL BSc
Chief Constable

Mr G W Rogers

Our ref:CC/AN
Your ref :

31 December 1998

Dear Garry,

I was delighted to hear that Her Majesty The Queen has awarded you the Queen's Police Medal for Distinguished Service and on behalf of all members of the Greater Manchester Police, might I send sincere congratulations.

I am sure that you and your family will be very proud and rightly so.

Once again, many congratulations and best wishes for 1999.

Sincerely

Chief Constable

Letter received from the late Sir David Wilmot, former chief constable of GMP, upon my eventual award of the Queen's Police Medal.

NORTH WEST REGIONAL CRIME SQUAD

North West Regional Crime Squad
Headquarters
18 Exchange Buildings
Exchange Quay
Salford
Manchester
M5 3EQ

Your Ref:
Our Ref: GN/LRK
Date: 15th November, 1996.

Tel: 0161-848-5050
Fax: 0161-877-6775

JEFATURA SUPERIOR DE POLICIA
PRIMERA REGION POLICIAL
SEGURIDAD CIUDADANA
MADRID

GARRY ROGERS

POLICIA INGLES

CASO DE INTERVENCION CONTACTA:
CON INDICATIVO . . MANZANARES

Dear Mr Marston,

OPERATION 'BLUEBELL' -

JUDGE's COMMENDATION -

DETECTIVE CONSTABLE V2642 G. RODGERS

Operation 'Bluebell' was a protracted enquiry undertaken by the North-West Regional Crime Squad with the assistance of the Covert Operations Section of the Greater Manchester Police, into the importation and distribution of controlled substances in the Greater Manchester area. It was a complicated enquiry and resulted in the arrest of a number of target criminals and successful prosecutions.

At the conclusion of the trial on the 20th August, 1996, Judge Owen, commended the Undercover Officers involved in the case stating that

'the public should be grateful to officers performing duties involving high risks such as these'

Incorporating the Police areas of Cheshire, Cumbria, Greater Manchester, Lancashire, Merseyside & North Wales

Judge Owen's commendation for my work after presiding over the trial of Operation Bluebell and my security pass while working in Spain.

Commendation for working on
Operation Boulder in Moss Side re
supply of heroin.

Certificate of
Chief Constable's
COMMENDATION

CONSTABLE 'V' 2642 GARRY WAYNE ROGERS

is commended for
outstanding Police Service
in connection with

"For his professionalism, bravery and great
personal courage shown in infiltrating with
criminals involved in serious drug offences,
thereby obtaining evidence and intelligence which
resulted in 3 persons being arrested and
convicted".

CHIEF CONSTABLE

Certificate of
Chief Constable's
COMMENDATION

CONSTABLE GARRY W. ROGERS

is commended for
outstanding Police Service
in connection with

"His tenacity, determination and personal
courage shown in infiltrating a team of
known violent criminals who as a result
were later charged and convicted of
serious criminal offences and sentenced
to lengthy terms of imprisonment"

CHIEF CONSTABLE

Commendation for working on
Operation Crocodile in Manchester and
beyond for numerous offences including
'Conspiracy to commit robbery'.

CERTIFICATE OF COMMENDATION

Commendation for Operation Lion working in the Granby Street area of Toxteth regarding the supply of crack cocaine.

Awarded to

Detective Constable Gary W. ROGERS

for

courage and dedication displayed whilst engaged in a highly dangerous situation collecting evidence. This resulted in the conviction of fourteen persons in the Toxteth area involved in dealing crack/cocaine.

Date __18th March, 1996.__ Chief Constable _____

At a private award ceremony receiving commendation from the late Sir David Wilmot.

Mixing with the locals in another pub on another operation with another name.

A stolen Porsche recovered from a lock-up garage in Staffordshire during Operation Crocodile. The targets trusted us enough to let us take it, on a promise to pay later.

A selection of expensive motorcycle leathers stolen by the team of ram-raiders, subject of Operation Vixen, which they brought to me after carrying out the burglary in Preston.

A further selection of expensive motorcycle helmets stolen during the same burglary and recovered with the motorcycle leathers and boots; Operation Vixen.

On tour with English 'footie fans', this time enjoying the delights of Amsterdam.

A day that was a long time coming, with many ups and downs along the way! Me and my wife at Buckingham Palace after receiving the Queen's Police Medal from Prince Charles. The stresses and strains show, but what I didn't know then was that there was more to come.

In full uniform with medals, still proud to have served as a police officer despite the 'back-stabbing' antics of certain members within the higher echelons of Greater Manchester Police and beyond.

NORTH WEST REGIONAL CRIME SQUAD

Chief Constable's Management Committee

COMMENDATION

This is to certify that

CONSTABLE GARRY WAYNE ROGERS

has been commended for

"his professional assistance, commitment and integrity during Operation 'Bluebell', a target operation into the core criminal fraternity in Manchester"

1997

Chairman _____ *Date* 26/2/97
Chief Constable

Commendation from the Regional Crime Squad for Operation Bluebell. This was the operation where the main targets were put on remand at Strangeways prison together with the targets from Operation Vixen, which then compromised my and my family's safety but with little concern from GMP.

CHIEF CONSTABLE'S CITATION OF MERIT

CONSTABLE GARRY WAYNE ROGERS

is commended for
outstanding police service
in connection with

**"the professionalism, commitment and dedication he
displayed during Operation Miracle"**

1997

CHIEF CONSTABLE

Commendation from Sir David Wilmot which had questionably initially been held back and classed
'Worthy of Nothing' by the head of the CID. Reinstated as being 'Worthy' five years later.

Chapter Sixteen

Don't Mention the Masons

At this point it's probably necessary to explain the attitude towards Freemasonry in policing at the time. The reality was that, among the lower ranks at least, it was common knowledge – and expected – that senior officers would be members of a Masonic Lodge. You then became more aware of other officers around you, at your own rank or below, who were also Masons.

As a serving cop, the main concern was that there were clearly officers gaining promotion who didn't seem to have the skills or experience necessary to do the job they were taking on. This meant that the question on everybody's lips would be how did someone who most people inside the job regarded as ineffective, incapable or simply a waste of space become a senior officer? Inevitably, a lot of people felt that in many cases (although not all), it was down to the funny handshakes and rolled-up trouser legs of the Masons.

That may in part be down to the way the promotion system works in the police service. Each promotion board would be made up of three senior officers; how you performed at the board would then determine whether you were ready to take up your promotion as and when the right opportunity arose. The particular concern about Masonic influence over appointments and promotions was that, if you can imagine a scenario where someone sitting their sergeant's or inspector's board was in the local Lodge and one (or maybe more) of the senior officers on the board were members of the same Lodge, what are the chances that they would treat a fellow Mason more favourably than other candidates?

It was no surprise then that a lot of officers viewed joining the Masons as a way to get on, but it didn't appeal to me. I'd previously been asked if I'd like to go to a Masonic night with my wife by an officer

I worked with in uniform. He'd already been invited to a Masonic do by a neighbour of his and had become a member of the Lodge in Bolton; now he was inviting me and my wife along to another evening event. To be honest, it really wasn't for me; I just didn't like the atmosphere or the attitude of a lot of the people there, and in the end we left early and went home.

* * *

It's also important to understand the wider concerns over the influence that Freemasonry had on policing in the 1980s and '90s. There was a backdrop of accusations and allegations of police corruption often linked to Freemasonry, the most high-profile of which stemmed from the investigations by *The Times* and *Sunday Times* newspapers into the Metropolitan Police CID units such as the Obscene Publications Squad. Operation Countryman, the subsequent external inquiry into corruption of policing in London, again led to further accusations over Masonic influences in policing, as the lengthy investigation led to just two prosecutions.

At this point the concerns over Masonic influence were not just centred on the police – there were suggestions that the wider legal system, local government, finance and other areas were also affected – and were not just confined to London. The publication of two books in the 1980s – *The Brotherhood* by Stephen Knight in 1983 and *Inside the Brotherhood* by Martin Short in 1989 – kept the issue of Freemasonry high in the public consciousness. In between those two volumes, the so-called 'Stalker affair' had spent many days dominating the news agendas.

John Stalker was the Deputy Chief Constable of GMP and had a lengthy career in CID; as a young detective sergeant he had investigated the Moors Murderers and in 1978, at the age of 38, he became the youngest detective chief superintendent in the country, heading up Warwickshire Police CID. Mr Stalker rose to public prominence after he was appointed to lead an inquiry in 1984 into an alleged 'shoot to kill' policy implemented by the Royal Ulster Constabulary (RUC) in relation to suspected members of the Provisional IRA. He was removed from the inquiry amid controversial circumstances two years later, just as he was about to make his final report. Mr Stalker had been accused of associating with criminals, something he strongly denied and for which there seemed little if any evidence. He was cleared of all allegations following an investigation by West Yorkshire Police, after apparently strenuous efforts by their senior investigating team to find him guilty of some wrongdoing. Despite being completely cleared, John Stalker was not reinstated as head of the inquiry; that job went to Colin Sampson, Chief Constable of West Yorkshire Police, the man who had led the investigation into the allegations! The findings of the inquiry were never made public.

At the time there was intense speculation in the national media that Mr Stalker had been the victim of false accusations and a smear campaign orchestrated by Masons in GMP and the RUC. Such was the level of interest that the Masonic Order of the North-West called a press conference to publicly deny any involvement in the Stalker affair.

Writing in his autobiography *Stalker*, published in 1988, Mr Stalker said he simply didn't know whether there were any Masonic links in relation to his own treatment, adding: 'I am not a Freemason, but I know many good and efficient policemen who are.' However, he also revealed a conversation he had on his return to work in the force with Detective Chief Superintendent Peter Topping, effectively the operational head of the CID in GMP at the time:

I asked him whether the press reports were true, that since his appointment to the CID, the Drugs Squad and the Fraud Squad had all come to be members of Masonic Lodges. I made it clear that I was not being critical; I merely wished to know. He said: 'They are all there on ability. I emphatically deny any wrongful influences.' I said to him that I was not suggesting there were any, but that some people might see it as unhealthy. He said: 'I would welcome any scrutiny of their activities. I choose people on their ability – nothing else – and I resent any inference that I do not.'

I asked him whether he would always exercise a preference for a fellow Mason, all other things being equal. Topping replied: 'Yes, I would and I do: and I see nothing wrong with that. In sensitive departments I need to know I can trust my officers. The ones I have chosen are all there on personal merit. I know without doubt I can trust them; others I only think I can trust.'

So that was the approach from the senior officer in GMP's CID in the late 1980s: that while all members of the team were chosen because of their ability, they were also all members of the Masons and that when it came down to an officer's word, Detective Chief Superintendent Topping would always take the word of an officer who was a Mason over one who wasn't, because he knew he could trust a fellow Mason ...

* * *

By the early 1990s the situation was starting to change, in part due to the fallout from the books by Stephen Knight and Martin Short. The focus on Masonry and corruption in the Met Police had prompted successive commissioners to advise against officers becoming Freemasons, although with varying levels of success. When Sir Kenneth Newman suggested in 1982 that officers 'forego the prospect of pleasure and social advantage in Freemasonry', the response from some was to set up a new Lodge, the Manor of St James. Several years later his successor, Sir Peter Imbert, made it clear that it would be best for public perception – and promotion prospects – if senior officers relinquished their membership.

The Home Affairs Committee inquiry into Freemasonry in the Police and Judiciary, which took place in 1996 and reported in 1997, underlined some of the public concerns most explicitly. Freemasonry as an organization co-operated with the inquiry, and while MPs found that there was plenty of 'unjustified paranoia' about the level of secrecy and influence held by Masons in the police and across the judicial system, there was significant and understandable concern among the public about the potential for abuses of power. The committee recommended that police officers, magistrates, judges and crown prosecutors should be required to register membership of the Freemasons (and any other secret society), stating:

> ... nothing so much undermines public confidence in public institutions as the knowledge that some public servants are members of a secret society, one of whose aims is mutual self-advancement – or a column of mutual support, to use the Masonic phrase. We note the claim by United Grand Lodge that Freemasons are not a secret society but a society with secrets. We believe, however, that this distinction is lost on most non-Masons.

However, there seemed little appetite for making it compulsory for all members of the police and judiciary to register Masonic membership. While new judges and magistrates were initially required to declare whether they were a Mason, that requirement was dropped altogether in 2009 after a similar compulsory register introduced in Italy had been declared unlawful by the European Court of Human Rights.

* * *

Despite the books and the media interest (the inquiry was still some years away), at this stage of my career the whole Masonic thing didn't really bother me because it wasn't affecting me. I was working on units or in jobs that I really enjoyed, and I'd been able to get transfers or new posts without being a Mason. Obviously I could see the injustice of someone being promoted apparently because of their Masonic membership as much as anything else, and there were plenty of stories going around about who was or wasn't 'on the Square'. Yet I suppose I was a bit blinkered and naïve: up to this point, as far as I knew, those sort of decisions or injustices hadn't directly had an impact on me.

Bearing in mind what was to happen later in my career, it's also worth pointing out that I didn't hate Masons, and in fact I still don't. I can see why people in some walks of life would want to join. For example, a neighbour of mine who had his own business was a Freemason and I imagine it was a great way for him to network, make contacts and build up that business.

However, I just don't think there's any place for it in policing. There's always going to be a conflict of interest: whether you're treating someone favourably inside the police or treating criminals differently because they're in the Lodge, it can't be right. There have been plenty of examples where that conflict of interest has proven to be a problem, from gangster-turned-murderer Kenneth Noye's ability to rub shoulders with senior police officers as a leading member of the Hammersmith Lodge in London to allegations of Masonic influence in the cover-up following the Hillsborough disaster.

It's also important to realize that, because of my general indifference towards Freemasonry at the time, my perception and understanding of how it eventually affected my own career is all with the benefit of hindsight.

Chapter Seventeen

From Strength to Strength: Dorothy and Malmo

The operations continued to come in, and the office went from strength to strength, especially under Harry's leadership. I was determined to learn as much as I could from him, so as to improve my own way of working in this specialized field of policing. There still weren't that many undercover police officers in the UK, but every year, those of us who were in the job had the chance to meet at an annual conference where we could share and exchange experiences. As far as I was concerned it was also one of the few opportunities where you could relax and enjoy the social scene with other officers doing the same job.

The event included guest speakers, and when I attended in 1992 it was Joe Pistone, alias Donnie Brasco. This was the famous FBI agent who infiltrated the New York Mafia for six years and whose work led to multiple arrests and convictions which sent shock waves through the Mafia, so much so that they took out a contract on his life. A film of his story was later released with Johnny Depp playing the part of Donnie Brasco. I got to meet Joe personally and had a good chat with him; he even signed my *Donnie Brasco* book. It was a pleasure and a privilege to meet him and to listen to what he had to say.

By this stage, GMP had really pushed ahead of a lot of the other forces in forming a dedicated undercover unit. As I mentioned before, the Met had SO10, but while the staff focused solely on undercover work, most of the officers came in and out of undercover operations as required. However, as we only took on undercover operations as a unit, we were effectively taken out of the regular police force. We all liked to think our unit was the best, but I can say with some confidence that GMP's Covert Operations Department was leading the way.

Also while there was some sharing going on at the conference, generally it was natural for me and other officers in the department to play our cards pretty close to our chest, even when dealing with other police forces. I'd previously been invited down to London on an operation, and the SO10 team was full of questions about how we did things and what we were up to. Harry had already briefed me to 'tell them nothing', so I duly answered all their questions without giving them any information at all. The next day, while still with the London team, I was handed the phone by one of their senior officers. On the other end was ACC George from GMP, wanting to know why I hadn't been more co-operative with our London counterparts. As far as he was concerned, if they wanted to know something, I should tell them…

However, he had no undercover experience, and I was more than happy to go along with Harry's philosophy. If I needed a reminder that confidential information should remain so, it came in the shape of Operation Dorothy.

* * *

Such was the success of the Covert Operations Department that outside forces now approached GMP with operations that they wanted us to take on. Operation Dorothy was one such job, instigated by Merseyside Police. It focused on the owner of a café in the Wavertree district of Liverpool; the information we had was that he was heavily involved in the supply of heroin and ecstasy across Merseyside. His business was immediately opposite Wavertree Police Station, and above the ground-floor café were several floors where he also provided accommodation, with many of the tenants receiving DHSS payments.

I was introduced to the main target and built up a good rapport with him. Once again, I was the first undercover officer to go in and I later introduced Reg as my brother. The target believed I was a villain from Salford who ran, among other things, an amusements business, and that I could get him the latest arcade machines for his café. He placed an order for some machines, and then we got round to what he could supply in relation to his drug empire. We were able to agree a deal for a large amount of ecstasy and an initial 10oz of heroin, and sorted out a time and date for the deal to take place.

When the day for the deal arrived, Reg and I turned up at the café in my supposed works truck and parked outside. We knew that a few hours earlier, several technical officers had entered Wavertree Police Station with the authority to set up an observation point within the lost property store, which faced the café. It had a brick wall with no windows, and they had to drill through the brick in order to install a camera to record everything that went on for future evidence. This was all done on a need-to-know basis, so as to keep what was going on a close secret. Unfortunately it's been known for some police officers to be in the pocket of villains – that applies throughout the country, not just on Merseyside – and the fewer people who knew about the operation the better.

The tech guys had set up hours before we arrived, and we were on film from the moment we pulled up. An interesting point that emerged when the surveillance footage was checked later was that the target and his team clearly had their own surveillance unit too. You could see certain individuals walking up and down the road from the moment we arrived, looking for anything untoward that might spook them or give them cause to stop the deal in its tracks. They could have been checking us out further, looking for any sign of the police, or just be worried that we might try to rip them off. At the end of the day, this was a business, and their approach highlighted how professional their criminality was. Nobody wanted to end up in prison.

As we walked into the café the target was there, perfectly relaxed, and we all sat down and had a brew. He made the call to get the gear brought over to the café, as naturally he didn't have it in the building just in case. We also made it clear that we were concerned about the cash we supposedly had stashed in the truck (if this was for real, they might try stealing our money), so respect was required on both sides. A short time later the target's phone rang and he had a brief conversation. As he put it down he had a worried look on his face and said to us: 'I have just had a call and been told that the police have a camera trained on my café from over the road as we speak.'

I was gobsmacked, and if ever I needed a change of Pampers, it was now. I was expecting him to say: 'And I know who you are. Now get the fuck out of here!' While that was going through my head, I also knew that it was important I didn't show it. The target's reaction is always going to be natural. He's just being himself, it's his environment, and whether he's cool and calm or a nervous sort of guy or someone prone to going into a rage, that's just the way he is. Reg and I had to carry on playing the role that we were in and, to a large extent, bluffing our way through it. I also knew what he was saying was true. However, he added that it wasn't a problem: he'd sent the gear back and he would ring me in half an hour to sort out a different location for the deal.

To say I was relieved would be an understatement. I knew in that split second that we were okay, that he wasn't overly concerned because the police were always watching him. More importantly, it also meant that whoever had made the call about the camera wasn't sufficiently in the know to be aware that Reg and I were police officers, although it did mean it was highly likely that someone at the police station was working for our target.

It then gave us another opening. I reacted by getting wound up, asking what the hell was going on and wanting to know what the police were watching him for: was he setting us up? Straight away he told us to calm down, that everything was okay, we'd just meet up somewhere else. Having navigated our way through a difficult few minutes, Reg and I exited stage left and, true to his word, the target contacted me a short time later. We arranged to meet and deal at the Rocket pub at the end of the M62. We made our way there and they arrived as promised; as the deal was going down we were all arrested and I was taken to Admiral Street police station where we were detained, searched and then held for questioning as the local police once again didn't know who we were. The welfare side of the office promptly did their job and we were released and free to go.

When the phone records from the police station were checked later, it was clear that a call to the café had been made, although it wasn't possible to say by whom. I wasn't overly surprised to find out that someone in the station – either an officer or a member of staff – was corrupt. Having worked on the RCS I'd heard plenty of stories going about regarding bent police officers, so I knew this sort of thing went on. It just underlined again why Harry was keen to keep everything tight, not to talk about the work we were doing, and only give people information if and when they needed to have it. There were those in the force, including some in CID, who thought we were being dramatic about it, coming out with all the 'secret squirrel' stuff and having a laugh. Yet I would have paid good money to watch them in that situation, having to react to whatever comes up and knowing that your safety – and potentially your life – could be on the line.

The target and another male both pleaded not guilty and appeared before Judge Wickham (known locally as 'whack 'em Wickham'), where once again I had to give my evidence from behind a screen. Both men were found guilty, and the target was sentenced to eight years' imprisonment.

For this success, Reg and I received the following commendation from Merseyside's Chief Constable Sir James Sharples:

For courage and determination whilst working in conditions of extreme danger when he, with another officer infiltrated a team of known criminals who were actively supplying controlled drugs throughout Merseyside, and who were later sentenced to lengthy terms of imprisonment.

The officer was also commended at the trial by His Honour Judge Wickham at Liverpool Crown Court.

* * *

By mid-1992 it was time for the European Championships and another job targeting the hooligans following the England football team, this time in Sweden. As usual, Reg and I, and the rest of the team, would be living and breathing with the rabble that were there solely for trouble. By now we had built up a good network and were known by many other travelling fans, which made life a bit easier but there was still the unpredictable behaviour of some that you could never account for, so you had to have eyes in the back of your head.

Our brief was the same as in Italy, with a control room, a telephone number to ring with a code, and then the chance to relay any important information or intelligence that could help to avoid or crack down on any planned trouble. The Swedish authorities, like the Italians before them, had done a fantastic job and had set up refreshment tents and entertainment for all in the main square at Malmo. The English fans, in the sun and heat of Sweden, would start drinking early, especially with the many beer tents situated all around the square, and it was soon obvious that it wouldn't be long before there was trouble.

The English fans proceeded to throw the hospitality of the Swedes back in their faces as they went on the rampage through the main shopping street, smashing windows and looting goods. I saw an ITV news cameraman attacked, his really expensive camera pulled off his shoulder and smashed to pieces on the road; there was nothing he could do but watch. We were able to identify those idiots and they were arrested, charged and locked up, but it underlined for me once again that the so-called fans we were mixing with were morons, complete animals. They had been provided with everything they could want – places to stay, places to eat and drink, entertainment – but all they wanted to do was fight and destroy things.

We were able to make a difference though. On one occasion, everyone was having a good time in the square when the word went round that they were going to have another 'do' with the authorities and opposing fans. The plan was that a couple of English fans would quickly get up onto the roof of the largest beer tent, and when the authorities made a move to get them down, this would be the signal for everyone to kick off and cause mayhem. We were able to get this information back to the control room, and the decision was made to leave them up there and send nobody in to get them down. When they made their move and began bouncing up and down on the beer tent roof, they were totally perplexed as to why no one wanted to get them down. To say the hooligans were deflated was an understatement; the idiots were left up on the tent, bouncing themselves to death, and nothing happened.

You only needed one thing like that to set off a whole night of trouble, so even something as small as that shows the benefit of having intelligence coming in from the ground. It was an example of why what we were doing was so important. When it came to football hooliganism, we knew we were never going to win the war and end it completely, but if we kept getting little victories, preventing as much violence as possible and locking up the ringleaders, we knew we were making a difference.

Quite often, you could see that there were just a few ringleaders, with a much larger group of idiots ready to follow them. The real problem was that for a lot of them, that group of idiots became like a family. It was the same at club level. However, as I've said before, these people came from all walks of life. Nowadays people would want to look at their backgrounds, their home lives, and try to work out why they were so focused on violence. Did they have a tough upbringing? Were they short of education or opportunities? In reality, though, they came from all sorts of backgrounds. Yes, some had a tough time and grew up in poor working-class communities, but there were plenty of others who had decent jobs, came from solid middle-class backgrounds, but who just seemed to enjoy the violence. When you're among a group of people like that, you can't help but think they are idiots.

Steve, our 'favourite' London fan, was a classic example. He was a postman, and used to fund his trips away by nicking credit cards and cash from the mail. He'd split up from his wife, left her with the kids and all the responsibilities, and fighting at the football – either with Tottenham or with England – was now the big thing in his life. He would have a skinful of ale, go to the game and have his back to the pitch for most of the ninety minutes, jabbering away and sorting out meet-ups and fights. All I could think was that he was a moron. I wasn't interested in the root causes or what made him the person he was; when it came to the football, he just behaved like an animal.

While we were working on the England football jobs, I never really felt like we were in danger of being identified or exposed as undercover officers, although, as I knew from what happened to the guys back in Manchester near the Grey Parrot, it was a constant possibility. I've always been able to scan crowds for faces, to spot them before they spot me, and it's something I still do today, but I'd never been in the situation on a football operation where I thought someone could have recognized me as a copper. I was also fortunate that, having been on the RCS, I'd spent a lot of time away from the usual uniform and CID operations before I joined the unit, so people were unlikely to have come across me in their day-to-day dealings with the police. I'd also been working a fair distance from the local area in which I was now based. So any worries about being recognized became less and less as the football jobs went on, and our credibility, networks and back story all developed.

Covering all the England matches with Reg worked out well too, because we were able to use the cover we had on other operations, as brothers who were villains. As far as anyone else was concerned, we were football hooligans who funded our lifestyle from crime. We just had to make sure we remembered all the stories!

As usual, though, operations like this had an impact on my family back home. They would have seen all the trouble that was happening in Sweden on the telly and my wife would have known that I was out there in the middle of it, but it was pretty hard to keep in touch on a regular basis. We were often out all day with groups of 'supporters', and we didn't know when we were going to be able to make a call. The priority also had to be ringing the control room to update them with any intelligence.

Sometimes I think it was probably a good thing that I couldn't get in touch with the family. For example, letting them know that I'd been in prison for the night or that I'd spent another day in the centre of rioting fans wasn't going to ease their worries. Looking back, I know it must have been tough on my wife especially, having to look after the kids on her own while not knowing what was happening to me. Fortunately, the two weeks in Sweden came and went pretty quickly, and it wasn't long before I was back at home, heading into the office where yet another operation was waiting.

Chapter Eighteen

Crocodile, Lion, and Reg Goes On to the Welfare

Not all operations were triggered by an informant or as a result of targeted intelligence. Occasionally, our work in tackling one type of crime or a certain gang would reveal another target to go after, and Operation Crocodile was one such initiative. The operation was completely self-generated as a result of our work in Middleton on another matter. We were originally there to look into the protection rackets that were rife all over the Greater Manchester area, in particular involving security staff on the doors of pubs and clubs, and Middleton had a significant problem. I moved into an address in the area and was drinking and socializing around the town. It was decided that Reg and I would, among other things, run a stall on the local market selling second-hand goods. Although everything had been purchased or acquired legitimately, much of it could appear to the outside world to have been stolen, which enhanced our criminal credibility.

Thanks to our frequent appearances at the market we soon started talking to other regulars and friendships grew. One in particular was with a local brother and sister who were selling all manner of top-quality power tools. They took Reg and me at face value, assuming we were operating on the same side of the law as them – i.e. the wrong side – and we were soon socializing in the Middleton, Manchester and Salford areas. It was not long before the guy was discussing all manner of villainy he was involved in, and confirming that most of the power tools on their stall were from burglaries. He introduced me to one of his brothers who worked as a security guard on a building site at North Manchester General Hospital, explaining that when his brother was on nights he would let him into the grounds to steal whatever he could take.

On one occasion he offered us a large industrial drill that he had stolen from the site. He let us take it with an agreement to pay for it later (when we checked it was identified as stolen from the site). He also claimed to have a Porsche car that he and his mate had stolen and had stored in a lock-up garage in Staffordshire. This latest bit of information prompted the office to focus on this as a job that had evolved rather than being pre-planned, and we were soon on our way to Staffordshire to take a look at the car. When we got there we were introduced to his mate in a local pub, and then went to the lock-up garage where, sure enough, a bright red Porsche was parked. His mate had a set of false number plates which they fitted in the dark, while our man off the market put in a new battery. We soon had the car started and out of the garage.

We agreed a price for it and, such was the level of trust, they let us take it back to Manchester and pay later; that was a good thing, as GMP wouldn't agree to let any money go for its purchase. It would also have been the wrong time to make an arrest as there had been further discussions about much bigger jobs than the car, so it was decided by the department to let it run, which meant that not having to pay for the car straight away worked out well for us. As we were driving back in convoy at night on the motorway we realized that they had fitted the number plates the wrong way round, with the white one on the rear and the yellow one on the front. If a sharp-eyed traffic officer had spotted them we could have had some explaining to do back at a police station, but we managed to get the car back in one piece and then stored it in our own lock-up.

We met our man the next day and told him we had a possible buyer for the car. It was at this point that he mentioned he was planning to rob the owner of a jeweller's shop in Eccles and asked if we would be interested. Obviously we were, but not for the same reasons as him. He said he was going to do the job with a mate of his from Salford who was from a well-known Irish family and well-connected in the criminal fraternity. A meet was arranged in a local pub on Rochdale

Road in Harpurhey where we talked to his mate; the robbery was duly discussed and we were recruited as the heavies.

Their information was that when the jeweller arrived each day at his shop, he always had up to £50,000 worth of jewellery hidden in the lining of his coat. The plan was to grab him first thing, throw him into the back of a van, tie him up and then take him onto the moors to find out just what he had on him and where he kept the rest of his money. Our man's Irish friend apparently knew the jeweller well, so his information was supposedly 100 per cent, although he couldn't take part in case he was recognized.

Some days later we all met up at the back of the pub on Rochdale Road and went to Eccles where the shop was pointed out. Our man, who had been to an all-night party and was still out of his head on some substance or other, became quite aggressive and unpredictable. He had brought a large iron bar with him and when we got near the shop he wanted to get out and do the job there and then. Fortunately Reg, the Irish guy and I were able to talk him out of it as this was totally the wrong time for what they – and we – had planned. Arrangements were eventually made for a later date. When we returned to the pub there were four of the Irish guy's brothers and we ended up staying and drinking with them, which, although adding to our credibility, was quite an endurance test.

When we left the pub we went to the Irish guy's girlfriend's house in Harpurhey, and from under the floorboards he took out an imitation handgun, a CS gas canister and two black ski masks. These were for me and Reg to use in the robbery. It had been decided in the pub that we would do it the following day, something we had pushed for, as now that we knew about their plans we couldn't afford to sit back and wait. There would have been a risk that they could have changed their minds to use us and then gone on to attack the jeweller another time, causing him serious harm or even worse. So the plan was to all meet at our man's flat at 6.00 am the following day and then make our way over to Eccles. The next morning they were there but we were not, and an arrest team went in our place. They were arrested and charged with conspiracy to rob. They were bailed to a future court date, whereupon

119

the Irish guy went on the run and was rearrested some time later. All were later sentenced to four years' imprisonment.

* * *

By the early part of 1993, Reg, for a number of personal reasons, had made the decision to stop working undercover. His young son hadn't been well and I think that the pressure of the job, as well as the fact that we were often away a lot, meant that something had to give.

Reg asked to move on to the welfare side of the department. When a job came into the office, the welfare officer was the person who would meet whoever was putting the job forward to see if it was viable for the team to take on. They would also work out who was the most suitable person for the job; we were all undercover officers, but none of us could be right for every single job that came in, nor would we want to do all of them. For example, I could never do a job going undercover as a paedophile – I just couldn't cope with that – and there would be no point in a muscle-bound undercover cop pretending to be a heroin user. So you had to have the right skills, the right temperament and the right look for a job. If Harry agreed, it would then be up to the welfare officer to put everything in place so that the undercover officer could do their job. However, no one from the office that put the job forward would ever meet the undercover officer; that was crucial for our safety, and it meant they could never give us away, whether inadvertently or deliberately.

Moving from the undercover side to either a welfare or technical role was the usual route for anyone who had come to the end of their time as an undercover copper, and everyone has an end date in that role because of the risks of becoming overexposed and also the inherent pressures of the job. Having gained all that experience as an undercover officer, being able to use those skills and that knowledge for the benefit of the unit was ideal and a natural progression. It was a move that was straightforward for Reg, but unfortunately was never offered to me.

* * *

I continued working undercover, and now a new job came into the office from Merseyside Police. Code-named Operation Lion, it concentrated on the Granby Street area of Toxteth, which had an ever-increasing problem with the supply of crack cocaine and heroin. Those dealing in these drugs seemed to think they were untouchable. Merseyside Police approached GMP due to the success we had had with Operations China and Miracle, which had both targeted the supply of cocaine and heroin around the Moss Side area of Manchester in the early '90s.

With Reg no longer involved, there were four undercover officers designated to do the job and each of us had to come up with a watertight cover story for being in that part of the city. At some point we would be going individually into the heart of Granby Street to buy drugs, while also getting the evidence needed to arrest and convict the dealers. I was still recovering from the shock of what happened the last time I worked in Liverpool, and the tip-off from a police station to the main man in that job. I didn't want any recurrence of that this time round.

It was imperative that we got the best evidence for the court on all of the deals, which meant trying to get video and audio recordings of each individual deal. However, that was much easier said than done. Granby Street was virtually a no-go area for strangers; if you were in the heart of it you were there for only one reason, and you could be sure that all eyes would be upon you. There was no way to set up an observation point on the street as the dealers would have sussed it in no time.

After giving it some thought, I came up with a plan that I hoped would give us the evidence we needed. I was going to make out that I was a rough and ready landscape gardener from Manchester who was working in Liverpool, and while there obtaining my gear from them. I had an old Rover car that had a tow bar on the back, and through a friend I bought an old caravan that was only held together by cobwebs and which I filled inside with gardening equipment. The technical team fitted video cameras into the front indicator lenses, as well as one on the side of the bodywork, so that whoever approached the car would be caught on camera. There was audio fitted in the car which would record whatever was said. The actual recording equipment was hidden

121

under the seating bench in the caravan and it was essential before I set off that I remembered to switch it all on.

As I said, the caravan looked right due to its condition (that went for the old car too) and a little bit of my own handiwork. It was a sickly mix of faded orange and beige, and I hand-painted the name of my gardening business in black on the sides. It was hardly a professional job and I don't think you would want me doing your grass or borders, but it looked good. The beauty of the caravan was that you could see it coming from the top end of Granby Street, so anyone dealing would soon get to recognize it and know why I was there, as long as the first encounter went well. All I had to do then was make sure my appearance and demeanour were suitable for the cover story.

The big day came and I was first to make my way into Granby Street. As I got to the shops on my right, one of which was a Caribbean food supplier, I noticed that there was a group of black men standing in and around the entrance, staring at my 'wares' and trying to take it all in. I wound the window down and one of them walked over and asked what I was after. My heart was pounding because I knew that if this went wrong it would be a while before any back-up could get there. It was basically shit or bust, so I told him I was after a 'rock' (crack cocaine). There were no pleasantries: they had the upper hand in this situation; I was just another user who needed them. Their empire on Granby Street had been running nicely for quite some time with limited interference from the police, so they had become a bit complacent and just wanted the money, all of which made it easier for me and those who followed. I was directed into a side street where I had to turn the car and caravan around (that was a task in itself). The same guy then came to the driver's window and offered me a rock wrapped in cling film from a larger bag with many more rocks in it. I took one, paid him and he went back to his mates at the shop. I drove away, just hoping that this was real gear and that I hadn't been ripped off with crap; if I had, I could hardly go back and complain to customer services.

I went back to the safe house, making sure I wasn't followed, and handed the rock, which was now an exhibit, to the exhibits officer. We then checked the footage from the caravan: it had worked well, the video clearly identified the supplier and all the conversation was recorded. The exhibit came back as good quality cocaine, and with the initial purchase having gone so well we were all set to continue at different times of the day over the next few months. To build the strongest possible case for the court, each undercover officer had to try to get a deal from the same target more than once to demonstrate that they were regularly supplying. The caravan set-up worked extremely well, and every time I went into Granby Street and bought cocaine or heroin, we got clear footage and audio of each deal. The camera on the side of the caravan recorded all the faces of the gang hanging around outside the shop so that they could also be identified.

As a result of our efforts, numerous targets who were supplying Class A drugs in Toxteth were arrested and convicted.

Chapter Nineteen

Vixen, and the Rot Sets In

By now the office had new premises: we'd moved out of the old Prestwich police station and were working from a private industrial unit just outside the city centre. To the outside world, it was just another private commercial company trading from an industrial unit; inside, the Covert Operations Department was beavering away, still under the wing of GMP's CID (known internally as the V Department), led by Detective Chief Superintendent Dave James.

We had received a lot of accolades for the successes that had been achieved so far, and working from private premises felt as if we were getting more like James Bond every day! We may not have thought about it this way at the time, but looking back it would have been difficult to imagine how anything could undo all the hard work, long hours and disciplined approach that had been put in place to ensure the greatest possible credibility and honesty in the jobs we had completed.

Unfortunately, amid all these changes, there was another rumour going round that DCI Harry was possibly going to retire from the police. Everyone on the team was a bit concerned about this; me as much as anyone. We were also wondering who would take his place and who could have the experience and expertise to take on that role. We didn't have to wait long to find out.

* * *

For most jobs we had an informant, who would introduce the undercover officer to the target or their associates. It was usually someone who had been arrested for a serious offence and who, in order to get a lesser sentence, would offer to introduce a police officer to an ongoing criminal conspiracy that someone they knew was involved in. If the information was good and helped in an investigation or led to a positive outcome for an operation, the police were then likely to speak up for the informant at their trial to say how he or she had assisted officers. If favourably received by the court, it meant they were likely to get a reduced sentence.

Operation Vixen was different. All we had was intelligence that a particular team from the Leigh area of Manchester was responsible for a series of 'ram-raid' type burglaries throughout the north-west. These involved using a stolen car which they would crash into the front of commercial or retail premises before stealing large amounts of property and getting away in other high-powered stolen vehicles. The raids were all done with military precision; the gang had great success, with scant regard for anyone's safety.

The intelligence said the gang regularly used a particular gym in Leigh where they worked out, pumped up their bodies and took plenty of steroids. As a result they looked even more intimidating when they donned the black ski masks they used when carrying out the raids. Without an informant, it was up to us to work out how we could infiltrate the team and that job was given to me. We knew from the start that as a police officer, I couldn't go into the job on the same level as them, as part of the ram-raiding gang. There were several reasons for that. There's no doubt that if I'd been sitting in a car with them, going out on raids, I would have got some great evidence. However, the potential scenario of a police officer being in a vehicle with a gang of ram-raiders which then ran over and seriously injured or even killed an innocent member of the public was completely unacceptable.

There are certain legal lines which you knew, as an undercover officer, you couldn't cross. For example, we couldn't incite or encourage someone to do something illegal that they otherwise wouldn't have done. The criminal activity had to be an ongoing conspiracy that would have happened whether you were there or not. That was the legal position, but professionally and morally it was also hard to justify a police officer committing a crime that could harm an innocent member of the public. It was a similar situation in Operation Crocodile, where first of all we had to make sure our drugged-up target didn't go steaming in to attack the jeweller with an iron bar, and then we had to bring our end of the operation forward to ensure that they didn't go ahead and carry out a violent raid.

In this instance the decision was that I needed to come into the scenario above the gang rather than on their level, and become a handler of stolen property. That would also mean we knew exactly which raids they had carried out, because if it all went according to plan, they would be bringing the fruits of their criminal efforts to me. So my job was to set myself up as someone who seemed to be making a living – and a very good one, if I was going to be convincing – out of dealing in stolen gear.

Also we had to be convincing, because this crew had little fear and could be pretty ruthless. I already knew of one witness who had been intimidated by the crew when they stole his car from his front drive, obviously intending to use it on a job. The man was woken up in the middle of the night by noises at the front of the family home. When he looked out onto the drive he saw this lot, all dressed in dark clothing and wearing ski masks, which frightened him to death, especially as he had his wife and young children in the house, but when the gang saw him, they didn't run off. Instead they told him to open the window, that they wanted his car, and that he should throw his keys down to make it easier for everyone. They also warned him that they had a scanner and they would be listening to police calls, so if he didn't comply or if he phoned the police, they would be back to sort him out. Understandably the guy wasn't prepared to argue; he threw the keys down and they left with the car, which was later used on a raid with false plates. This was the arrogance of them: they believed they were invincible, which is one of the reasons why they were targeted for this operation.

I started to build up my cover as someone who was handling stolen property and making plenty of money from my illegal enterprises. I lived in a flat in Leigh and had the use of several luxury cars, including a Maserati that was a stunner. After a while I started going to the gym in Leigh that we knew they used and began chatting to the owner. I got to know him pretty well, and then made a point of going in some afternoons, which was when the gang was likely to be in. However, I made no attempt to converse with them, as they kept themselves to themselves. I did my training sessions, would have some banter with the owner and others who were training and then leave. I always left my car in the car park opposite, and the Maserati certainly caught their eye. One particular day, as I left, I was aware that they were all at the window, watching me. I still hadn't spoken to any of them, but I'd built up a good relationship with the owner and occasionally I'd taken stuff into him that we'd bought legitimately but which I was selling on at a price that would suggest it was stolen. They were obviously listening to some of this and were aware I was open to handling the sort of stuff they might want to get rid of and also – thanks to the Maserati – doing fairly well at it.

We had to run with this build-up for quite a while but eventually I was able to break the ice with two of them, which was a big moment. From then on things moved pretty quickly. The conversations we had confirmed that I was someone with whom they could possibly do criminal business. The relationship went from strength to strength, until eventually they were happy to bring their stolen gear to me at the flat. On these occasions I had to be on the ball as the flat had been kitted out with audio and video equipment to catch them at it and record the best possible evidence for any future court date. It was essential that all the recording equipment was switched on prior to their arrival, and sometimes that meant me dashing from home to the flat if I suddenly got a call saying they were on the way.

* * *

Operation Vixen had begun in October 1993, and by the time we got into 1994 we were making real progress. However, while it was good news on the operational front, much more worrying things were going on in the background. Halfway through Vixen, Harry retired and it was a sad day. His replacement was Detective Chief Inspector Ken Seddon from Oldham. He had no experience of undercover work, and made it pretty clear from the start that he had no love for Harry. In fact, his exact quote was: 'I don't want any Harry clones in the office.'

To be honest, I was more than happy to be a Harry clone because as far as I was concerned his track record spoke for itself. I tried to keep my professional standards high the same way he had done, but this seemed to cause friction between DCI Seddon and myself from the start. An example of this was that I refused to go to police social functions, even those organized by my own office. As I've said before, I never socialized with the team and that was part of the rules that Harry had been keen for undercover officers to stick to. Being an undercover officer wasn't just an eight hours a day job; you had to constantly think ahead and be careful where you went and who you were seen with. As an undercover cop, working among hardened and often violent criminals, the last person I wanted to be associated with was a known police officer. I wasn't prepared to put my own safety at serious risk, or jeopardize any current or future operation. Also it wasn't just about safety and professional standards. The job was demanding enough as it was, and with a young family I felt like I was already spending too much time away from home.

At this stage I was out of the office most of the time anyway, as Operation Vixen had well and truly taken off. The gang was regularly contacting me and bringing stolen property to my covert address, which meant that I was spending a lot of time at the flat. On one occasion, due to the department's commitments to the FA and the policing of all the England matches, we had to travel to London for a home game while I was still trying to keep on top of Vixen. Although it was a juggling act, it was also an opportunity to enhance my credibility with the targets as I knew they were about to commit another burglary.

I never knew where they were going to raid as they would always ring me after. As always, it was crucial to get the best possible evidence, so as I was going away I told them that I would be in London for a few days and that if anything came up they could ring me at the hotel where I was staying. En route to London they rang me and confirmed that they had something they wanted to shift. I told them to ring me back later when I could talk properly (and by which time I would be in a position to record the conversation). As soon as I was at the hotel I set up the recording kit in my room and hoped they would ring before I was due to leave to meet up with the England 'fans' at pubs in and around Wembley. The undercover staff had travelled together to London, as had the welfare and the technical teams. DCI Seddon was due to arrive later.

When he did show up he wanted everyone to go to a pub down the road and drink as a group. I stayed in my room and waited for the call; when it came through the ram-raiders told me what they had on offer and we made arrangements to meet when I got back. It was another good piece of evidence, and with them ringing me at the hotel, it proved as far as they were concerned that I was in London doing a bit of business. By now it was time to set off for Wembley and I left for the match with the other undercover officers, returning to Manchester the following day.

Not long after, I was called into DCI Seddon's office, where he told me in no uncertain terms what he thought of my stance on socializing outside of the office. For me, this just confirmed that he didn't have a proper grasp on what was required to do things properly and, more importantly, safely. After all, it would never be him who could possibly be stuck in a compromising and dangerous situation; it would be me and the other undercover officers like me. I had no idea what previous experience DCI Seddon had that made him suitable for head of the undercover team and to this day I still don't (unless, in my more cynical moments, I regard Masonic membership as a qualification for CID progression). To my knowledge, his only specialist area up to that point had been as head of the HOLMES computer system, which was a far cry from operational undercover work.

A few weeks later I was called into DCI Seddon's office again. It was Friday, 11 March and it felt like we were now moving towards a crucial point with Operation Vixen. I was hopeful that we would have all the evidence we needed within the next few weeks, so that we could safely arrest the gang, but DCI Seddon didn't want to talk about the job. Instead, he informed me that I had been in the department too long and tenure of office (which restricted officers' ability to work in certain departments to a specific period of time) was going to be applied. I was being moved on. He was going on holiday for a week and he told me to come and see him again on his return to discuss it further.

I was stunned. Even more concerning was that at no time during this conversation was a re-entry programme discussed. This was an essential step for an undercover officer to be able to return to normal policing after a protracted period of undercover work. There was also no consideration given to the idea of me transferring to the welfare side of the department to pass on my experience to up-and-coming officers, just as Reg had been able to do and others before him. As mentioned before, this transition to welfare was always the normal progression. There were other officers, both within the welfare and technical sections, who had all been there longer than me, yet there appeared to be no tenure of office being applied to them.

To cushion this blow, DCI Seddon informed me that both Reg and I were being put forward for the QPM because of the success of the work in which we had been involved together. This in itself was unusual, because as far as I knew, officers were not usually told they were being put forward for the QPM: they only found out that they would be receiving it a few days before the Honours were announced.

I left the office with a feeling that all was not well.

Chapter Twenty

In or Out?

Having pondered over what I had been told all weekend, I decided that I would go and see Detective Chief Superintendent David James, the head of CID, on the Monday morning to clarify the situation. I was worried about what DCI Seddon had told me, and now that he was on holiday, I wanted to find out exactly what was going to happen. I assumed Mr James would know. It wasn't a decision I took lightly, especially in view of the ban on undercover officers going into police stations. To head for GMP's HQ that Monday was a big step to say the least, so I rang the Covert Operations Department first to tell them where I was going and then headed for Chester House.

I made my way to the CID command and sat outside Mr James's office. I hadn't been there long when I was approached by Albert Yates, another chief superintendent, who asked me what I was doing there. When I explained, he invited me into his office. I told him what DCI Seddon had told me on the Friday and what my concerns were as a result. Mr Yates stated very clearly that I wouldn't be moving from the office and that I should carry on as normal.

I walked out of Chester House with mixed feelings: party elated, because it looked like I would be staying in the job I loved, but mainly perplexed because what I had just been told was so at odds with what DCI Seddon had told me. It couldn't be a misinterpretation or a slight mistake. Someone wasn't telling the truth, and I had a good idea who.

I resumed my undercover duties and threw myself back into Operation Vixen and our ram-raiding burglars. The subject of my departure – or lack of it – wasn't mentioned again, even when DCI Seddon returned from his week's leave the following Monday. Actually, nothing was mentioned to me by DCI Seddon when he returned because, apart from the fact that he was clearly very angry, he decided to totally ignore me.

* * *

Just before the Easter of 1994, the gang raided a well-known motorcycle shop in Preston, stealing a whole host of leather motorcycle suits, helmets and boots. After the raid I received a phone call asking me if I was interested in them. Obviously I was, and we made arrangements for them to deliver to my flat, where it would usually be cash on delivery. It was decided that we now had enough evidence to arrest and charge the whole gang. The only problem was that it was the day before the Easter long weekend, and to make the arrests then would mean GMP having to pay an awful lot of overtime to officers required to work, once the detention clock had started ticking. The force wasn't prepared to pay that, so I was asked to try to put them off until after the holiday for their payment.

I'd put a lot of time and effort into this job, and – luckily, as it turned out – I'd been able to build up a lot of trust with the gang. So I was pretty pissed off to be told that there was no way GMP would be paying officers double time over the Easter weekend to process and interview this group of violent criminals. As a team, it was up to us to get enough evidence together, but we wouldn't be the guys arresting, interviewing or carrying out searches. That was down to whoever put the job forward, and so was any decision to delay the arrests for budget reasons. It was okay for them to say we had to persuade the gang to wait until after Easter for the payment; they didn't have to try to do it. It would have been easy for the ram-raiders to take all this stolen gear to their original contact to deal with, which could then have risked the whole job; much easier perhaps than leaving it with me with no payment for it, knowing there was always the risk that they might never see it or me again.

The one thing in my favour was the trust we had built up. I came up with a story about having a problem down south, and that I would have to shoot off to London for a couple of days to sort it out and to collect some money that was owed to me. I assured them I would be back in the next few days with full payment and they agreed. They were recorded delivering the entire stock they had stolen in Preston to me.

That Easter weekend was a complete washout for me and the family. The flat was only 3 miles down the road from my home, which had always been a bit too close for comfort, but now, having told the gang I needed to be down in London for a couple of days, I couldn't risk being spotted by them in Manchester. So anything my wife or the kids had planned for the bank holiday weekend couldn't involve me. Added to that were all the phone calls I had to take to keep reassuring them all was okay but that I would not now be back until Tuesday, so if they wanted to call round in the afternoon I would be there.

Easter came and went, and on the Tuesday everything was set up at the flat for their arrival. There was an arrest team in one of the bedrooms, with a back-up team outside in the shadows ready to move in when I gave the signal. All the audio and video was switched on, so it was 'lights, cameras, action'. They arrived, and I let them into the living room where they thought I was on the phone as I was talking about all sorts of mischief just for their ears; in fact, nobody was on the other end. After the call we discussed my trip to London and they asked me if I was interested in a full set of alloy wheels they had for sale from a BMW they had recently stolen; I told them I was. After a while there was a knock at the front door, which they thought was my mate with the money for them. I got up to answer the door, leaving them seated and talking among themselves. The actual caller was a police officer, and opening the door was the signal to strike and arrest. I ran off down the street, leaving the gang in the house being arrested by the teams in the bedroom, with support flooding in through the now open front door.

The gang was arrested, charged and put on remand to Strangeways Prison; a fact that was to become much more important further down the line. I wouldn't see them again until I gave evidence at their trial in Manchester Crown Court.

* * *

Despite the way the job had progressed, and the outcome, I'd had no comments, criticisms, encouragement or praise (not that I particularly expected the latter) from the head of the Covert Operations Department, DCI Seddon. In fact I'd had no meaningful contact with him at all. I was clearly still off his Christmas list. The month following the targets' arrest I spent in isolation in the attic area of Prestwich Police Station, our recently vacated old offices, painstakingly transcribing all the video and audio recordings that had amassed during the operation to ensure we had the best possible evidence for the impending court case.

Once all this was done, I returned to work in our new unit. It was now early May 1994, and finally, more than seven weeks after we'd last spoken and since my visit to Chester House, I was called into Mr Seddon's new luxury office. Having told me before he went on holiday that I would be leaving the office – without any plans for a move to the technical or welfare side – and then to find out from a more senior officer that this wasn't the case, I had serious concerns over who was telling the truth and, ultimately, who I could trust. I knew that my time as an undercover officer would be coming to an end; as I said before, you only have a certain shelf life in that role before you become over-exposed. I also knew that DCI Seddon and I didn't like each other. That was pretty clear early on. However, I've always believed that you don't have to like someone to respect them or be able to work for them. If they are professional, fair and good at the job, I'll happily work for anyone. I just didn't think he was any of those things.

Bearing in mind that lack of trust and indifference, I also started to wonder whether he was trying to set me up for something. Since coming back from holiday he'd barely acknowledged me, but he knew I'd caught him out telling one set of lies already. I decided to protect myself in the best way I knew how. I began to covertly record our meetings. I'm glad I did; if I was to claim afterwards that he had said this or that, he would have simply denied it and I would be left with nothing. He had no idea that I was recording them though, and it was something I was to do with almost every meeting I had from then on.

So I arrived at his nice, plush office just before our meeting was due. He then kept me waiting forty-five minutes past our appointment time, just sitting outside. This was not because he'd been called away or because anyone else was in there with him; it was the old management technique again: 'I'm more important, so I'll see you when I've got a minute.' When he did call me in, his demeanour was at best frosty. He acknowledged and made no apology for not having congratulated me on the success of Operation Vixen. His reasoning was simple: at the time he had been 'extremely angry' that I had been to see 'not only your but my Chief Superintendent'. He said that his anger had only just started to subside, but that he had 'never been frightened to grasp the nettle' and that he had considered 'mixing me a right bottle and sending me down the road' – which I took to mean stitching me up in some way and throwing me to the lions – but had later thought better of it.

So it went on. DCI Seddon claimed he had never thought about what to do with someone as long as he had with me, and pointed out that no matter who I spoke to, he was a DCI and I was only a DC, so they would always side with him because 'that's the way the system is'; a phrase that would later come back to haunt me.

He moved on to the London trip, and how I had stayed in my room when he arrived rather than going to the pub for a drink. I explained again the situation as it was then with Vixen, but he wasn't interested. I was already feeling fully justified in having recorded the conversation. I would have been foolish not to, especially when he made the classic comment of 'no matter who you speak to, they will always side with me'. He may well have been right – at least, without any sort of recorded evidence – because, as he'd just pointed out, that's the way the system is...

Finally, he declared that he had stopped me having any overtime and had declined my attendance at the annual undercover conference. This one-sided meeting ended with me being told that I would still be considered for future operations, but with a thinly-veiled threat that I should never speak to anyone above his head again. I knew my cards were marked, and for me it proved that what he had told me seven weeks earlier was simply his first attempt to get me out of the office, despite my 100 per cent record as an undercover officer. Now I knew he wanted me out, one way or another.

That first attempt had failed. I could have gone away after our first meeting, come back the following week and said 'this is where I want to move to', and that might have been it, job done. Yet I didn't want to move anywhere and I didn't think he was handling it right, so I'd gone to Force HQ and questioned it. That wasn't the way things were done in the police and I knew it would have riled him, even more so because he had turned out to be wrong. However, I really felt that, having taken on the jobs I had and got the results, both on my own and with Reg, I should have been treated with a bit more respect than that.

*   *   *

I'm the first to admit that I never liked or trusted DCI Seddon, and I felt that he was the wrong person for this position, but it concerned me just as much that the high standards of the Covert Operations Department, which had been held in high regard, were now seemingly being lowered because of one man. It was also becoming clear that he wasn't beyond abusing the system for his own purposes, which could indirectly affect the safety of officers. The situation about the cars bought for undercover officers was a case in point.

All undercover officers needed transport, usually a car, and it was essential that these cars couldn't be traced back to the police. The answer was to purchase all covert vehicles from different auctions and then register them accordingly. When DCI Seddon took over, this practice stopped; instead, all vehicles were bought from a car dealer friend of his in Oldham. This obviously raised serious concerns for some of us. We were buying vehicles for use by undercover officers, or in undercover operations, which were traceable back to one dealer who we didn't know and who hadn't been vetted by the police. Was that dealer, and anyone who worked for him or was involved in his business, really trustworthy enough to be armed with that sensitive information? It was a farce, and a dangerous one at that. I was also suspicious about how the cars were being paid for and who was getting what. I was right to be, as when DCI Seddon finally met his downfall, his car dealer contact was charged alongside him, but more of that later.

Such 'unusual' practices proved too much to bear for one member of the team. One of the two officers who were on the wrong end of the beating by the Manchester United hooligans near the Grey Parrot had also taken on a lot of the admin work for the unit. As the number and range of operations had increased, so the level of admin requirement had grown, and having had such a rough experience on the football job, that officer had now moved on. Harry had then brought a sergeant into the unit who focused solely on the paperwork. He was good at his job too – always looked a bit red-faced when he became under pressure – but handled it well and everyone knew they could rely on him. When DCI Seddon took over the team, the working atmosphere changed pretty quickly and the admin sergeant was clearly not happy with the way some things were being done. He was worried about the way some processes were being handled, concerned that the right procedures weren't being followed – such as procuring equipment and buying cars – which then put him under a lot of pressure.

DCI Seddon called our admin sergeant into the office one day, where another officer was sitting with him. Seddon told the admin sergeant: 'I want you to show this officer everything you do in your job.' When he asked why, Seddon simply told him: 'Because you're going' and that was it. The new officer was a particular DS who was a close friend and ally of Seddon, and who had been transferred in at his request. It was actually difficult to train him because he would never leave Seddon's side, in or out of the office.

Eventually our hard-working admin sergeant was out; not through choice, but forced to leave. They put him in a new CID role and piled the work onto him, so he was regularly working till 11.00 pm, and in the end he just couldn't take it. He kept telling them that he was overloaded but no one took any notice, and in the end the pressure got to him. He was on the verge of becoming suicidal before he finally went off sick.

Of course, none of this seemed to deter DCI Seddon from his approach to business, and by this stage he had bought a silver Saab Turbo, a blue Jaguar and a red Ford Sierra 4x4 as vehicles for the unit. A short time after the Sierra arrived, so too had our admin sergeant's replacement. This DS had previously been under a cloud in a different department, having been suspected of running a business on the side. As his new duties covered the administration of the office finances, this raised a few eyebrows, again, as it turned out, with some justification. Our new admin sergeant soon bought an identical red 4x4 Ford Sierra and it was common knowledge in the office that when it needed jobs doing to it, it was booked in and paid for with GMP funds as if it was the covert operations car.

Having spent the last four years watching my back from villains outside the job, I knew I now had to keep my eyes out for the dishonest chancers on the inside.

Chapter Twenty-One

Operation Bluebell and the End of the Road

Not long after my dressing-down by DCI Seddon, Operation Bluebell began. It was offered to the office by the RCS – which underlined the reputation that the department had built up – and it involved a major crime family from the Manchester area who were allegedly importing ecstasy from southern Spain. The crime family was connected to Manchester's infamous Quality Street Gang, and had also been linked to the inquiry concerning John Stalker and his association with Manchester businessman Kevin Taylor. Taylor was financially ruined by GMP as a result of the investigation and subsequent court case, but was completely cleared and later received compensation. He went on to publish a book, *The Poisoned Tree*, about his experiences.

It was clearly a big job, bearing in mind the people involved, and it needed to be tight, which is why they came to us with it. Initially, I would imagine because of DCI Seddon's desire to see me out of the department, I wasn't considered for the job, but it soon became apparent that there were operational problems. As always, the job revolved around building a good relationship with the informant. Whether you liked him or not was irrelevant; you were dependent on them to get the job going so you had to make it work, but for whatever reason the informant didn't get on with the undercover officer deployed in this case and refused to work with him. This now placed the Covert Operations Department in an embarrassing dilemma as they had been brought in by an outside agency that was paying for their professional services, and now the operation was at a standstill.

I was approached by DCI Seddon's number two, DI Tony*, who told me that I was to take over Operation Bluebell. I was to meet the

---

* We have opted to only use this individual's first name to help conceal their identity.

informant and see if we could build up a relationship and move the job forward. However, there was a problem. As I've mentioned before, one of the strict rules of undercover work is that once an operation has concluded, the undercover officer involved mustn't use the same false identity in any further operations. They should be allowed to go away and create a new false 'legend'. I explained to DI Tony that since completing Operation Vixen and having become 'persona non grata' in the office, I hadn't been able to create a new legend. He said he appreciated that, but maintained that on this occasion it would be okay to use my old Vixen identity as the plan was very clear: I was only going in to achieve the initial infiltration and build a relationship, but I was to introduce a second undercover officer who would take over. I would then be able to distance myself, and the evidence would start from the second undercover officer. I would never be divulged to the defence, and only the judge in any future trial would ever know that I was a police officer.

On the face of it, this seemed okay. Bearing in mind what had just happened between me and DCI Seddon, I didn't want to rock the boat more than necessary and, having pointed out my concerns, I'd been reassured that it would be safe. I believed that not only would I be protected, but it would also protect the informant because it would take the evidential part of the case one step further away from them. Also it was an opportunity to get back in the fold, to carry on working undercover, until such time as I could move elsewhere in the department. So I went with it.

I met with the Operation Bluebell informant and fortunately we got on well. I was able to infiltrate the main target and some of his associates, which involved a trip to Spain to meet other contacts and suss out a potential deal, and I was then able to introduce the second undercover officer, just as planned. The operation rolled on, and required long hours and lots of commitment. I had to be based down in Newquay, Cornwall for this job – I couldn't carry on living in Manchester as it would have been far too easy for them to check me out, such were their connections – so it meant lots of time away from home. By chance, while living down there I met and became friendly with the owner of the local fun pub who, spookily enough, turned out to be Kevin Taylor's nephew.

We were still waiting for the delivery of the ecstasy from Spain, so in the interim the main target was now supplying our second undercover officer with batches of heroin. I hadn't been able to take a back seat yet. I was present when the deliveries were made, and the main target was insistent that we let him know when we got safely back to Cornwall, which meant that no matter what the time was, we had to drive to Cornwall and then ring him from there to put his mind at rest. This may seem ridiculous now, but if we had telephoned him from anywhere else, for example Manchester, and he for some reason had wanted to ring us back on the landline, he would have instantly known that we were not where we should have been. Today the technology is in place to make it look like you are ringing from anywhere, but it wasn't then.

I would ring the office each morning to make contact and DCI Seddon's new admin sergeant would ask me what time I finished the night before. If, for example, I said 11.00 pm, he would book himself off at the same time, making out he had been covering for me in Manchester while sitting on his backside in the safety of his own home. Once again, this was a dangerous operation, due in no small part to the nature of the targets involved and the commodity in which they were dealing. These weren't people pinching bottles of milk from doorsteps, they were dealing in the quantities and types of drug that could send them to prison for a long time. What they especially wouldn't have liked was the thought that a police officer had fooled them, had joined their clique, and that they had taken them on board as someone with whom they could do business. Having to deal with that level of risk and threat was part of the job. Doing it in a situation where you were taking additional risks – such as not having a new legend in place – added to the pressure. Knowing that some lazy, corrupt copper was sitting on his fat arse back up in Manchester, profiteering from the risks I was taking, just incensed me.

Operation Bluebell came to a successful conclusion with the arrest of several main targets. This included the arrest of a GMP officer from Stockport, who was accused of assisting the gang with vehicle checks on the PNC among many other things. Numerous addresses were searched and evidence seized. After being charged, the main players were placed on remand. A headline in the *Manchester Evening News* read 'Cop held in probe on links with drugs ring', and stated that a dozen guns, ammunition, thousands of pounds in cash, amphetamine-based rave drugs and heroin were seized in the swoops.

So what happened next was a major disaster – both for me and for the informant in Operation Bluebell – and should have been foreseen by those running the operation. I didn't know it at the time, but all the defendants from Operation Bluebell were placed on remand in Strangeways, the same place where they had put the defendants from Operation Vixen, and what do people on remand in prison do? They talk, and talk they did. It must have soon become apparent to them that the undercover police officer in Operation Vixen was the same one as in Operation Bluebell.

Having been told by DI Tony that only the judge would know I was a police officer, someone in the department – whether it was him, as he knew the whole story, or someone above him – should have been liaising with the judge, the CPS and the Prison Service to make sure that they weren't remanded to Strangeways. What should have happened was that the two sets of defendants should have been kept apart and remanded to different prisons, and the two should never have had the opportunity to meet, let alone talk, but it didn't happen. All those assurances about the only person who would ever know I was a police officer would be the judge in the trial came to nothing.

The knock-on effect was that this totally blew the informant out of the water as he had introduced me to the main target. A massive damage limitation procedure eventually took place and the informant was suitably compensated and, as I understood it, he went abroad. No such operation was put in place for me and my family, and at this point I didn't know for sure whether my safety, or theirs, had been compromised. I was only to find that out while giving evidence at Manchester Crown Court.

* * *

While on the face of it Operation Bluebell had been deemed a success, things were far from happy in the department. Some of DCI Seddon's behaviour was starting to cause concern – not just for me, but among the team as a whole – and several incidents stood out.

One particular day DCI Seddon informed the office that the RCS wanted to use one of our covert properties in Constance Gardens, Salford for one of their operations. He told us that no one was to visit the property, and even asked for all the keys to be handed in. Everyone complied, except one officer who was on annual leave. When this officer returned he unwittingly went to the flat and tried to go in. As he put the key in the front door he realized it was locked from the inside, so he knocked several times. Eventually the door was opened and he was met by a man standing in the hallway in his pants. The officer had no idea who he was, nor the female who was there with him. It transpired that this was DCI Seddon's brother; he was a fireman, not an undercover police officer, and had no official authority to be in the flat. The woman with him was his wife and they were staying apparently rent free in the covert flat; a property paid for by the police authority, solely for the use of undercover officers on covert operations.

A caravanette that was also the property of GMP and which had been purchased for the sole use of the Drugs Squad as an observation vehicle on operations was flagged by customs leaving the country and checked back with the force. It emerged that DCI Seddon had taken his young family on holiday to Italy in the vehicle.

When officers from the department were infiltrating the England hooligans during home matches at Wembley, there were times when DCI Seddon brought members of his family to London and put them up in the same hotel as the undercover officers. A police officer from the unit was then asked to drive them to and from Wembley in the office Jaguar; again, a vehicle intended solely for the use of undercover officers on covert operations.

As a unit we got together one day at one of our other covert properties and discussed what had been happening, particularly regarding the flat in Constance Gardens. There were many concerns that officers in the unit could have their safety compromised by what had happened at the flat.

Had DCI Seddon's brother been seen leaving the property by certain unsavoury characters who also lived in the block – particularly if he was wearing part of his fireman's uniform – they would not automatically assume he was a fireman, but may well instead have thought he was a police officer. If there was any chance that suspicions could have been aroused and that the property could then have attracted their interest, the flat at that point would have been compromised for future use by undercover officers.

No one was happy about it – in fact, someone suggested we needed to write a letter to the force about it – but neither was anyone really prepared to put their head above the parapet, so nothing was done. The most worrying thing was that, as head of the illustrious Covert Operations Department, DCI Seddon allowed all this to happen in the first place and in some instances was actively engaged in this unprofessional behaviour himself, but then he would never be the officer at risk.

* * *

After what felt like a much-needed Christmas and New Year holiday, I returned to work on 9 January 1995 and headed in early to our office as I was due to give evidence at Manchester Crown Court against the defendants from Operation Vixen. It hadn't been the best of festive breaks as I was concerned about a number of things. The main one was that I had no faith in the way the office was now being run, particularly with regard to safety. Throughout my time on the unit the mantra 'loose talk costs lives' had been well and truly drilled into me, but now there seemed to be a lot of loose talk taking place.

I sat briefly at my desk and opened my private drawer, where I found a memo to me from the department management. It said that I would be leaving the department, and there was a list of items that I would be required to hand in, such as keys, driving licence and passport. I was completely stunned. Despite the disagreements with DCI Seddon in the past, I'd stepped back into the breach, taken on a job for them which was clearly in danger of falling apart, spent weeks travelling up and down to Cornwall trying to get the evidence we needed to put this pretty hardened family gang away, and managed to pull it off and get some of them arrested.

I thought I might actually get a message or a memo or just a conversation along the lines of 'Well done on that; that was a great result considering the situation we were in.' Instead, I get a memo left in my drawer – they didn't even have the balls to tell me face-to-face – saying you're out and here's a list of all the things we need you to hand in. There was still no mention of any sort of re-entry programme. Returning to 'normal' policing is not something that can be done overnight. You can't finish an in-depth, covert policing role on a Friday and stroll back in to resume normal uniform duties on a Monday. That doesn't work on a number of levels.

I'd only come into the office because it was the first day of me giving evidence in the Vixen trial. I now had to get up into the witness box, which is a stressful enough situation in the first place, with all this going around in my head. I headed off to the court, but as soon as I got chance, I made an appointment to see the force stress counsellor, Keith Jones, who I'd hoped might be involved in the process. The appointment was set for 23 January. In the meantime, my main concern continued to be the trial, and throughout the rest of January and into February I carried on giving evidence as best I could, with everything else going on in the background.

I was driven to the Crown Court each morning in a plain police car, which went straight into the underground car park. Once there, I was allowed to use the judge's entrance to enter the courtroom when it was time for me to give evidence. Every time I took to the witness box in the trial, I was giving evidence from behind screens to protect my identity from the public gallery, which was full most days with friends and family of the defendants, all keen to see who the undercover officer was. The screens allow an officer to continue in this dangerous field of police work. It's only the public gallery who are unable to see the officer; they are visible to everyone else, especially the defendant. In trials such as this it's up to the judge to rule on whether the undercover officer can give their evidence from behind the screen and under the pseudonym – the legend – that they used in the particular operation. Only the judge would know the officer's true identity. If this permission was refused, the prosecution would have to decide whether to continue or discontinue the case. Having been granted permission, using the judge's entrance enabled me to enter the witness box and get behind the screen that had already been erected without being seen.

Despite these safeguards, a number of bizarre and ultimately worrying incidents took place which, added to everything else that had already happened, eventually pushed me over the edge. One particular day, after lunch, I was following the usher back through the judge's quarters to take up my position in the witness box to resume giving evidence. As I came through the door into the court I heard someone shouting for me to get back, and as I looked up I could see that the screen had been moved from its position in the morning session, fully exposing me to everyone in the public gallery. There was no logical reason for the screen to have been moved during the lunch recess. I went back into the judge's quarters and the screen was repositioned, but by then the damage had been done.

On another occasion, again after returning to the witness box after lunch, I was standing in position waiting for the judge to return. In front of me were two men who I hadn't seen before, but who I realized were a solicitor and his runner, who kept on looking up at me and taking notes. I was starting to wonder what was going on as nothing was actually happening in court; we were just waiting for the judge to come back in. It turned out that they were representing the defendants in the Bluebell case, and they were writing down my description. They had the file from the case, which included a statement with my name on it. That wouldn't normally have gone to the defence as it wasn't relevant, but the crucial point was my name: the same name I had used in the Operation Vixen case. Up to this point, these 'names' were just people who were giving evidence against the suspects in the case. There was no confirmation or description of me as an undercover police officer in the case papers. However, with the same name appearing in two separate cases, they were starting to put two and two together and come up with Garry Quinn, undercover copper…

The judge then entered the courtroom and everyone stood while he took up his position on the bench. Almost immediately, one of the defence barristers in Vixen, Mr Glassman, was up on his feet and asking the judge for the jury to be excused for a short period as there were some points he wanted to raise in their absence. His request was granted, and Mr Glassman proceeded to ask me three questions, one of which was had I ever, during Operation Vixen, been involved in an operation code-named Bluebell? This obviously hit me right out of the blue, but when I assessed the questions I could honestly say that no, I never had, as I didn't get involved in Operation Bluebell until after Operation Vixen had ended.

After I had answered his questions, Mr Glassman again addressed the judge and vehemently argued for the trial to be stopped, saying that I was a liar and my evidence could not be relied on as being the truth. He stated he had asked me three questions which I answered, under oath, as having no connection to Operation Bluebell; yet he had a copy of a prosecution file for Operation Bluebell in his hand and in there was a statement from me using the same false name as in Operation Vixen. How could the court now rely on my evidence as being the truth?

The judge now reassessed the questions I had been asked and then the answers I had given. He was happy that I had indeed been truthful with my answers and allowed the trial to continue, rejecting Mr Glassman's request. However, if Mr Glassman's question had been 'Have you ever been involved in an operation code-named Bluebell?', my answer would have been totally different. At least I was able to answer, and answer truthfully. Yet in many ways the end result was the same: here was the confirmation, if we'd needed it, that the defendants in both cases had been talking. They now knew that the same officer had been involved in both cases, under the same pseudonym, and they had a description of that officer: me. It was an incredibly uncomfortable feeling, and straight away I became increasingly concerned about the safety of my family.

After another full day of giving evidence the case was adjourned until the following day, and I returned to the car in the basement and we left the court building. As we did so, the driver was aware that another vehicle appeared to be following us. It had emerged from a side street as we left the underground car park into the heavy traffic. The driver made a few manoeuvres to try to confirm this, after which he said he wasn't happy. Eventually he was able to lose the car and we changed vehicle the following day and made sure, as best we could, that it didn't happen again.

*　　*　　*

The meeting with Mr Jones, the force counsellor, took place as scheduled on 23 January, in the attic office of Prestwich Police Station, and once again I taped the meeting covertly. I'd started to employ the same techniques I had been trained to use to trap the criminal fraternity against my own organization, which I had started to mistrust. When I asked Mr Jones why he didn't know I was leaving the department and why, given the circumstances, he wasn't involved in the process, he simply replied that the organization only told him what they wanted him to know, and that what they say is not always what they do. Something similar to this was said to me later down the line when I went to speak with the civilian head of police personnel, Andrew Marston. I left this appointment with even more concerns than when I went in.

Around this time and out of the blue, I received a telephone call at home from a DS on the RCS at Manchester. He asked me if I was interested in a job as a surveillance motorcyclist, the role I had previously covered in the mid-1980s. I hadn't heard from him for several years, and he didn't know – no one really knew at that stage – that I was supposedly looking for a job, apart from DCI Seddon and a couple of other senior officers. I didn't let on, told him I was happy in my present role and that my next move would be in a welfare role to pass on my experience to other undercover officers. I didn't think about it too much at the time – in fact, not until much later – but how did an officer from a national organization like the RCS know that, almost a decade after I'd left, I might need to find another role? The only link I could see was that, just like DCI Seddon and our new admin sergeant on the department (neither of whom had any experience in or connection to the RCS), the RCS officer was a Mason from Oldham. It's a small world...

Shortly afterwards I was again summoned by DCI Seddon, who finally told me verbally of my impending move from the department. He mentioned that he knew I had made enquiries about a position with the RCS. I told him that this wasn't true, and that I had been approached. It seemed pretty obvious that the call had been orchestrated by him. Despite my denials, he said it would be a good move as no one would be able to see me under the helmet. I thought that not only was this comment crazy, but to consider sending me to the RCS office was madness as this was the originating office for Operation Bluebell. Anyone looking for the officers concerned in their demise would look there first, even though they were not supposed to know anything about me.

A few days later, I opened my desk drawer to find another unexpected report, only this time it had been left by someone who had my best interests at heart. It was a copy of a report marked 'Strictly Confidential' from DCI Seddon to Detective Chief Superintendent James, dated 26 January 1995. It stated that I had been allowed to carry out undercover operations for too long, that I had become overexposed, and that the department was now in a position where it did not know what to do with me. Most worrying of all, it said that there was intelligence that some of the defendants in the Operation Bluebell case had taken on the services of a private investigation company from Stockport to identify who the undercover officers involved in their case were and where they lived.

I've got a pretty good idea who had put the report there, and I'm very thankful that she did. Clearly, neither DCI Seddon nor Detective Chief Superintendent James were going to tell me about it because they didn't know I had seen a copy of the report and they never discussed it with me until I brought it up several months later. Surely that was something the job should have made me aware of, even if they weren't going to take any action about it?

I had already worked out that my safety, and the safety of my family, was not their top priority. This just made me realize that I could probably count the number of people I could actually trust on one hand. I was starting to feel pretty isolated in a unit and a job that I'd loved doing.

The report concluded by stating that I had actively sought a move from the office and had identified a position with the RCS as a surveillance motorcyclist, albeit with the caveat that this would be a short-term secondment. Once again it confirmed that not only did DCI Seddon want me out, but that this would be the extent of any re-entry programme after five years as a full-time undercover officer.

I also knew that Merseyside Police had been setting up their own undercover unit run by a Chief Inspector Jones, based on our model. He had contacted GMP and requested that I be seconded to their unit to help them set things up. As far as I was concerned, this would have been a great move; it would have taken me out of the GMP area while the dust settled from the aftershock of Bluebell and I would have been on the welfare side rather than in an operational undercover role, so it would have ticked all the boxes both for me and, I would have thought, the force. Those requests were turned down without any consultation.

By this time I had started to feel pretty rough, physically and mentally, and only now began to realize that the stress was making me seriously ill. I had completed five years as a full-time undercover officer on regular, long-term operations, both at home and abroad. I had a 100 per cent success rate and throughout all of this not one complaint was made against me or the official practices that I used. The methods and tactics deployed on undercover operations are only used as a last resort against target criminals when all other methods have failed. It's the last tool in the policing toolkit, but needs to be used correctly and safely for all concerned. Throughout those five years I never had a problem doing the job; in fact, I thrived on it. Yet I'd never previously felt stress like I was feeling now, and that was not because of the nature of the job I was doing.

From the moment DCI Seddon had taken charge of the Covert Operations Department, standards and long-term working practices – essential for the safety and security of ongoing and future operations and operatives – were, as far as I could see, being seriously compromised.

Because I would not be party to that compromise, he wanted me out; not just out of an undercover role, but out of the department. The non-existence of any structured re-entry programme, despite the suggestions to the contrary, just exacerbated the problem. To top it all off, the confidential report from him to the head of CID acknowledged that my family and I were at risk, yet they had no intention of telling me that.

The day I was released from court in the Operation Vixen trial, I knew that was it. My head was in bits, and there was no way I was going back into the office to try to talk to that idiot again. I was all over the place. I knew I would be going off sick the next day. It would be eleven months before I was back in work again.

Chapter Twenty-Two

Sick of It

In February 1995 I went on sick leave from work, suffering from stress and anxiety. I was fearful both for my own safety and that of my family. I was still struggling to get my head around the thought processes, or lack of them, that had led to gangs from two different undercover jobs being put on remand in the same prison. Clearly, officer safety now came a long way down the list of priorities for the force. In response to my concerns, all they were prepared to offer was an alarm on the side of our house, which linked directly through to a police station. That was little comfort when I knew that at least one bent copper had been arrested in relation to these cases, so who else was on the gang's payroll? When I pointed that out, I was told – not for the first time – that I was just being paranoid. Yet you can imagine the psychological effect that all of this was having not just on me, but also on my wife.

The situation wasn't helped by the fact that a close associate of the targets from Operation Bluebell, who I had met during the job while down in London, lived only 3 miles away from my family home. Remember, I wasn't meant to be involved in the evidential stages of this case; that should all have been passed through to the second undercover officer going into the job, so it really shouldn't have been an issue. However, it wasn't long before I found out, when visiting my local doctor's surgery, that we shared the same GP. Fortunately I saw him first and took evasive action, although by this stage, it's doubtful if he would have recognized me anyway.

Throughout my time as an undercover police officer I always portrayed the persona of an armed robber. I had been 17 stone with a shaved head and pierced ears, but my change in appearance was becoming pretty dramatic as I was losing weight really quickly. At the time I was helped a lot by my own GP, the late Dr Brian Sides, who arranged for me to have basic counselling once a week via his practice. I was also prescribed Prozac for depression. I started to cut myself off from people – work, family and friends – and my relationship with my wife suffered greatly as there seemed to be no end to what was going on. All I knew was that I was ill, and my depression spiralled. I was referred to Dr Leslie Faith at Wythenshawe Hospital who diagnosed that I was suffering from Post Traumatic Stress Disorder (PTSD). She admitted that what I was suffering from was beyond her treatment and that I really needed to see a specialist. She was still willing to see me, and it was good for me to be able to talk to her to offload, but she said from the outset that she wouldn't be able to give me the sort of specialist support I needed.

My health continued to deteriorate and after several weeks I was contacted by a DCI Trevor* who, I was informed, had taken over from DCI Seddon at the Covert Operations Department. DCI Trevor came to see me at home and told me that DCI Seddon had been moved almost overnight due to his mismanagement of the department. He added that Seddon had been doing things that he should not have been and that had he, DCI Trevor, been in charge before, things would have been handled differently. He admitted that I had been something of a guinea pig as far as GMP were concerned in relation to undercover policing, and that the so-called re-entry programme had been virtually non-existent but that it would be set in stone for all new undercover officers who came into the department. This confirmed much of what I already believed, but it was like closing the stable door after the horse had bolted. I was obviously not surprised to hear about DCI Seddon as I knew he couldn't continue to use and abuse the department forever and get away with it.

By this stage though, I was more concerned about my own health than DCI Seddon's problems. To be honest, being off sick was much more stressful than doing the job. You've got the financial worries all the time: how you're going to pay the mortgage, the threat that you will

---

* We have opted to only use this individual's first name to help conceal their identity.

be going onto half-pay after six months, and if you are still on sick leave much longer after that, the prospect of no pay at all. Our income had been reduced so much that, when I was put on half-pay, at one point I actually received financial support from the Benefits Agency for a few weeks. So we were seriously struggling.

The PTSD was now really kicking in. I knew I was ill, not because of being an undercover officer, but because of the way the force had treated me. I knew the way I was feeling, and some of the things I was doing, weren't right, but it becomes harder and harder to get out of the hole you're in. I felt like I should have been able to cope with anything, but I really couldn't.

I was still rapidly losing weight – I eventually dropped from 17 stone to 12 stone – which was down to stress. That must have been quite frightening for the kids too; to see me change from this big 17-stone guy to a really gaunt, 12-stone bloke who didn't look like their dad and who was basically miserable and pretty scary most of the time. I don't know what goes through a child's mind. For all I know, they could have been thinking that I was on my way out, that I was dying, because I certainly looked ill. It wasn't good. I'd be jumping out of bed at night in my sleep, trying to get into the cupboards because I thought they were doors and I could escape through them. My wife would have to try to wake me up to stop me panicking but as I say, even when I was asleep my mind was in turmoil.

I was also still very reclusive. I'd cut myself off from everyone, other than the obligatory visits from DCI Trevor, I didn't want to go out anywhere, and I started to shut off from friends and family too; I didn't tell my wife everything that was going on, partly because I wanted to protect her from as much as possible. I'm not sure that helped, because understandably she felt I was being secretive and not telling her the whole story. However, I also mainly wanted my own company. I later found out that this is a relatively common symptom of PTSD, but at the time I didn't understand it; I just felt like that was what I wanted.

As I wasn't doing anything each day, my mind was going over and over what had gone on and mentally I was all over the place. Also I knew I was out of 'the club'. The force and policing had been there for me since I was 16 years and 6 months old, and for the vast majority of that time it had been good. When bad things had happened in the past – losing Dad, Tony dying, whatever else – I'd had people around me in the job. I may not have been the biggest socializer in recent years and I liked working on my own, but I was still part of the force; I was in that club. Now I wasn't: I was outside of all that. I'd done nothing wrong, but I was really struggling, and I was on my own.

I was asked to see Dr Deighton, the force medical officer, who was keen to get me back to work, and I was offered counselling with Vera Waters who had an office in Oldham. She had previously worked for GMP providing stress counselling before setting up her own private practice. She had obviously been very friendly with the GMP hierarchy, especially Detective Chief Superintendent James, who arranged the offer of counselling. At this stage I still thought he was okay as a boss, so I took them up on the offer.

I didn't know what to expect when I got there, although I did hope that our conversations would be confidential. I'm also not someone who gives away a lot of information easily, so I let her talk quite a lot and it was soon clear that she knew a lot more about me than I thought she should have known, including some details that could only have come from Mr James. It made me uneasy and I started to wonder whether this was an indirect way for him to have some control over me, to work out what I was thinking. Our conversation was supposed to be confidential, but I thought there was a real likelihood that, as soon as I left, she would be on the phone to the force. Given how little trust I had in GMP by this stage, I made my excuses, left and never went back. It frustrated the force hierarchy even further, but they really shouldn't have been surprised.

On 28 March I received an unexpected visit from a Superintendent Bill Fernside who was from GMP's Internal Investigation Department, the Y Department. He informed me that he was investigating DCI Seddon for so–called 'irregularities within the Covert Operations Department' and that he was speaking to everyone from the unit. Little did I know at this stage that they were also underhandedly investigating me.

* * *

As I was approaching six months on sick leave, I was warned that I could be put on half-pay. This remained a massive worry, particularly for my wife, as we had a young family with the normal everyday bills to pay. My perspective was that I was truly ill, not just swinging the lead, and it was GMP who had caused my illness. I was in a hole that I was finding it hard to get out of, and at that stage paying the bills was not one of my main concerns. Nevertheless, I wrote to the chief constable and, with the help of my GP Dr Sides – who was one of the few people I felt I could rely on – he relented and left me on full pay, with the caveat that if I did not return after nine months I would then go on half-pay. Whenever DCI Trevor visited my home, he would discuss how I could return to work, although every time I asked for the attachment to Merseyside, it was refused point-blank. He suggested an attachment to Sedgeley Park Training School on the undercover courses to make the most of my experience. I didn't feel safe doing this, as to get credibility on such a course you would have to talk about your own experiences, and with what had just gone on and the threat of private investigators, I didn't want to highlight anything about myself. The force didn't appear to have any sympathy with those concerns, and I think by this stage they had simply labelled me as awkward. DCI Trevor also expanded a bit more on what had happened to DCI Seddon. The quick move was as a result of his indiscretions coming to light, apparently after an anonymous letter was sent to the force and the *Manchester Evening News*. He had been moved to the CID on the C Division at Grey Mare Lane.

Eventually I was called in to see Assistant Chief Constable David McCrone at Chester House in his capacity as head of personnel. At the meeting on 10 July (which again, I recorded[1]), Mr McCrone agreed that there wasn't a re-entry package in place as standard for undercover officers, and that 'without making you feel like a guinea pig, in a way you are'. I tried to explain some of the struggles I was having: the fact that nobody wanted to sit down and talk through what I could do in the future, the frustration I felt at seeing the officer arrested as part of the last job simply walk away with his pension intact, and the anger and despair at DCI Seddon's behaviour in putting officers and the department at risk. How much of this he actually took in I don't know, but the conversation ended with him promising to look at my situation and identify a suitable position for me to return to.

The next three months came and went, and I was still off work and as ill as ever. When the move to half-pay kicked in it crippled us financially and I was forced to cash in some insurance policies I had with the Police Federation in order to survive. I looked dreadful, and I was losing weight so quickly that at one point I had to go and have a camera investigation of my gut [colonoscopy] as the doctor was worried I had cancer. By September of 1995 my health was still poor, but my finances were drained and I knew things were not going to get better. It felt as if the organization was against me and, as they say, 'no-one is bigger than the club'. DCI Trevor came to see me with three prospective job placements that had been identified as suitable for me to return to work; at least, as suitable as any policing can be for someone suffering from PTSD and depression and having spent the last nine months on Prozac. I was in a corner, because if I stayed off work any longer than twelve months I would receive no pay at all. With the benefit of hindsight, I now realize I was still extremely ill and as I wasn't receiving any specialist treatment my PTSD continued to fester, but I had to go back to work, come what may.

I sent a handwritten letter outlining my situation to the chief constable as a last-ditch attempt to get some sort of understanding from the force, but again it fell on deaf ears. To be fair to Mr Wilmot, at this time he didn't know the full story about what certain members of his senior staff had been up to. When he later did find out, he made moves to rectify certain matters and for that I thank him.

It was made perfectly clear to me that I would not be allowed to utilize my experience as an undercover officer in any shape or form. The three positions offered to me were the following:

- Video analyst within the Video Imaging Unit located in the basement at Chester House, GMP HQ
- Taking statements for the Civil Litigation Department
- Computer Section.

None of these positions interested me at all, but they were all that was on offer. No one within the GMP Command Team had any clue about what it's like to be a full-time undercover officer and the effects it has on you as an individual. They didn't understand the 24/7 nature of the job, the fact that your real persona has to take a back seat to the sometimes damaging personalities and the intimidating appearance of the characters that you play. They didn't understand that, unlike the everyday criminals who saw being arrested by CID or uniformed officers as all part of their job, the gangs we had infiltrated now hated us with a passion because we had been able to win their trust. After all that, I was left to my own devices to try to sort things out, and after being off work seriously ill for nine months, the best they could come up with was these three posts which psychologically would make me worse.

Out of the posts offered to me, I had no knowledge of computers and I couldn't take the risk of going out and about in public as a police officer taking statements for civil litigation, so the only option was the Video Imaging Unit. I notified Mr McCrone that reluctantly I would accept the Video Imaging Unit, but also stated that I would not be able to return to work until after Christmas and the New Year as I could not face all the merriment and party attitude that would be taking place due to my stress and depression. It was agreed that I would return to work on Monday, 22 January 1996.

The crazy thing was that, after all this time, and especially now that DCI Seddon had been moved on, no one could tell me why I couldn't stay in the department as a welfare officer. Everyone was pushing the fact that I had to go anywhere but remain in the Covert Operations Department, despite my exemplary service. I was being cast aside, yet the real villain in this tale was being looked after left, right and centre.

* * *

There was more depressing news to come. In the Chief Constable's Orders Issue 96/48, dated 26 November, the following announcement appeared, listed as Item 6:

An officer appeared before the Chief Constable in formal disciplinary proceedings and was found guilty of the following offence:

Improper disclosure of information – Caution
The officer revealed information about operational policing matters to a person not authorised to receive such information.

That, it transpired, was the entirety of the action against Seddon, following an inquiry that had been completed discreetly, and leading to his appearance in front of the chief constable earlier in November 1996. The caution was in relation to Seddon allowing his brother and sister-in-law to stay in the covert flat at Constance Gardens. I couldn't believe that was it.

I didn't know what had gone on at the time, but I subsequently obtained a copy of the official briefing notes for HMI Sir John Steven's inspection of GMP in 1997/98 which were prepared by his then Staff Officer, Superintendent John Tapley. Mr Tapley met with Constable Gerry Millington (then the Joint Branch Board Secretary of the Police Federation) who acted as Seddon's 'friend' at his disciplinary hearing after the eighteen-month investigation. He told Superintendent Tapley that Seddon was found guilty of a 'technical' offence regarding the use of the covert flat as it was no longer being used by the department. Seddon's brother apparently occupied it only for two days, and the defence argued that it was better to occupy the flat than draw attention to it by leaving it empty.

The conversation between Superintendent Tapley and Gerry Millington also revealed that, according to Seddon, he was apparently selling the caravanette on behalf of the force at the time it was used for the holiday. He also made a retrospective payment for his family's stay at the London hotel.

Once again, I was gobsmacked. Seddon's 'defence' just didn't stand up. The property was still being regularly used by undercover officers, until Seddon asked us all to hand our keys in. Even if it had been sitting empty – which it hadn't – why didn't he tell us what he was doing with it? More importantly, why didn't he just openly go to the ACC or even the chief constable and explain that, to make it look like the flat was permanently occupied, he was going to ask his brother and sister-in-law to stay there? I'm guessing that if he had done, he would have been chased out of police headquarters carrying his P45. The force would know that was unacceptable; even if they didn't recognize that having his brother there could compromise our safety, they would have understood that if the property itself was ever compromised, Seddon's brother and sister-in-law would have been at risk of attack and GMP would have been responsible for their safety. So there was no way that could have happened legitimately. Yet that defence was accepted by the chief constable.

Equally, had he also gone to see the chief constable to seek his permission to take his family abroad on holiday in the Police Authority-owned caravanette, bought exclusively for the operational use of the Drugs Squad, I don't think the chief would have wished him 'bon voyage'. Was this not a clear case of taking the vehicle without the owner's consent?

Actually, when I say I was gobsmacked, that's probably an exaggeration. By this time I'd started to realize that there seemed to be one law for one group of people in the job and one law for everyone else. I'm pretty sure, if I'd moved my brother into a vacant covert property, I would have been off the department and out of the force. So it just confirmed what I been thinking about everything else, and brought back to mind Seddon's prophetic words from a couple of years before: that they would always believe him, because 'that's the way the system is'.

* * *

Christmas 1995 was not a particularly happy occasion at our house. It was always a difficult time because of the anniversary of my dad's death on Christmas Day, but this year my depressive mood swings made it even worse.

After Christmas, with at least my financial problems addressed due to my impending return to work on full pay, I decided out of the blue to contact my former undercover partner Reg. I hadn't spoken to him or anyone else from the department for eleven months. I hadn't fallen out with any of them; it was just part of the illness I'd been suffering from that made me want to withdraw from normal contact with everyone. What made me ring him I still don't know, but I gave him a call. We exchanged all the initial pleasantries, and I explained that he was the first person I had spoken to for some time.

He then said to me in a low voice, 'Have you got it?' I replied: 'Have I got what?' 'The QPM.' I thought he was having a laugh as it had been a joke between us ever since Seddon told us, but it was no joke. He had been awarded the QPM. I can't even remember what else was said, apart from him apologizing to me. It wasn't his fault, of course. Reg had made the right move for him, from operational undercover to welfare; later he went on to a training role, and then eventually into Special Branch. Like me, he knew what had been happening on the unit under Seddon wasn't right. He chose not to rock the boat, just to get on with it; he had a young family at the time and that was the right choice for him. I didn't feel I could do that, and while I didn't feel I had done anything wrong, I was now having to live with the consequences.

To say my mood took a nosedive was again an understatement. I felt even lower than I had before and, knowing I was going back to work in a couple of weeks, it felt like being punched twice. I'd been punched and knocked down once, had just got back on my feet and was trying to get my head round going back to work, and now I'd been punched again. The New Year was even less of an event at home as the thought of this ate away at me. Why had he received the QPM and I hadn't?

Chapter Twenty-Three

Taking Action from the Basement

By the time Monday, 22 January arrived, I had been off work for more than eleven months. When I woke up that morning, the thought of having to go back to work – knowing deep down that that was the last place I wanted to be – was unnerving to say the least. I was going back mainly for financial reasons, and also in the hope that I could get my life back on some sort of even keel, not out of any sort of enthusiasm for the jobs I'd been offered. Out of the three posts they had found for me, I knew the video analyst role was the best option because at least I'd get to see tapes coming in from operations, and I had a bit of an understanding about the jobs they were doing and what they needed for the recordings. Yet realistically, as far as I could see my career was over.

Due to those difficult financial circumstances, my transport was now a bike, so I cycled the 8 miles from my home to Chester House. I had a backpack with clean clothes as I would have to shower when I got there, so with that in mind I set off early. I had been told that a lot of thought and effort had been put into this placement by a lot of people who only wanted what was best for me. I was also told that I would be met on the first morning at 9 o'clock by one of the main staff at the Video Imaging Unit, DC Ian Jakeman. I soon discovered that he liked to give out his details as DCI Jakeman, letting people believe that he was a detective chief inspector and not just a detective constable.

I arrived in plenty of time, got showered and was in the reception of the Imaging Unit for 8.50 am. I told the lady on reception who I was, that I was starting there that morning and that I had been told to ask for Ian Jakeman. She looked a bit bewildered, and explained that while he was in today, he wouldn't be around until lunchtime as he had been on holiday to America so was starting late. No one else could help, so

I had to hang around like a bad smell until he arrived several hours later. It wasn't a good start, and in my state of mind I could have easily got changed and gone home, but I knew I had to stay and endure it. I remember thinking that a lot of people may have put a lot of thought and effort into my placement, but apparently they'd all forgotten to tell DC Jakeman.

Once he finally arrived I was shown where I would be working and what I had to do. I was the only police officer among around a dozen civilian staff who worked at the unit. I was told that no one in the department knew where I'd been working or what I'd been doing, and that officially I was on attachment to the office. I felt from the start that everyone was staring at me; my personality had become very introverted and I only spoke when I had to.

I worked in a windowless room in the basement of Chester House, with banks of video machines. When tapes came in and they needed eight, ten or however many copies for a future court case, it was my job to copy them. It soon became obvious that the department had been told they were having me, whether they liked it or not. I hadn't filled a vacant position; I was surplus to requirements.

My mood swings were forever up and down, and I found it very hard to get into a friendly conversation with anyone, even my wife. On one particular day after I had been there for several weeks, the fire alarm went off at Chester House and the whole building was evacuated. I heard it, in my little room with no windows, and waited for it to stop, thinking that it was a test. When it was still going a little while later, I opened the door and looked into the main office: it was deserted and there was only me there. I hadn't been told what the evacuation procedure was, but as I realized that everyone had left, I went out of the building and onto the front concourse where there were large groups of people standing around. I waited there as the fire brigade turned up, and eventually the all-clear was given and everyone made their way back to their relevant departments.

I was standing in the main office, with staff slowly beginning to reappear, when the Head of the Imaging Unit Pat Davies came over to me and said loudly in front of the whole office: 'Where the hell have you been? In future come into the rear car park.' This took me by surprise, and I initially apologized and explained that when I looked out of the tape room no one was there, so I'd made my way to the front of the building as I knew no different. I initially accepted it, but as he walked away down the corridor to his office, I was aware that everyone in the office was looking at me as a result of what they had just witnessed.

Suddenly a red mist came over me. I followed him to his office and told him in no uncertain terms that while I may have been in the wrong place, ultimately it was his responsibility to ensure I was briefed properly when I started, for health and safety reasons, which he'd failed to do. I added: 'And another thing – don't ever speak to me like that again in an open office, in front of other people. If you want to have a word with me, get me in your office and speak to me on a one-to-one.' I turned round and walked away. Our relationship after that was never a good one, as I knew from the start that he hadn't wanted me in that office. There may well have been other reasons for that, as I was to discover later.

The biggest problem for me at that time, which nobody else seemed to understand – especially the 'do as I say and not as I do' types – was that I was suffering from unresolved and untreated PTSD. This was being fuelled by the environment in which GMP placed me to keep me quiet and out of the way. As it turned out, putting me at Chester House and in among them was the worst thing they could have done: it allowed me to ferret away from within and ask questions that they didn't like.

* * *

I knew I would have struggled to adjust to working as part of a civilian team at the best of times, having spent all my career as an officer and much of it undercover or on CID, so it was no surprise that I was finding it difficult now, bearing in mind what I was going through. It wasn't helped, though, by the attitude of both civilian managers and senior officers to having me working in their team. As a police officer I was subject to the annual appraisal system, whereby your immediate line manager or supervisor would appraise your work over the previous twelve months. The appraisal form consisted of a written comment section and also a 'tick box' section, ranging from 'A' for outstanding to 'E' for totally unsatisfactory. As I started back at work on 22 January, my appraisal was due on 2 April. Because I had been off sick for eleven months I had accumulated a large amount of outstanding annual leave, and as I was not well and was already starting to hate where I worked, I took this leave almost immediately. By the time my appraisal came round I had only been in work for about six weeks. My civilian line manager was Pat Davies and we'd already clashed over the fire alarm incident, so I wasn't sure how my appraisal would go. A lot of the marks and comments were matter-of-fact, but one in particular jumped out at me. I'd always previously got an 'A' for my appearance, but he'd given me a 'D'. I was now down to 12 stone and with my shaved head and being so gaunt, I looked like a Belsen survivor. However, I felt that I couldn't help my appearance – it was a look that I'd had to adopt for work in the first place – and I was being unjustly marked down.

I took this matter up at my appraisal interview with the next person up the line manager ladder, Detective Chief Inspector Geoff Keeling. I explained my position and the point that I would have scored 'A+' for my appearance in my last department and that this seemed to me to be a little harsh. His response was quite revealing: 'If we are putting our cards on the table, when we heard you were coming here, we thought why are we getting this monster?'

Again, I couldn't understand this attitude towards me, which only served to fuel the illness that was smouldering inside me. I wasn't sure how many people knew what I'd been through, although I would have thought that the workings of the Omega Unit and the Covert Operations Department would (or should) have been kept pretty confidential, but then I'd been off for eleven months, during which time Seddon had been removed and I'd been awkward. DCI Keeling, like Seddon, Detective Chief Superintendent James and most of the other senior-ranking CID officers always stuck together so just how much I was discussed within the CID hierarchy was anyone's guess.

Clearly he knew enough about me to have formed this opinion before we'd ever met.

* * *

It had been confirmed that Reg had indeed received the QPM. As this situation continued to eat away at me, I also became aware that a number of other awards and chief constable's commendations that I had been due to receive in relation to undercover operations had, for some reason or other, never materialized. Like everything else that was happening, I couldn't understand it. However, whenever I tried to delve a bit deeper, I couldn't get anywhere: either people said it wasn't their responsibility, or they weren't sure how the system worked, or that things were still being considered, many months and even years after reports had been submitted. Eventually, as a result of all the negative responses, I decided to instigate the In-Force Grievance Procedure in relation to three specific matters:

- Why had I not been awarded the QPM for my distinguished undercover work when my ex-partner had? I explained that we had both been informed of our nominations, and that I had been a full-time undercover officer for five years, while he had completed two.
- Why had a Chief Constable's Commendation for Operation Miracle never materialized, despite it having been submitted?
- Why had a Chief Constable's Commendation for Operation Crocodile never materialized, despite it having been submitted by DI Terry Brown?

The full grievance procedure form[2] spelled out my conversations with DCI Seddon and subsequent departure from the department, my work on various operations – Miracle and Crocodile in particular – and why I felt that instigating the grievance procedure was necessary. The aim of this internal procedure was supposedly to honestly and objectively right any wrongs. I took advice on what to do from GMP's in-house Equal Opportunities Advisor, Roz Caplan, who immediately told me that as my situation was somewhat unusual – being the only police officer working among civilian staff at the Imaging Unit, and with a grievance focused on police awards – then I should miss out Stage One of the procedure, which would have been to go to Head of the Imaging Unit Pat Davies, who wouldn't have a clue what to do with the grievance report. Instead I was told to go straight to Stage Two, as this would see the report placed in front of a police supervisor.

I took her advice (after all, she was the expert on this), typed and signed my grievance report and on 24 April submitted it by hand in a sealed envelope marked 'Private and Confidential', addressed to Detective Chief Superintendent David James, Head of GMP CID. I left it in his personal pigeonhole in the CID Admin Office at Chester House.

Several weeks went by and I heard nothing. I contacted his secretary, and later she came back to me to say that he hadn't received my report. I resubmitted it, once again by hand. On 23 May I received a memo from Mr James, headed 'Grievance Procedure'. It read as follows:

> I refer to the above in respect of the current grievance you have instigated. Unfortunately, I was unaware of your intention as I have never had sight of your correspondence until I obtained a copy from the Equal Opportunities Unit after receiving their memorandum that you had taken out a grievance.
>
> Nevertheless, I now intend to expedite the matter, but as you have avoided Stage One of the procedure (e.g. through your line management) it will be a matter of say two weeks before I will be in a position to discuss your grievance with you and your representative if required.

This seemed to me to be a delaying tactic; after all, I was keen to get answers, so why would I have said that I had taken and delivered my report if I hadn't? I had nothing to gain by doing that, but they did: time. Also I couldn't see where else the first report could have gone. It was addressed directly to him and put in his personal pigeonhole, so how could that go missing?

My view was that Detective Chief Superintendent James had got the first report, and gave himself some extra time to try to work out what to do about it. He would have received that on or shortly after 24 April; by saying he hadn't received it before 23 May and then asking for time to deal with it, he gave himself until the grievance interview to decide exactly what to do.

I was also concerned that he seemed to think I had tried to 'avoid' Stage One of the procedure. I'd simply followed the advice of the force's Equal Opportunities Advisor; I wasn't being a maverick or deciding to ignore proper procedure.

I immediately sent a memo back to Mr James, dated 24 May, which explained all of this in what I described as an attempt to 'clarify any ambiguity'. I was still giving them the benefit of the doubt.

* * *

Another couple of weeks went by until I was granted a grievance interview with Mr James at Chester House on Tuesday, 6 June. I was accompanied by Gary Tobin from Russell, Jones and Walker, the Police Federation's solicitors. During the initial introductions and explanations of the procedure, Mr James mentioned once more that I had not gone through the correct procedure by missing out Stage One. This meant that yet again, I had to explain that this is what I had been advised to do by the force's Equal Opportunities Advisor. For a senior officer he seemed to be a bit slow in absorbing the information I was providing, which was slightly worrying given that this initial meeting was, as he described it, his opportunity to gather more facts so that he could investigate my grievances and report back at a later date with his conclusions.

He told me that in relation to the award of the QPM, I should never have been told of my nomination, but despite that I shouldn't worry; I was still in the system as he had personally recommended it. This later turned out to be less than accurate but as I say, I was still giving them the benefit of the doubt. The following is a transcript from a tape recording made at that time:

GR: 'So in effect are you confirming that I have been put in for it [the QPM]?'

DJ: 'What, recommended? You were recommended for the QPM.'

GR: 'And that as you understand it, I'm still in there?'

DJ: 'As I understand it, the way the system works is that every time someone is recommended for the QPM, that goes down. The next year you have the same format, it says please address the issues in relation to awards, and the Chief Constable via Personnel will submit recommendations for whichever award. That basically is the system. They say please do not resubmit previously recommended persons, and all they do is check up to see if you are still serving.

He eventually moved on to the other aspects of my grievance, such as the awards that I believed had mysteriously gone missing or had now been classed as not worthy. His argument was that I had been well served by the award system, telling me how many chief constable's commendations I had received to date and that I should be grateful for them. I pointed out that I had earned every one of those awards, thanks to my success as an undercover officer, but that I now found it strange that for some reason all remaining recommendations seemed to have been blocked. I argued my corner, and the meeting ended with me being told that the next meeting would take place on Monday, 26 June.

I was still covertly recording these meetings, both as an accurate record of what had been said and also for my own protection. I'm not sure if Detective Chief Superintendent James suspected I was recording the conversations – if he did, he hadn't asked me about it – but I don't think he was happy with me being accompanied by a 'non-police' outsider in the form of Gary Tobin. He was there to watch my back as I no longer felt I could trust the organization, but I believe Mr James didn't say as much as he would have done had Gary not been there. As I waited for the meeting on 26 June, I was slightly buoyed by the fact that according to Mr James, the head of CID, my QPM nomination was safe and I was still in the running to receive what I'd always regarded as a prestigious award.

The meeting on 26 June was cancelled by Mr James and a new date of 31 July was allocated. The grievance procedure seemed to be designed to wear you out in the hope that you might turn round and say forget it, as weeks were turning into months and I did not seem to be getting any answers. I was never given any explanation as to why this was changed, but it meant I had to fester away in the basement of Chester House, copying video tapes in my windowless room.

* * *

When the date for the second meeting finally came round, I arrived at Mr James's office together with another representative from the Police Federation, Geoff Barber, and once again, I was recording the conversation.[3] Mr James started by saying that my grievance in relation to the QPM was something that the force had 'no control' over, so he hadn't followed it up. He also went on to say that, as far as he was concerned, Operation Miracle wasn't worthy of a Chief Constable's Commendation and reminded me again how many I'd already received. I explained that it was my understanding that, rather than not being worthy of recognition, the award for Operation Miracle had been held back while I was off sick (and, as it would later turn out, under investigation), and that because so much time had elapsed, it would have been more embarrassing to put it in front of the chief than to let it disappear, which is what had happened. I also told him that, just as the recommendation for the QPM had apparently been held back by the force, the same seemed to have happened with the original Operation Crocodile report, although Mr James once again claimed that Operation Crocodile hadn't been worthy of a Chief Constable's Commendation.

It was at this point that the meeting became very interesting. As we were talking, Detective Chief Superintendent James produced a report about Operation Crocodile that had supposedly been re-submitted by DI Brown earlier in the year. As I read it, there was something not quite right about it. I knew that the report had originally been submitted in June 1995, four months after I went on sick leave. This report was again from DI Brown, with a submission date of February 1996, twelve months after I went sick but around the time I instigated the grievance procedure in relation to it. On the bottom left of the front page there was a date stamp from DCI Trevor, which clearly showed 18 February 1996 together with his signature. So the front page of the report seemed to show that it had left DI Brown on 15 February, been received and dated by DCI Trevor on 18 February, and then ultimately landed on Mr James's desk for his consideration and decision. All well and good.

However, when I turned to the second and concluding page, Mr James had handwritten his comments on the foot of the page about how this operation was worthy of nothing. He then date-stamped it with his own personal stamp and signed it. The date read 21 January 1996, almost a month before both DI Brown and DCI Trevor's supposed dealings with it. This in effect meant that he had received the report before Mr Brown had even created it!

I had returned to work from sick leave on Monday, 22 January 1996. This date stamp of Mr James also meant that he was working on Sunday, 21 January. I pointed out the irregularities and he responded by flippantly saying that his date stamp must have been wrong. There was no doubt about this, but was it wrong for all the wrong reasons?

I held the report up to the light and I could immediately see that the date on the top right of the front page had been typed onto Tipp-Ex fluid; looking closer I could see the original date of June 1995 underneath. Mr James said he knew nothing about this.

As a police officer you're obviously trained to try to pick up on things like that; you look for evidence. So if you show me a report, I'm going to look at the detail, taking in as much information as possible, and the fact the dates had been changed jumped out at me pretty quickly. The reality was that this was DI Brown's original report, which for some reason had been stored somewhere gathering dust until I raised my grievance. As a result of that, they had a knee-jerk reaction to try to disprove my claims, quickly coming up with a false story about the first report and recommendation being lost and making out that a new one had been submitted. They were arrogant enough to think that a pretty amateur attempt at deception would be enough. They didn't even bother to create a new report; they just falsely altered the original. It was clear that, once again, someone wasn't telling the truth; the question that still remained was why?

Below is an excerpt from the full transcript of my conversation with Mr James and Geoff Barber. It seems that I may have touched a nerve:

GR: 'I had a discussion and said what is happening with the report for Crocodile because I was aware it had gone in; I was then told that it had been held on to with the other thing to see what happens.'

GB: 'Well I agree with Mr James that's not your problem is it... you deal with it when you get it...there is a five-month gap, I agree with you and someone is to answer for that.'

GR: 'No, the person told me that you, sir, had it and you held on to it.'

DJ: 'I mean I'm not going to have it, send it back and then ask for another report.'

GR: 'What I'm saying to you is that I am basing my belief on what I have been told.'

DJ: 'I know you tend to feel this is against Garry Rogers, and no one is going to persuade you it is other than that.'

GR: 'So that one you got in February: did you ask for that, or is Mr Brown saying that he put that one in because the other one got lost? Why would he suddenly take it on board to put another one in?'

DJ: 'Well you may have started it.'

GR: 'That's got January 21 on it.'

DJ: 'Yeah.'

GR: 'Which is before I came back; I came back on January 22, 1996.'

DJ: 'I mean, that's another issue there, that's stamped January 21, 1996, and that's dated February 15, 1996. I can't give you an explanation for that.'

GR: 'So he has not put in that report further to my other report...
that's the original?'

DJ: 'Yes. Now, whether you have stimulated that or not I don't
know...I know I dealt with that as soon as it came on my
desk.'

GR: 'Strange.'

DJ: 'I could have fucking altered that by now if I had done that!'

GR: 'That was obviously a Sunday because I came back on the
22nd, a Monday...that report...just the stamp...'

DJ: 'Clearly the stamp was wrong...you sometimes see things
that are not there, there are a lot of people have done a lot
for you!'

GR: 'Well I would like to speak to them, present company
excepted.'

Mr James might have been right about one thing: I was starting to feel
that this was all against Garry Rogers. I just didn't know why, because as
far as I could see, I still hadn't done anything wrong. It would be seven
years, several jobs and plenty more anguish and depression before I was
to discover that the answer to that question was sitting in a file, several
floors above my basement office in Chester House.

I told Mr James that, as he had clearly made up his mind, I was going
to exercise my right to take my grievance up to the next level. Then I
went back to my windowless room and continued copying video tapes.

Chapter Twenty-Four

Due Process

So that brought an end to Stage Two of this endurance process they called the grievance procedure. I was determined to carry on with it, despite the ramifications of this decision. While there were plenty of times when I felt like giving up, particularly in my lowest moments when I was off sick, I just couldn't handle the thought of rolling over and letting them get away with it.

This has never been about one incident, one problem, one single thing that wasn't fair. Everyone knows that sometimes things go against you, or you don't get what you're entitled to or what you deserve, but this was about a whole series of decisions and actions that, from my perspective, seemed to be part of a coordinated effort to either discredit me, silence me or persuade me to give it all up. As a result, my anger and frustration were increasing and my illness was getting worse, but I was never tempted to give up. Never.

I knew I was slowly being labelled as a troublemaker, and certain members of the Greater Manchester Police 'club' no longer wanted me as a member. Even at this relatively early stage I felt I couldn't trust the organization or certain key members within it. It was pretty obvious that things weren't right, although I was still trying to work out exactly where they had gone wrong and why.

One thing that my meeting with Detective Chief Superintendent James had finally confirmed was that I needed to look at him in a different light. Having thought he was a solid boss, I'd then spent quite some time trying to give him the benefit of the doubt and maybe accepting that whatever was going on, he wasn't directly involved in it. However, now I could see that he'd lied to me about still being in line for the QPM (I didn't buy the idea that at his rank – only one step down from becoming an ACC – he didn't know how the system worked). He had held on to submitted reports that recommended me for commendations, effectively putting a stop to them. It was only when I returned from a long period of sick leave and started to use the grievance procedure that he was forced to resurrect those documents, and then concoct stories about original reports being lost. He'd also rubbished the work that we'd done on Operation Crocodile.

There had to be a reason for this behaviour, and surely something more than just me falling out with DCI Seddon or going on long-term sick leave. I made up my mind to continue to Stage Three with Andrew Marston, the new civilian head of personnel. However, before I did, I thought it was important to get hold of a copy of the Operation Crocodile commendation report that had so obviously been altered. Shortly after leaving Mr James's office I submitted a request to him for a copy of the report. He came back the same day (31 July), saying that his written response would include 'the relevant parts of that report, the full contents of which I do not intend to release for obvious reasons relating to confidentiality.' So that was that, although he did say he would consider a request from 'any other adjudicator' wanting to see the report in the future.

To me it was pretty obvious that he didn't want to release the report because of the clear alterations that I'd pointed out during my grievance interview with him. The only good thing now was that, having discovered those changes, I'd put him on notice that I wanted to see it again. Hopefully it wouldn't go missing as, according to him, these reports sometimes do...

Andrew Marston, as Director of HR, was the first civilian head of personnel in GMP, the post having previously been filled by a chief superintendent. My first meeting with him (which, as always, I recorded) took place on 13 August 1996 at Chester House and also included Roz Caplan (the Equal Opportunities Advisor), Geoff Barber of the Police Federation and a secretary, Sandra Firth. I went through all of my concerns, highlighted all the points I had raised with Mr James and left Mr Marston in no doubt what had gone on to date. The meeting concluded with him promising to go away and look into all the matters, and that we would have a further meeting to discuss his findings. By now I knew not to hold my breath.

The next meeting took place on 11 September, with me, Mr Marston, Roz Caplan and Sandra Firth present. Mr Marston began by informing me of his lengthy discussions with Mr James and his efforts to research files and paperwork to establish details regarding the awards and other issues, particularly the QPM. Unfortunately he hadn't been able to find out anything; I told him I wasn't surprised. However, he did confirm that, contrary to what I'd been told, for me to get the award now I would have to be put forward again separately by the force. The joint submission with Reg, if it was ever made, was no longer relevant.

It was also clear that he had struggled to get any straight answers. Mr Marston said:

> My understanding, based on what little I have been able to find out – and I acknowledge it is a little – is that it would seem unlikely now that the original [QPM nomination] could go forward. As far as the force appears to be concerned, that issue is now a closed issue. It's not been progressed for whatever reason, and I haven't been able to work out why. Nobody that I have spoken to could actually shed any light on that – or if they knew, they weren't telling me. My impression is the only way that that could go forward now would be a fresh application going in.

I couldn't believe what he was telling me, especially if that was the answer to my grievance. He explained that he had found it 'extremely difficult to get any information at all', which would clarify what had happened, despite trying everything he could think of. Mr Marston continued:

> I am admitting I have run into the same brick wall that you have. I don't seem to be able to progress it. What I am saying is that if, putting the worst perspective on it, you were both up for the QPM originally, and somebody pulled it from this end, then I can't establish that.
>
> I can't find anybody who will a) admit to that, b) verify that, or c) even admit the possibility of that happening could exist. I have to say that I'm embarrassed. It's an unusual set of circumstances for

me to be in. Normally when I do this sort of thing, it's not difficult to get hold of the information; it's unusual to find yourself in the position where there is no information. I can't get at it, I really can't, and I admit to being embarrassed about it.

This was the newly-appointed civilian head of GMP's Police Personnel Department who took on my Stage Three grievance to investigate thoroughly and report back to me with his findings. What happened? GMP command refused him access to sensitive files and reports to block him from getting to the truth. This wasn't just another old-time senior police officer who had been through the mill, ending up at this elevated position and singing off the same song sheet as the likes of Dave James and Ken Seddon. This was a civilian who would not or could not be manipulated to cover things up, so all they could do was prevent him from getting to the truth.

I could understand why he was embarrassed, although he wouldn't be the last person to be wrongly refused access to personnel files by the force's senior command team, as Her Majesty's Inspectorate of Constabulary (HMIC) was later to find out. At least he was able to confirm that my nomination for the QPM was now dead in the water. The question I still needed answering was why this was so, and just what had happened to cause it?

Because Mr Marston was unsuccessful, I now moved on to Stage Four of the grievance procedure, which involved a meeting with ACC David McCrone, the Head of Police Personnel.

*   *   *

Despite feeling deflated by the process so far, so strong was my belief that I was right that I had been looking for all manner of ways of trying to get my grievances answered. With this in mind I'd submitted a report to ask for an audience with Her Majesty's Inspector (HMI). Every police force is inspected each year by an HMI, who are all senior-ranking officers seconded to the Home Office. This year the GMP inspection was to be carried out by Sir Geoffrey Dear, the former

Chief Constable of West Midlands Police. To my surprise I received confirmation that my request was granted, and in the August I'd had a face-to-face meeting with him at Chester House, where I had the opportunity to express, to someone outside GMP, the full extent of my grievances. He listened to what I had to say, although he didn't fill me with any great hope. All I could do was wait and see.

The following is a letter that was sent by Mr Dear to Mr McCrone on 5 November 1996 following our meeting and his inspection of GMP:

Dear David

Detective Constable V2642 Garry Wayne Rogers

You will be aware that during my recent inspection of the Greater Manchester Police I saw the above named officer at his request in respect of his concerns regarding his relationship with the Force.

Having now had the opportunity to consider the contents of DC Rogers' file and based on the material it contains, I feel that GMP do have a responsibility to this officer to ensure that he is reintegrated into the Force as soon as possible, in employment which recognises both his experience and his unique contribution to policing.

I note also the comments of yourself dated July 11 pertaining to the officer's potential to sue the Chief Constable and requiring that matters relating to this officer should be carefully documented; yet there is no update or further reference to the development plan contained in the file.

Clearly DC Rogers has been difficult to deal with, but I am keen to support him for the reasons I articulated to you during the inspection.

Yours Sincerely

Geoffrey Dear

This was a letter sent from a source outside GMP, and for the first time someone appeared to be listening to what I had to say as opposed to the way certain senior elements within the force were treating me. Unfortunately this was all taking place behind the scenes and I didn't get sight of this letter until some time later, so I was never aware of its contents while my grievance continued to Stage Four. While it was encouraging to see that he'd written it, he didn't do any more than that. I subsequently wrote to him more than once and never heard from him again.

*   *   *

From first meeting Mr McCrone he had always reminded me of the former Conservative MP Norman Tebbit, as depicted on the *Spitting Image* TV programme but without the leather jacket. He never ever seemed to smile and was always miserable whenever I saw him. Maybe I brought out the worst in him!

Stage Four commenced on Monday, 30 September at a meeting between myself, Mr McCrone and Peter Hands, who was my Police Federation rep. I started off by explaining why I had taken my grievance to this level, which was basically because no one to date had given me any feasible explanation or answer to the points I had raised, particularly in relation to the QPM nomination.

Mr McCrone was clear that he didn't want to go over all the detail again as he had seen the papers from my grievance meetings to date and he was aware that Mr Marston hadn't been able to come up with any answers. Instead of offering to look for the answers himself, he wanted to know if there was 'anything further in relation to what you want to say', and also to discuss my current job down in the video tape room as he said I seemed to be 'unhappy' in that post.

I wasn't sure what he meant about having anything further to say; I still had exactly the same questions as I had at the start as none of them had been answered! I asked him whether this meant that effectively the grievance procedure had come to an end and he assured me that it hadn't. However, I still didn't know what he expected me to say, so I outlined my grievances again, starting with the QPM: why, having been told I'd been put forward for it jointly with Reg, had I not received it and he had, and whether Mr James or Mr Marston was right about my chances of still receiving the award. His response was less than encouraging: 'My comment at this stage is that you should not have been aware if there was a recommendation.'

Undeterred, I then told him the full details of my conversations with Mr James and Mr Marston about the other missing award recommendations, including how Mr James had produced a clearly doctored report. This went in one ear and out the other. He just didn't seem interested in anything I had to say. The conversation ended with Mr McCrone telling me that he needed to make 'further enquiries' and would 'probably' see me again in several weeks.

So it was back to the basement of Chester House and back to copying video tapes while I waited and waited for a phone call or memo telling me that Mr McCrone wanted to see me again, all the while hoping that what I had said to him may have been looked into properly and some previous decisions changed. The wait became another endurance test but eventually, on 6 December, I was summoned to see Mr McCrone once again (and as always, I recorded the meeting).

I would have thought that he'd had plenty of time since 30 September to do this properly. He basically told me that he agreed with Mr James, no one else in the force had as many commendations as I had for undercover work, and that I should be happy with them. As for the QPM, I should not have been told. This was the result of his nine-week inquiry: he came across as still not being interested; he just wanted to say what he had to say and that was the end of it. He completely glossed over the alteration to the Operation Crocodile report, which once again left me thinking, would he have done the same had I been altering official police reports?

I tried to bring him back to the issue about the report, but it was a struggle to get anything sensible out of him. The tapes of those meetings with Mr McCrone make for interesting listening. He's pretty hesitant throughout, and doesn't really say anything; it's like listening to a politician who doesn't want to answer a question. Remember, this is the same officer who, a few months before, was pointing out to other senior staff that I might be in a position to sue the chief constable, and that all matters relating to me needed to be properly documented. Well, there wasn't a lot to document from these meetings as he never actually said anything! Having sent me away for ten weeks and effectively done nothing, he was about to send me away again, before finally telling me that not only had he done nothing but that there was nothing to be done. The following excerpt is part of the longer transcript[4] of our meeting:

GR: 'Just a couple of points there Sir, about something you said. I appreciate you have looked into it and you agree with Mr James. Just a few things though. The report that I am saying was submitted in February, what was the result of that? When I was saying the original report was submitted in June last year, yet there has been another report that I am saying has been falsified?'

McCrone: 'I've seen the original report and the wording in that report and the wording is not exactly...'

GR: 'Is this the report from June?'

McCrone: 'This is a report from, I am trying to think...the report you are suggesting recommended you for the commendation.'

GR: 'It's a report from Mr Brown from June. I've spoken to Mr Brown; it was put in with a note from himself recommending a Chief Constable's Commendation. That report went missing and a further report was submitted in February with February's date on, which has been made out as if it was put in by Mr Brown in February. I've spoken to Mr Brown who says he did not put that in.'

McCrone: 'I've seen that report. There is a confusion really, one part of the report is dated February and the later part is dated January, it's clear that one part...something is wrong...'

GR: 'The main thing is that none of it was submitted in February.'

McCrone: 'No, well I...however the wording in that doesn't actually...'

GR: 'I fully appreciate what you are saying there Sir. That the wording doesn't say Chief Constable's Commendation, but the point I am making is...what is the bottom line on that report, how was that report...'

McCrone: 'Well I, I can't find any more than that I, I, I don't know the answer...from that sense...I can't believe that anyone...er...if there was anything so untoward on that report which is quite glaring...one part in February, one part in January, as opposed to a deliberate cover up, well I mean it is incredibly inept.... I understand what you are saying and I will further explore that part...'

GR: 'Because if it's the one from June that is missing, there should not be any other report.'

McCrone: 'No, there shouldn't be.'

GR: 'But someone has put that together?'

McCrone: 'Unless of course it's a copy that has been changed, I will look at that aspect and respond to you...but I want to try and concentrate on...I won't sweep that aside, don't worry...'

Mr McCrone then tried to convince me that it was 'not unusual' for papers to go missing, for reports to be copied and for copies of reports to be passed off as originals. To be honest, by this stage I was struggling to know what to say. I felt like I was banging my head against the same brick wall that Andrew Marston had already run into, and that I'd come up against before, only this time I couldn't see how I could take the grievance any further. I gave it one last shot with Mr McCrone. Knowing that a meeting with the chief constable was not part of the strictly defined grievance route, I asked him if that option was closed to me. His answer was still that of a politician: 'Well, anyone can ask.'

The interview ended a short time later with Mr McCrone saying he would look further into the mysterious 'second' Operation Crocodile report; the one that DI Brown had already told me he had no knowledge of and that I'd already raised with Detective Chief Superintendent

James, Andrew Marston and now Mr McCrone himself. While part of me was hopeful that I might finally get an answer, I think deep down I knew that they had closed ranks and they weren't going to come back with anything new.

As it happened, that wasn't quite true. I was called back in to see Mr McCrone two weeks later, and he had some news for me. The report that I'd been shown in my meeting with Mr James – the one with dates from January 1996 and February 1996, the report that was resubmitted because the original had been lost, yet that still had the June 1995 date on it, the one that I couldn't be given a copy of because of 'confidentiality' issues – that, said Mr McCrone, was actually the *original* report. However, in that original report, DI Brown's recommendation had been for a commendation and not a Chief Constable's Commendation; Mr James hadn't thought it worthy of either, and that was that.

Again, I was at a loss for words. I tried to explain that I already knew it was the original report but doctored to look like a new version, that – far from being lost – I'd been told by DCI Trevor that it had been held onto by Mr James, along with my QPM nomination, and that none of this was normal behaviour, so why was it being done? Mr McCrone's response was simply to repeat what he'd said before: none of this was unusual or underhand.

I realized now that those outstanding awards were never going to materialize. I was persona non grata. Mr James, DCI Trevor and now Mr McCrone had colluded to discredit me. Why? The only answer I could think of was a certain DCI Seddon and my willingness to question his practices. They seemed happy to protect him, while hanging me out to dry.

If I was right, then certainly part of it was to make sure there was minimal fallout for the Covert Operations Department. If his behaviour had got out into the public domain and it was known that the man in charge of the unit that tackled serious crime and major criminal gangs was himself guilty of corruption and deception, that could call into question the credibility of the unit itself, which would have been a major embarrassment to the force. A lot of the successful jobs we had done may have been re-examined, tainted by association with a corrupt senior officer. So to discredit the only person inside the job who, as far as I knew, had been happy to highlight his malpractice – me – was perhaps part of their plan.

However, there were also people who were part of Seddon's other 'club': they were his fellow Masons, and I believe they were pretty keen to make sure no harm came to him. It's hard to think of any other reason why he would be so well protected, why he escaped serious punishment for activities that would have quickly ended most careers and could have effectively wrecked one of the force's most prestigious units. After all, it would have been pretty easy to sideline him somewhere in the force, banished to a role that would have meant he had no influence anywhere, without creating any bad publicity, but that didn't happen. He was just moved to another office and got on with his career, while his 'misdemeanours' were watered down before he went in front of the chief constable. Also, as I was soon to find out, he was about to become an ambassador for GMP overseas.

Chapter Twenty-Five

Stepping up the Fight

The internal grievance procedure stopped at this point, as from what I understood there was no right to see the chief constable as part of the process, although as Mr McCrone had flippantly pointed out, 'anyone can ask'. His view seemed to be that they'd looked at what I had to say and decided there was nothing in it. Yet I was sure that they knew what I was saying was true and, more than anything else, they were now embarrassed; they couldn't let what Seddon had been up to become public knowledge.

While I felt dejected by what I saw as something of a sham process, I was still determined that things should be put right, so I wrote a letter to Gary Mason, editor of the national policing magazine *Police Review*. I suppose the letter was the real start of my attempts to take my grievances and raise my concerns outside the force. I realized I wasn't going to get anywhere within GMP, at least not at that stage as there were too many lies being told, so I thought I would look outside our organization to see what I could do.

To my great surprise, I was contacted by the magazine which, rather than wanting to run it as a letter, wanted to do a feature on it. That was music to my ears. A reporter came up to Manchester to interview me, and at the end of May a two-page feature entitled 'Identity Crisis' appeared in the magazine. It outlined my work as an undercover officer, how I'd been told that I'd been over-exposed and not offered any sort of re-entry programme or alternative role, the effect on me and my family, and the threat to our safety. It also detailed my period off sick, that I was currently working in an administrative job (the only post open to me), the fact that I had been seen as a 'guinea pig', and my efforts to try to rectify the situation and find out why my QPM and commendations hadn't materialized, although it didn't go into details about my experience of the grievance procedure to date.

I was over the moon that the article had been published. When I had sent in my original letter, I'd used a pseudonym – David Burton – as the magazine was available for anyone to buy and I couldn't risk exposing my real identity. However, I had given the editor my real name, and we agreed that the article would appear using the same pseudonym.

The initial response from the force was to try to stop publication of the article with the threat of a possible libel action. I was later able to obtain a copy of the following memo about the article, sent to ACC McCrone on 29 May 1997 from the head of GMP's Press Office, Dave Metcalf:

RE: *POLICE REVIEW*

I have still not heard from Gary Mason or the author of the article Keith Potter. They have gone ahead and printed the story despite the warning which I issued them that you were seeking legal advice over inaccuracies and possible libel action.

Jason Bennetto of the *Independent* has got hold of an early copy of *Police Review*, and is planning to run a story on Saturday. He has asked the Press Office for a response and I have briefed him on the legal implications.

However, he would like an on-the-record response to the article to balance up his story.

Police Review went ahead with the article and the libel threat was never followed through (there was nothing libellous in the article). It was also picked up by one of the national Sunday newspapers and the *Manchester Evening News*, although again, the use of the pseudonym (and the obvious lack of any pictures) meant that my identity was safe.

However, Mr McCrone did give a response the following week on the magazine's letters page which, among other things, criticized me for using a false name, but said they had now been able to identify the officer concerned. As I explained in a follow-up letter also printed in the *Review*, the pseudonym was crucial to protect me and my family, but the force senior management team should already have known who I was. There were only half a dozen undercover officers out of a force of more than 7,500 and, as far as I knew, I was the only one who had spent the last year going through a grievance procedure! My letter also made it clear that someone was telling lies and that I would welcome an independent inquiry into these matters as I had nothing to hide and everything to gain.

The strange thing was that while all these written exchanges were taking place in the printed pages of a national magazine, nothing was said to me personally at work, despite the fact that I was incarcerated in the basement of Police HQ and the command team were all above me on the top floor. Of course, psychologically this obviously enabled them to crap on me from a great height.

* * *

As part of my return from long-term sick leave and ongoing diagnosis of PTSD, I'd occasionally been going to the police convalescent home at Harrogate after Dr Faith had said the breaks could help with the effects of stress. When I was there I would go for a long run first thing in the morning, then have my meals during the day and, in between, just try to relax. I would read a lot for relaxation, and one of the books I read while I was there was *No Way Up the Greasy Pole* by Alison Halford, the former ACC of Merseyside Police. She was the first woman in British policing to hold that rank, and her book described the problems she had faced within that force and how she had fought back.

I was inspired by her story. Spurred on partly by my own illness and low mood, but more importantly my belief that I had done nothing wrong yet things and individuals within GMP appeared to be working against me, I decided to write to Alison Halford. I contacted her publishers who passed my letter on, and a short time later she got in touch. We arranged to meet for lunch in North Wales, where we had a long and interesting conversation about what had happened to me, as well as her own experiences. As a result Ms Halford, who was by then a county councillor and went on to become a member of the Welsh

Assembly, wrote directly to GMP Chief Constable David Wilmot on my behalf.

Having been through so many struggles of her own with the police, including having her phones tapped, she may have been able to empathize with me more than most. Her letter[5] said that I had a 'serious grievance' with the force, that she was worried by the treatment I had received so far, and that 'knowing how police management frequently leaves much to be desired', my story had 'a depressing ring of truth' about it. She added:

> I have a clear recollection of that interview room in March 1983 when fate cruelly decreed that the Merseyside ACC's promotion should be mine. In my short acquaintance with you then, I rather rated you and felt you were a cut above the rest.
>
> It seems a great wrong has been perpetrated against Garry Rogers and that you as his Chief Officer are the only one capable of finding a solution. It is a sad fact of life that despite extensive training and seeming commitment to change for the better, the sensitive and compassionate management of many junior officers by the service's senior echelons leave much room for improvement.

I would like to say that when David Wilmot read this letter he instantly understood what had happened and who had been involved, and immediately took steps to put matters right. I was awarded the QPM straight away, and all those involved in this conspiracy were disciplined and duly sacked without any pension rights. I'd like to say that, but I can't.

Mr Wilmot replied to Alison Halford stating that I had not told her the whole story, that they were doing everything they could to integrate me back into policing but that I was causing them problems, and that he could not discuss the QPM. Mr Wilmot was pretty clear that he thought I was being difficult and that the force was doing everything possible to help me.

Of course, I was just a name and number to him. He had never met me, and I'd never been able to explain my side of the story, which is one of the reasons why I wanted a meeting with him. I felt that if we could talk about this on a personal, one-to-one basis, maybe I could get somewhere.

I wrote to Alison Halford again, thanking her for her support. She was a lovely person, seen within the job as a bit of an eccentric, but one of that handful of people I felt I could trust. She'd done as much as she could for me, and she wished me well for the future.

* * *

Although Mr Wilmot's response was less than positive, the knock back seemed to spur me on once again and I requested to see the chief constable. Unsurprisingly, this request was turned down. I was increasingly keen for my allegations to be heard and investigated independently from someone outside of GMP. I knew I had nothing to worry about, but I was pretty sure the force didn't feel the same.

I continued in the Video Imaging Unit, despite my health and personal life being in turmoil. I was still, due to financial circumstances, riding my pushbike to work and I became obsessed with my health, fearing I had something drastically wrong with me. My attempts to get justice, both inside and outside the force, were largely going on behind my wife's back. I wasn't being deceitful; I just think she would have been even more worried about what I was doing. She would have felt that, by going against the authority of the force, I was digging myself an even bigger hole.

I could understand why she would think like that, but the reality was that this battle to clear my name and get some sort of justice was what kept me going. As far as my working life was concerned, it was just an existence. I knew I shouldn't be in there, but I couldn't afford to go off sick again; I would have been straight onto half-pay, and that would have crippled us financially. So I would come into work every day, hating what I was doing, but also trying to think of ways I could prove that I hadn't done anything wrong. The alternative was to give up completely and I think that would have been more damaging to my health, but it did mean it was on my mind 24/7, trying to sort all this out while keeping quiet about it at the same time.

I was being pretty blinkered. I thought this was just affecting me: it was my fight, no one else's, and I could win it, but the reality was it affected the whole family. Mentally I was still in a really tough place, and I could lose my temper at the drop of a hat. It meant that my wife and I would end up arguing, which was my fault, but she would then go away to her mum's for a few days to get some space between us so that things could calm down. Although we never separated for a lengthy period of time, that could easily have escalated and ended our marriage.

There were times when I must have been impossible to live with. There were certainly times when I felt it would have been better for me, and for everyone else, if I just wasn't around. I've said I never wanted to give up trying to prove that I hadn't done anything wrong, and that I was wrongly being targeted, and that was true. Yet the constant pressure of that, of feeling like I was taking ten steps forward and twenty back, of knowing – or feeling – that no one in this big organization believed me...that was difficult. Add to that the way I was behaving at home, and the whole sense of injustice and frustration that I felt, and yes, there were times when I felt suicidal.

All of this came out further down the line when I got to see a good PTSD counsellor. However, my wife wasn't a counsellor. She couldn't have been expected to understand what was going on in my head; at that point I didn't understand it myself. What I did know was that, as much as this fight to try to prove I hadn't done anything wrong was damaging my health, it was also the thing that was keeping me going.

*　*　*

On 12 August 1997 I sent the following letter to the then Home Secretary, Jack Straw:

Dear Home Secretary,
Further to my letter of June 23, 1997, which you subsequently passed on to Mr O'Dowd, the Chief Inspector of Constabulary,

to which I enclose copies of his correspondence to me, I am writing to you once more in a continuing state of frustration. I am grateful to Mr O'Dowd for the time he has spent on this issue but it is quite clear that the main theme of his letters is that the HMI cannot interfere with the operational independence of the Chief Constable.

My question therefore is who can? Or does the Chief Constable have total autonomy to cover up what he or she likes? I, through yourself, would like to air all the facts to whoever you so wish providing that person can interfere!

I hope that by writing directly to you once again, you realise how strongly I feel about these issues and that my resolve is strong.

Thank you for your time

Yours Sincerely

G Rogers

I sent this letter by recorded delivery so I could prove that they had received it. Four weeks later I had still heard nothing, so phoned the Home Office and was informed that they had received my letter on 13 August but that the first department it went to had refused to accept it, and that because of its content it should be sent elsewhere in the Home Office. The new department had accepted it on 23 August and I was told to expect a reply in the next ten days.

My continuing letters to the Home Office had borne some important fruit though. I was granted an audience with the new HMI, John Stevens, who later went on to receive a knighthood and become Commissioner of the Metropolitan Police. I initially met Mr Stevens' staff officer, Superintendent John Tapley, on 15 August 1997. He was a breath of fresh air, and is another person who takes one of the fingers on my imaginary hand when I count the number of people who really helped me. Despite his unique position and rank, he was someone who I felt happy talking to in that he actually listened and genuinely looked into the points I raised, in spite of the obstacles put in his path by GMP. Superintendent Tapley pushed a lot of things forward for me because, having met face-to-face and been able to explain everything

I'd been through, he felt that I had a strong argument. If he hadn't felt that way, or someone else had been in that role who didn't want to see me, I would never have got to meet Mr Stevens. Things could well have turned out very differently and I might not be sitting here today.

Mr Tapley had to be satisfied that what you wanted to speak to the HMI about was relevant and not likely to waste his limited time while on his inspection of the force. I had one more meeting with Mr Tapley before my appointment with Mr Stevens could be confirmed. During this meeting I also discovered that the QPM nomination for my former undercover partner, Reg, had been sanctioned and processed on 25 March 1995, but that all the paperwork for my nomination was now non-existent. So in the course of a few weeks back in 1995, I had gone off sick, Seddon had been removed overnight as head of the Covert Operations Department and my nomination for a QPM had been shredded, while the nomination for Reg – who I had been told was put forward jointly with me – had sailed through. Little revelations like this helped to spur me on because, although in one sense they were annoying or depressing, they proved that I had been right to believe that something underhand was going on.

I met with Mr Stevens during his inspection of GMP at 6.00 pm on Wednesday, 10 September 1997. We met at his hotel (the Old Rectory in Denton) and I'm pretty sure that, after a long day of meetings and assessing the force's activities, all he really wanted to do was to go and have some dinner. However, he put me at my ease and the meeting was informal from the start. There were no private lounges in which to speak, so we went to Mr Tapley's hotel room and I explained everything to Mr Stevens as clearly and concisely as I could, while – slightly bizarrely – he lay on the bed and Mr Tapley took written notes.

After a while he intervened and said: 'You need to see the Chief Constable.' I explained that this wasn't an option in the GMP grievance procedure, but he told me to submit a report requesting to see Mr Wilmot anyway. He likened my situation to an air bubble that appears under some newly-laid lino – no matter how many times you stand on it, it pops up somewhere else – and that was his way of saying that no matter how many times GMP stood on me, I was not going to go away. The force had to sort it out.

The following morning Mr Tapley came to see me at Chester House and we went to a quiet area of the canteen. He told me that he had checked GMP's grievance procedure policy and that I was right: you don't get to see the chief constable; it stops at the ACC.

However, Mr Tapley also revealed that the force had refused to give him access to my personal file, something he described as 'highly unusual'. He'd made a request to GMP on 18 August (shortly after our first meeting) in his official role as the HMI's staff officer for copies of my personal file, grievance procedure report and all other documentation relating to my case. He was acting under the delegated authority of Mr Stevens, which allowed him to go anywhere in the force and to see any relevant documents in relation to the inspection. His request in relation to my case was perfectly legitimate and was made to the GMP HMI liaison officer.

The Deputy Chief Constable (Mr Cairns) apparently refused this request, without explanation. Mr Tapley said that it was the first time in his four-year career that this had happened, and it wasn't something he had heard of taking place before. All HMIs act under the authority of a Royal Warrant, and Mr Tapley's view was that if the force carried on down that route and refused to give the HMI access to the records he needed to do the job, then eventually he would have to invoke the Royal Warrant. This would force GMP to give the HMI access to whatever information he wanted to see.

Mr Tapley said that Mr Stevens didn't wish to 'push the issue' and would try to talk through a way to avoid that when he met directly with Mr Wilmot on the formal inspection. Yet the fact that the force would even put itself in this position was disconcerting, and once again raised the question why? It convinced me even more that I was doing the right thing, and so did a further revelation by Mr Tapley. He told me that I had never been put forward for the QPM, only Reg had, and that this was a 'travesty of justice' that could blow up in the chief constable's face.

So had I never been nominated for the QPM in the first place, or had it never got past Detective Chief Superintendent James? Had it never reached him, or had it reached him and been shredded? Either way, it had never gone above him. Yet several months earlier he was telling me to my face, in a formal grievance meeting, that I was 'still in the pot' for the award.

At 2.15 pm the same day I submitted a report requesting an audience with Mr David Wilmot, Chief Constable of GMP.

Chapter Twenty-Six

Time to Go to the Top

As well as requesting a meeting with the chief constable, I made arrangements, should my request be granted, for a representative from the Police Federation to attend with me, but there was now a personal issue for me with the Greater Manchester branch of the Federation. Gerry Millington, who was General Secretary of the Joint Branch Board, had been DCI Seddon's 'friend' when he had appeared before the chief constable and received his laughably lenient disciplinary action. Mr Millington was also a good personal friend of Seddon's.

John Tapley had given me a copy of the report he had prepared as a brief for Mr Stevens, which investigated my situation and what I was saying about the way I had been treated. The report included details of his meeting with Gerry Millington. Mr Millington had been highly critical of me, saying that Seddon was sure that I had been behind the anonymous letters to the force and the *Manchester Evening News*. He also said that Seddon had explained to him why he wanted me out of the unit – because apparently I had been 'taking liberties in the downtime' between operations and going drinking while I should have been in the office.

Nothing could have been further from the truth – in fact, that was what I was getting in trouble for *not* doing – but this is what Seddon had been saying behind my back to his friends and Masonic mates. He even claimed that I was 'well suited' to being an undercover officer because I was a 'Walter Mitty character'!

I was by now becoming increasingly alert to the fact that Seddon had seemingly done a good job in convincing a number of people that I had been responsible for the letters exposing his unprofessional, corrupt behaviour. CID Command, headed by Detective Chief Superintendent

James, had been forced to take action to move Seddon before that behaviour could be confirmed in the public domain, but that doesn't mean they were happy about it or the way it had been exposed. It was quite conceivable that Mr James had shredded my QPM nomination (if one had ever been made) in response to what he wrongly believed I had done, having taken the word of his DCI and fellow Mason Seddon rather than asking me directly.

Seddon had used his friends and Masonic contacts to make it appear that I was looking for a job in the RCS when he had first tried to move me out of the Covert Operations Department. He had also called on the support of his friend Gerry Millington to not only avoid serious disciplinary action but to plant lies about my own behaviour, which were then being fed back to the HMI as truths and 'facts'.

I had also now been made aware of a note attached to the altered 'original' commendation report in my personal file regarding Operation Crocodile, the operation which Mr James had said was not worthy of any recognition. The note, handwritten by Mr McCrone, said the report was being held back not because the operation wasn't worthy of recognition but because of an ongoing Y Department investigation. So aside from the questions this now raised about Mr James's comments, I'd also begun to wonder whether this investigation was into Seddon's activities – as Superintendent Bill Fernside had suggested when he'd first visited me back in March 1995 when I was off sick – or whether in fact the investigation was focusing more on me...

I now strongly believed that certain individuals – Seddon's friends and Masonic mates – were pinning the anonymous letter on me. If I was right, not only was this Masonic kangaroo court totally off the mark, but it was also largely responsible for the sudden nosedive in my career, the treatment I had received since and the stress, frustration and sense of injustice I was feeling now. This was a police force supposed to uphold law and order, prosecute offenders and protect the innocent, yet they were willing to ruin my life and my career to protect one of their own. They did these things only suspecting me of being responsible for Seddon's downfall to date. God knows what they would have done if I really had sent those letters, and they could prove it...

With all of this going around in my head, I was inevitably concerned about where the allegiance of the Greater Manchester Federation office would lay: would it be with serving rank-and-file officers like me, or with officers who were friends and possibly fellow Masons? I felt that Gerry Millington had already made his views clear, so I asked to be represented by Lancashire Joint Branch Board.

* * *

On 17 September I received a reply to my request for a meeting with Mr Wilmot. The chief constable had agreed to see me at 11.30 am on Wednesday, 24 September and had allocated fifteen minutes for the appointment. This was great news, as I felt I now had my opportunity to speak face-to-face with the most senior officer in the force and tell him everything that had gone on, rather than relying on those below him to only tell him half the story. I wasn't worried about the fifteen minutes; I knew we'd be talking for longer than that, as I had to make sure that after 24 September he knew everything. Then it was up to him.

While things seemed to be starting to move inside the force, my efforts to get my voice heard outside GMP were proving less successful. I'd still had no response to my previous letters to the Home Office or the Home Secretary (I knew Jack Straw would never see it, it would just go to one of his minions, but I figured I might as well start at the top), so on 18 September I rang the Home Office and spoke with a lady by the name of Sally. She told me that my letter had now been sent to a further department which dealt with police awards and that she would contact them and get someone to ring me back. True to her word, twenty minutes later I had a call from a Pauline Laybarn, who now told me that she didn't know exactly where my letter was, but that she would make further enquiries and come back to me.

It seemed to me that no one was listening and that they were passing me from pillar to post. The next day I had a call from someone else in the Home Office, Lynn Cousins, about my letter of 12 August to Mr Straw. She told me I would get a reply. She was also aware that I was seeing the chief constable on 24 September (good news travels almost as fast as bad!) and said that if nothing was resolved I was to ring her on her personal office number.

Throughout my efforts to get some justice from GMP and my dealings with the Home Office, I was repeatedly told that it was against protocol to discuss certain issues or to be given certain information as it was confidential. On that basis I'd always expected my correspondence to the Home Secretary to be confidential. So imagine my surprise when I discovered the following fax, sent on 19 September 1997 to Chief Superintendent Chris Cross of GMP from Les Owen at the Home Office, in response to his obvious previous request to obtain my letters to the Home Secretary:

> Chris
> I cannot send the letters he has sent to the Home Secretary, apparently this would breach protocol. If you need any detail from them please give me a ring and I can paraphrase.

They were therefore getting confidential correspondence from me to the Home Secretary behind the scenes. Imagine what I would have been told if I had telephoned GMP or the Home Office and requested information from their correspondence? It certainly felt like this wasn't a level playing field.

*   *   *

When 24 September arrived I duly went up to the Command Suite on the top floor of Chester House with Norman Briggs, my Federation representative from Lancashire. We were met by the chief constable's secretary, who seemed perplexed that I had someone with me; she said the chief constable thought I would be on my own. She went away and returned a short time later with the civilian head of personnel, Andrew Marston, who I had seen earlier in the grievance procedure. He had a tape recorder with him and took us into a conference room. He explained that the chief constable was a bit uneasy at Mr Briggs being present as this was not an extension of the grievance procedure. He also warned us that while the chief constable would see us, he might not actually say anything about my situation today. Finally he asked if we minded the conversation being tape-recorded. I had no problems with any of it being recorded, as long as I could be given a copy of any relevant tapes (which he agreed). It made a nice change for a meeting to be recorded openly rather than covertly.

We took our seats in this grand conference room that very few officers at my level ever get to see, and the chief constable arrived a short time later. In the end, as you can see in the full transcript[6] of our 'conversation', apart from an opening comment about the meeting not forming any part of the formal grievance procedure, Mr Wilmot said less than fifty words.

However, more importantly, he did sit and listen. He listened to both Norman Briggs and myself going through the various aspects of what had happened: the non-submission of the QPM nomination; the lies about what had happened to it; the obvious doctoring of the Operation Crocodile commendation report; the apparent Y Department investigation; and Mr McCrone's lack of action over any of it. He also listened to my impassioned plea that, far from wanting to waste anybody's time, I just wanted to have an opportunity to tell him the truth and explain to him what had gone on and that it would have made me ill if I hadn't taken that opportunity.

As stated, Mr Wilmot said no more than fifty words, but one sentence from those fifty words stood out for me:

Okay, at the end of the day I cannot comment apart from what was initially said by asking me to agree to look into the procedures within the force and to possibly investigate the procedure that led to this meeting today. It raises some significant concerns.

This last phrase was, once again, music to my ears. To me it meant that if the chief constable found what I was saying to be true and credible, then something had gone badly wrong. This was the first time that any officer within the force at any sort of senior level (and they don't come much more senior than the chief constable) had taken my concerns seriously. I would have loved to have been a fly on the wall at some of the follow-up meetings that Mr Wilmot had.

* * *

Throughout this whole process, alongside the recordings of meetings and telephone conversations, I kept accurate records on a daily basis of all relevant events that took place. It was what I had done throughout my police career, so it was second nature to me.

At 10.00 am on Tuesday, 30 September I had an appointment to see Andrew Marston in his office. I had earlier been to collect the audio tape and typed transcript of my conversation with Mr Wilmot from his secretary Sandra Firth. At this meeting he told me that the chief constable had listened to what I had to say, and he felt that I told Mr Wilmot things of which he had not been aware. In my notes at the time I made the following comment: 'What will happen in the future is a big??? Chief Constable won't confirm or deny anything.'

While talking with Sandra Firth she gave me a copy of the following poem that was on her wall:

Don't Quit

When things go wrong as they sometimes will
When the road you're trudging seems all up hill
When the funds are low and the debts are high
And you want to smile, but you have to sigh
When care is pressing you down a bit
Rest if you must but don't you quit.

Success is failure turned inside out
The silver tint of the clouds of doubt
And you can never tell how close you are
It may be near when it seems so far
So stick to the fight when you're hardest hit
It's when things seem worse
That you must not quit.

Chapter Twenty-Seven

A Man of Letters

I was now in limbo. I didn't know what was going to happen next, or what I should do for the best. I felt as though to date I'd tried almost everything I could to get someone who cared, or who could make a difference, to listen to what I was saying. At the start of October I sent a letter to Mr Tapley, asking whether Mr Stevens' involvement in my case was now effectively at an end. If so, I needed to know now so that I could work out what to do in the long term. A few weeks later Mr Tapley called me and basically told me that Mr Stevens had done as much as he could; that was the end of it.

I was grateful for his help so far, but I wanted to have something in writing to confirm the issues we had discussed and Mr Stevens' views, as the HMI, on what I had told him. I immediately sent a letter[7] to Mr Tapley, asking for that written confirmation of three key points: the discussions we had at Mr Stevens' hotel, particularly about the doctored report; that Reg's signed QPM nomination had been submitted to the Home Office in March 1995; and that DCI Seddon had been disciplined for his actions by the chief constable. Mr Tapley called me back the following week to say that Mr Stevens was away in South Africa but that I would get a reply when he returned at the end of November.

It was now a month since my one-to-one with Mr Wilmot and I'd heard nothing. You never really saw him around Chester House (or at least I hadn't), and he wasn't a particularly 'sociable' chief constable, but I guess like any chief officer, up there in those ivory towers, those below him would let the good stuff filter up while trying to bury the bad stuff. Having spoken to him though, I got the feeling that he had genuinely listened to what I had to say. Unlike Mr McCrone, who may have heard my words but had no intention of acting on them, Mr

Wilmot seemed to believe what I was telling him and was prepared to do something about it. At least, that's what I hoped. I spoke to Norman Briggs, who had accompanied me to the meeting as my Police Federation representative. He wrote to Mr Wilmot on 23 October[8] asking if he could update us on revisiting the circumstances around my case, as well as the investigation into the doctored report.

I was still looking for ways to try to get some sort of justice, and any avenue that I felt I could use to further my cause was worth a try. *Manchat* was the monthly GMP Federation magazine which featured news and articles about both national and local issues, and I read in the October edition that the editor was leaving. He proudly stated that throughout his editorship, if a subject had needed to be broached it would be published without fail. This caught my eye, so at the start of November 1997, I sent him a long letter[9] outlining the sequence of events that had happened to me.

I wrote about everything, including my view of the grievance procedure: that it was one-sided, that paperwork would go missing, that senior officers were seemingly allowed to alter reports to their benefit, and that even when you discovered this, nothing was done about it. I also compared my experiences with those of a 'certain senior officer' who was simply reprimanded for serious abuses of authority that would have got any other officer sacked. I knew that might touch a nerve, as obviously the Federation had been instrumental in enabling Seddon to escape serious punishment – and at the same time, helping him to blacken my name – but if I was going to talk about everything, I felt I should make that point too.

My letter appeared in December's 'You say, You say' section of *Manchat*, all 800+ words of it; except, of course, for the paragraph about Seddon. I made the following note in my diary of events at that time:

Manchat published article 'Our Force' edited with section re Seddon left out? Response by ACC McCrone in his usual tone of everything has been done – makes my blood boil – no news re QPM – have decided to press forward and have outside force investigate my complaint.

By the end of November I had received a reply[10] from Mr Stevens, who had now returned from South Africa. It certainly made encouraging reading. While he was clear that he was only acting in an 'advisory capacity', he confirmed that he had told Mr Wilmot about my concerns. He also knew that I'd already met with the chief constable and that I was receiving advice from the Federation, and suggested that I might want to talk to the Federation about further action if the chief couldn't resolve things. He confirmed our conversations about the doctored report (in detail), Reg's QPM, and Seddon's disciplinary. While he also said that he had pursued his advisory role 'to its limits', it was not necessarily the end of his involvement, as he encouraged me to contact him or Mr Tapley 'if there are further developments'.

To me, this was fantastic. Here was the HMI, not telling me to go away as I was imagining things that were not there but clearly stating everything we discussed in a letter that confirmed what took place. He then sent a copy to Mr Wilmot for his information. I couldn't really have asked for much more.

On 28 November, Mr Briggs received a reply[11] from the chief constable. It was much more concise than Mr Stevens but, to my mind, equally encouraging. In it, Mr Wilmot said:

> Firstly I now have a report regarding Constable Rogers' achievements and as per my policy with any other officer I do not intend to say how I have dealt with that report. I can, however, assure you that it is comprehensive.
>
> Without wishing to be pedantic in respect of the wording of your penultimate paragraph, I do not recall agreeing to 'initiate an investigation' regarding the date change on another award recommendation. I have, however, looked into the matter and a report is with the Awards Committee of the Force.

While I was quite happy with this, Norman Briggs wasn't so sure. He wrote to me explaining that we now had a bit of a dilemma. As Mr Wilmot said that a 'comprehensive review' had taken place, I now had to decide whether I left things for six or twelve months to see what the outcome of that review was, or whether I looked at taking another course of action.

I was now pleased that at last, things seemed to be moving, so I wasn't sure whether to sit and wait or try something different. A while later, as I sat in the Chester House canteen a week before Christmas Day, I bumped into my old undercover partner, Reg. He told me that DCI Trevor, the DCI of Covert Operations, had telephoned him at beginning of November asking him about the operations we had done together as he had to put in a report about them as a result of me being to see the HMI and the chief. He also wanted to know about the commendations we had received.

It was clear that Mr Wilmot had been asking questions, so maybe my feeling about him had been right. When I had come out of our meeting I felt great. The idea that I had explained what had happened to me and that situation had raised 'significant concerns' was pretty encouraging. However, I still couldn't be 100 per cent sure that this wasn't just his chief constable's façade: that he hadn't gone away, looked at it and decided I was seeing things that weren't there. The fact that he was now asking the right questions of other people seemed to suggest that he was actually doing something. It still took a while though; things moved a lot more slowly in the force than they did with, for example, the HMI. Reg finished our conversation by saying that he felt the QPM was really mine. That was good of him to say. I didn't want to take anything away from him as he deserved it, but my argument was simple: if he deserved it, so did I.

*   *   *

The year 1997 became 1998 and I returned to work on 5 January. I received a letter from the Personnel Department informing me that the chief constable had awarded me his Citation of Merit for Operation Miracle. This award had been stopped when I went off sick in 1995 and was in relation to an operation that we had concluded in 1993. Here we were, five years later, receiving a Citation of Merit for that job and only getting it because I'd gone through the grievance procedure.

Mr James had said our work hadn't been worthy of recognition, but, like the commendation for Operation Crocodile and the QPM, it had really been held back because I'd made my feelings known about DCI Seddon's behaviour, then gone off sick, and Mr James and others believed I was responsible for alerting the wider force and the media to their corrupt mate. Of course, unlike the QPM, they hadn't been able to hold my award back on its own while giving everyone else on the job theirs – that would have been too obvious – so they decided that no one would get it. They were prepared to take away the recognition that other officers deserved just to make a point to me; that wasn't fair to me or the rest of the team.

Following on from our meeting, the chief constable had looked at the operation (up to that point the citation report was clearly going nowhere); unlike Mr James, he felt that the work was worthy of recognition. So now the whole Operation Miracle team would be getting a Citation of Merit. I and the rest of the team were invited to a private presentation ceremony in the Officers' Mess at Chester House on 15 January. It was a bittersweet moment, as while I felt it proved I was right to start the grievance procedure which in itself gave me a much-needed boost, it reinforced the fact that there were elements within the force that had been determined to make sure that my career was effectively over. I didn't feel like celebrating: I rang Personnel and told them that I wouldn't be attending the presentation. Instead I collected the award from Personnel on 14 January, without any fuss.

* * *

While it looked like things were starting to move in the right direction at work, I still felt as if I was in a battle where the odds were stacked against me. After all, the force would always be judge and jury on itself; the only way to get a completely unbiased viewpoint was to get someone involved externally. So I was still pushing for someone outside, someone independent of the force, to look at what I was saying. With hindsight I was still suffering the effects of the PTSD for which I had yet to have any specialist counselling. Emotionally I was on a rollercoaster, and while every now and then we took a step forward, that was quite often followed by at least one step backwards. I must have been almost impossible to live with, and inevitably all this was taking its toll on my wife too. Unbeknown to me, she had decided to write a letter[12] to the Police Complaints Authority (PCA) in London to see if she could help my situation.

The letter went through all the details of what had happened to me before I went off sick, the reprimand for Seddon, and my subsequent return to work and experience of the grievance procedure. She spoke about the 'lie after lie' I'd been told by the GMP senior management, the support I'd had from Alison Halford, and my conversations with both HMI John Stevens and the Chief Constable Mr Wilmot. She also explained that she was writing the letter 'as a member of the public' to bring the matter out into the open. Below is an extract from the letter:

> I apologise if my letter is disjointed and hard to follow in parts, but we have suffered so much and I have so much that I want to say that I find it hard to put it into words. As a result my husband and myself have both received counselling...
>
> It is to you, therefore, that I am writing, without may I add my husband's knowledge, as I feel enough is enough and these matters must be investigated by an entirely separate, unbiased body who will investigate these matters correctly.

She sent this letter on 9 January 1998. Even reading it today is difficult, realizing just how tough much of this was for her. A week later she received a response from Mr Merrell of the PCA, explaining that responsibility for recording a complaint against a police officer fell to a chief officer of the force involved (in this case ACC George), and checking that she was happy for him to follow the usual route of referring the letter to the chief officer, given the nature of her complaint. My wife immediately replied to Mr Merrell, confirming that she wanted him to forward her letter to ACC George.

On 3 February she received a letter[13] from Superintendent K.S. Homan (another name worth remembering) from GMP's Discipline and Complaints Department. It was pretty straightforward: as far as they were concerned, the issue had been fully investigated through the grievance procedure, and I had also spoken to both the HMI and the chief constable about it, so that was that. Additionally, he pointed out that the complaints legislation didn't allow for her, as a member of the public, to make a complaint on behalf of a police officer.

Yet again, there were no surprises here, but the disappointment prompted my wife to tell me about her attempts to help me and get these issues out in the open. To be honest, and to my shame, when she first told me I was annoyed, because – blinkered as ever – I felt that it was my campaign, I was trying to put things right, and in my own way I'd been trying to protect my wife and family. Yet deep down I was very grateful. I knew she was doing it to try to help me; she could see the frustration that was building up in me and she wanted to see if she could change things. It again made me realize that this wasn't only affecting me, but was stamping its mark on others who were innocent bystanders.

It also underlined how bad things were becoming. We'd both had to have counselling, and the stress that I was suffering was putting my family life under incredible pressure too, but as far as the job goes, you're just left to deal with that. All GMP were talking about were the practicalities of my working life: don't go off sick again or you'll be on half-pay; there are plenty of jobs that you can do to keep you out of the way; and we may even be able to sort out some of those awards for you. Don't worry, this won't happen to anyone else, and we're sorry you were treated as the guinea pig. However, my overall health, my PTSD, and the effect on my family and on my wife were never really considered.

Fired up by the response to my wife, I decided to write to Mr Merrell directly. I explained that I now knew she had been trying to help, but that the response from GMP had been less than sympathetic, and requested a face-to-face meeting with someone from the PCA. It was a waste of time though. Mr Merrell wrote back, pointing out again that the relevant legislation didn't cover complaints made by or on behalf of police officers, only complaints by members of the public against police officers. We'd come up against another brick wall.

With the frustration continuing to increase, at the beginning of March I wrote to both GMP and Home Secretary Jack Straw. My letter[14] to the force set out my dismay with the grievance procedure and asked for a copy of my comments disputing Superintendent Homan's claim that my 'complaints had been fully investigated and aired' to be placed on my personal file. I added that I would be looking to instigate a new grievance procedure in the near future.

The letter[15] to Mr Straw set out my 'utter dismay' about what I'd been through, much of which I'd already explained in two previous letters. I also highlighted my concerns about the contents of what I considered to be confidential letters to the Home Secretary, then being shared by phone with senior officers in GMP. I included a copy of the fax from Les Owen to Chief Superintendent Chris Cross, adding:

This fax implies to me that information I felt was confidential was passed by phone to assist senior management at GMP to be armed with certain information at the time of my audience with the Chief Constable. If I were to ring the Home Office and ask for information to be given to me over the phone, I wonder what the reply would be?

This type of back-door attempt to keep one step ahead turns justice into injustice. This is one further example of not what you know but who you know, and raises a lot of questions over the system.

The reply[16] came on 31 March from an Ian Smith at the Home Office and again, was straight to the point, saying that he didn't understand the basis of my complaint, and that there was no 'back-door' collusion. Instead, there was 'a fair amount of work by people solely concerned with dealing fairly and properly with your grievance.' Mr Smith added:

This was done entirely professionally and properly with the sole objective of facilitating a meeting between you and your Chief Constable with a view to resolving your grievances.

I hope that this explanation reassures you that nothing improper whatsoever took place and, in particular, the actions were designed to serve the interests of justice, not, as your letter might be read to imply, to promote an injustice.

So that was me told. I hadn't really expected them to say anything else, although I still couldn't see how supplying details of letters sent in confidence – not to the HMIC, but to the Home Office – could be right. If it was so right, why didn't they just fax them? If sending the letters across in their entirety was against protocol as Les Owen had claimed, how could disclosing all the information in them over the phone be within protocol? Besides, all of that information was already with both the Home Office and GMP as I'd written many letters to both of them over the previous months and years. Maybe they just hadn't read them...

I sent one final letter[17] back to Ian Smith – as much in anger and despair as in any sense of hope – pointing much of this out. I didn't expect a further reply, and I wasn't disappointed.

Chapter Twenty-Eight

Farewell Seddon, Hello Harrogate

During 1998 the Video Imaging Unit moved from Chester House to Bradford Park on Ashton New Road. I was still able to cycle from home to work and back, but my new work room now had windows! So while the work was no more interesting, copying video tapes and producing stills for court, I at least had a bit of a view.

One particular day, I happened to look out across the car park to the CID building opposite, when to my horror I saw DCI Seddon and his wife come out of the building, followed by a small group of people. I hadn't seen Seddon since I'd gone off sick three years earlier, so it was a real shock; I couldn't really comprehend what I was looking at. Fortunately the windows were one-way: you couldn't see in from the outside, as I probably stood there, dumbstruck, just staring I think; but now, at just 12 stone and pretty gaunt, I doubt he would have recognized me anyway.

Seddon and his wife had their kids with them too. They stood chatting to a group of people on the steps before everyone hugged them and then they got in their car and drove away, with everyone waving them off. At the time I didn't know what was going on, but I was also a bit intrigued. It took a little while, but I found out that he was going off on secondment to Australia, effectively as an ambassador for the force.

I think what I felt was a mixture of disbelief and anger. It was like being back in that emotional boxing ring again. When I saw him it felt like I'd been punched; when I found out he was going to Australia as an 'ambassador' for the force, it felt like I'd been punched again. Here was the man who had been removed overnight from an elite, high-profile, professional undercover unit, which was at the forefront of police techniques. He was removed for irregular activities, and later appeared before the chief constable in disciplinary proceedings where he pleaded guilty to a disciplinary matter (which, to this day, seems to bear no resemblance to what actually took place). With that track record, surely he should be the last person on earth to send to Australia on such a prestigious secondment?

Meanwhile I was still ploughing on, still trying to get some sort of resolution to my grievances, while this bastard was swanning off to Australia, being waved away like some sort of GMP hero.

*　*　*

I continued to press on in the same vein, keeping my head down at work, doing what I had to do and no more. I was still having regular appointments with the Force Medical Officer Dr Deighton every couple of months, which was traumatic in itself. When I first went to see him, he was pretty convinced I was trying to swing the lead. He was used to people going into his office who just wanted to get out of the job on medical grounds, so his first approach was always to try to get people back to work as quickly as possible.

However, my situation was a bit more complicated because I didn't walk into his surgery with a broken arm or a dislocated ankle or any sort of injury that you could see. So as well as assuming initially that I was telling lies to get out of the job, he didn't understand the illness I was suffering from. He had very little (if any) experience of PTSD, so after a while, although he may have begun to realize that I was genuinely ill, he didn't have the first idea what to do about it.

He would just ask me how I was and then send me away for another couple of months before my next appointment. It wasn't the first time the force had sent me to see people who couldn't really help me. In fact, until much later when I eventually got to see Professor Gisli Gudjonsson, a PTSD specialist in London, I felt like they had all been playing at it. Still, I doubt they had any experience of dealing with officers suffering from PTSD anyway; or at least no experience of PTSD that had been diagnosed.

I didn't realize it at the time, but by now I had also developed an inner hatred for the police and everything associated with them. That's a strange thing to say, given my length of service and all the good times and success I had had, but due to what had taken place, I no longer trusted the actual service I had joined with such pride. I'd witnessed and experienced first-hand the lies and deceit, and the feeling was irreversible. Being among them every day fuelled my anger and my ill health as it was a constant reminder of what they had done.

Dealing with those sorts of emotions wasn't easy, so I tended to shut off, especially when it came to any contact with senior officers or management. I had as little as possible to do with Pat Davies, the civilian boss of the unit, or with DCI Keeling, the officer who wanted to know why he was being landed with a 'monster' like me. However, I got to know other people in the unit, civilian staff, who knew nothing about what I'd been through. Many of them were nice people with whom I got on well.

I knew I was still surplus to requirements though, and I also realized that I had to look ahead and try to get out of the rut I was in. I decided to apply for a public speaking course at the Force Training School in Prestwich, my idea being that if I was successful I could possibly get on a Police Trainers Course, get out of GMP and go to work at the National Police Training Centre at Bruche, near Warrington. It wouldn't have been my first career choice in previous years, but I knew someone who worked at Bruche who told me that it was a good place to be, and I felt I still had a lot to offer and just not within GMP.

I successfully completed the public speaking course, which opened up the next door: the Trainer's Development Programme, a course of around ten weeks at the National Police Training Centre in Harrogate. I was still going to the police convalescent home in Harrogate for occasional breaks, and as I'd always found that to be like a breath of fresh air, I hoped the 'train the trainers' course would be much the same. I couldn't cycle to Harrogate and back though, so I invested in a small 125cc motorcycle. I looked a bit like a circus act as I set off with my large bag strapped to the back and me seated on it. From certain angles it looked like I was floating along as you couldn't see the little bike beneath me, and it could be pretty hairy tackling some of the roads between home and Harrogate.

I enjoyed the course, although I still didn't socialize much, even though most of the officers I was with were from outside GMP. I wasn't much of a drinker anyway by then, and I was trying to concentrate on staying fit and healthy, so I'd go for a decent run every morning, and another guy and I used to go to the gym or do some sort of fitness activity in the evenings rather than heading for the bar every night. It didn't go completely according to plan though.

One Sunday afternoon I was at home, getting ready to go back to Harrogate that evening, when I became aware that my heart was beating extremely fast; it felt like it was coming out of my chest. I thought I might be imagining it, but to be safe I went to A&E at Salford Royal Hospital, where they connected me up to a heart monitor. That soon proved it wasn't in my head: the alarm was continually sounding and I was immediately taken to the Heart Care Unit and admitted as a patient. I couldn't believe what was happening.

The machine I was attached to continued to sound its alarm as my heart carried on racing. That night I didn't sleep at all, and a nurse on the ward came to talk to me; she was telling me how they could work wonders these days with heart bypass operations, but that wasn't what I wanted to hear and it depressed me even more. My wife had to ring the instructors at Harrogate to tell them the news. I could only afford to be away from the course for a few days, otherwise they would fail me. That particular Monday was the day the course had the official 'class' photo, which is why I am nowhere to be seen on it: I was laying in the Heart Care Unit at the Salford Royal.

The doctors carried out several tests and eventually concluded that my condition had been caused by the Prozac that I was still taking for depression. The doctors told me that they hadn't seen a reaction like that before and I was immediately taken off the Prozac. Having realized that I wasn't going to have to go through surgery, my spirits lifted, and pretty soon after changing my medication my heart rate returned to normal. By the Wednesday I was back at Harrogate.

The course was quite intense and stressful, but in a positive way. You constantly had to prepare and then present different topics to an audience of instructors and your peers, and you were critically marked on each presentation. As well as successfully completing the Trainer's Development Programme, which allowed me to become a National Police Trainer, while I was at Harrogate I also completed my City and Guilds accreditation: the Further and Adult Education Teachers' Certificate.

* * *

I had also, through the Police Federation, been advised to seek legal advice on everything that had taken place. I was directed to Russell, Jones and Walker, the Police Federation solicitors in Manchester, where my case was dealt with by William O'Brien. They began proceedings against GMP, and soon documents were flying backwards and forwards between the force and Russell, Jones and Walker, with claims and counter-claims being made. Mr O'Brien contacted DCI Harry, my boss in the Covert Operations Department before Seddon took over, to provide a statement about my work and my character. Below is some of what Harry had to say:

I first met Garry Rogers in about 1982, when I was a detective sergeant on the Regional Crime Squad and he was a surveillance motorcyclist. We worked together on a number of operations and in particular on two highly sensitive 'supergrass' operations for which I had responsibility. I would actively seek out Garry to work on my operations as I found him to be thoroughly professional. I found Garry Rogers to be very professional in his approach to his work, although somewhat single-minded. He had exceptionally high standards, which he was not prepared to lower. This was exactly the attitude and approach I sought from my officers as it was these high standards and good practices that maintained the safety and integrity of the covert officer, and the success of the operation.

At times I saw him as a mirror of me in the way that he would approach and work during investigations. Garry was a very intense person and was very reliable; because of his attitude and approach he was not always a good team player but in my opinion he was the best undercover operative in the department. I have no first-hand knowledge of Garry Rogers' re-integration into normal policing duties. I do, however, believe that with his abilities and talent he should have been utilised as a welfare officer or in the training of undercover officers, in an effort to pass on his considerable knowledge and experience. In fact it is within my knowledge that another police force, within the north-west area, was interested in setting up an Omega-type operation. This force had requested that Garry Rogers be attached to them in an effort to pass on his experience and assist in the training of their officers. Together with Garry I planned an operation for this force, which had been running for about one month when I retired.

Prior to my retirement the unit had been inspected by Her Majesty's Inspector of Constabularies, Sir Geoffrey Dear. He was so impressed by the dedication and skill of the unit that he felt the officers deserved to be recognised. He instigated the procedure for a Queen's Police Medal to be awarded to officers from the unit. I recommended Garry Rogers and believed that this was to happen.

Garry Rogers had been exposed to such a high number of criminals and over such a wide area of the Greater Manchester Police that there should not have been any question of him returning to normal operational policing. I have been made aware that Garry was offered his old job as a surveillance motorcyclist with the Regional Crime Squad. With my knowledge of Garry he would see this as being a step backwards and just wasting the skill, knowledge and experience he has acquired.

With my knowledge of Garry Rogers, and my experience of having worked with him and the type of work that he has been involved in, I believe that he will feel let down. People do not appreciate the dangers that he has put himself in. The standards he maintained needed to be high so as to protect himself, his family, and other officers involved.

Garry would find it very hard to accept and would voice his concerns if the standards he expected of himself were not reflected or sought by his supervisors and other officers on the Omega unit. I believe that they would see this as Garry just being difficult.

I hadn't prompted that letter – it was something for which the solicitors had contacted him – but considering he was my old boss it was a real boost to see him saying those things about me. It was gratifying that he had agreed to give a statement in the first place. His line that he saw me 'as a mirror' of himself was, for me, a huge compliment. I knew Harry well enough to be sure that he wouldn't have said anything that he didn't feel was true; he wasn't just going to say nice things to please me, which made his comments even more powerful.

There were other things that Harry had said which had relevance to the situation I was in now. For example, the fact that he thought I was very professional, single-minded and not prepared to lower my standards was, according to him, crucial to my success as an undercover officer. They were also traits which he, as someone with a lot of experience of undercover work, recognized as valuable in ensuring such operations were successful.

By comparison, someone like Seddon, who had no knowledge or understanding of what the undercover role really entailed, had seen those character traits as problematic, to the extent of stating that he didn't want 'any Harry clones' in the unit. I suppose that single-mindedness and the belief that things should be done in the right way was now evident in my battle with GMP and my desire to see things put right.

The letter also confirmed one other thing: that Harry had recommended me for the QPM. At the time this would have been quite a departure from the usual process, as the Queen's Police Medal tended to reflect a promotion to a particular rank – such as ACC, chief constable, assistant commissioner or commissioner in the Met – or, in fewer cases, signified especially long service to policing. It was much less common for it to be awarded to lower ranks who were seen to be doing a really successful job or achieving great results. However, HMI

Geoffrey Dear had been so impressed by the unit when he inspected GMP that he instigated the process by which we could be recognized through the award of the QPM. This meant that when Seddon and Mr James decided to thwart my nomination, they were going against the wishes not only of Harry, but also HMI Geoffrey Dear.

Chapter Twenty-Nine

A Christmas to Remember

On 10 July 1998 I sent another letter[18] to David O'Dowd, the Chief HMI at the Home Office. We'd already had one exchange of letters in which I'd expressed my views and feelings about what had gone on, and he had responded with an in-depth explanation of the awards system but little else. So now I wrote back to him, thanking him for his previous reply but saying that I was 'saddened' that the Home Office didn't seem interested in the 'irregularities and deceit' that had taken place, or the treatment I had received for speaking out, and signing off with the promise to 'take these matters elsewhere', although at this stage, to be honest I was running out of places to go.

Rather than prompting another letter, this time I got a phone call at home from Mr O'Dowd's Staff Officer at the Home Office, Les Owen. This was the same Les Owen who had previously paraphrased my letters to the Home Secretary – which, up to that point, I had considered to be totally confidential – over the phone to GMP. By now I was recording all incoming telephone calls and this one was no exception. He went on to tell me that Mr O'Dowd had done a lot of work on my case and that he had a good idea of what had gone on. He then gave me the following warning:

> I suggest it would not be in your interest to keep shouting. The more you shout, the more you come to notice for the wrong reasons. The people who need to know now know…when you and I retire, I'd like to meet up with you and tell you what I think has gone on.

This was the first time that anyone in a position of authority had acknowledged that not only had something irregular gone on, but that someone was going to do something about it. I interpreted his comments as him basically giving me the nod that things were about to be put right, as long as I stopped making so much noise about it all. I told him that in view of what he had said, I would now – for the immediate future at least – keep quiet and see what happened. I stopped writing letters, stopped making follow-up calls, and waited. I knew that, if nothing changed over the coming months, I could go back and say look, this is what you told me at the end of July, what's going on? However, things did start to happen...

A couple of days later I received a letter from Fred Broughton, then Chairman of the Police Federation of England and Wales, again responding to an earlier letter I'd sent to him. He said he'd taken my comments very seriously, adding: 'I'm assured that everyone who matters believes these matters have not been dealt with as they should have been. I believe in the near future they will be resolved to your satisfaction.'

Clearly, he had spoken to someone at a higher level about what was going on; the fact that he had been 'assured that everyone who matters' had been made aware of what had gone on and would now be putting things right was another boost. However, considering how long all of this had been going on, I was determined not to get my hopes up too much.

* * *

The days passed slowly, and on 30 September, William O'Brien from Russell, Jones and Walker wrote to me. He explained that GMP had made a payment into court of £5,000 as an initial settlement offer of my legal claim against them. It was up to me whether I accepted or rejected it. If I accepted it, I would get the £5,000 and all my legal fees would be paid. If I rejected it, the case would go to court and, if I was successful in my claim, a judge would then decide what damages I'd receive. If the judge ruled that I was to get more than £5,000, then again I would receive that and my legal fees would be paid, but if the judge decided the damages should be £5,000 or less, I could end up paying the costs for both sets of lawyers, which could be considerable. So it was a gamble. William went on to say that the Federation's barrister thought the damages might be higher and suggested we went back to GMP's legal team with a counter-proposal of £8,000.

Here we were in September 1998, two and a half years on from when I started the grievance procedure and nearly four years since I'd had to go off sick, and only now did it seem that people were sitting up and listening to what I had to say. It started to feel like we were getting towards the end of a long process and things were finally starting to move, although this whole legal action was only about the damage that I had suffered because the force hadn't put the proper procedures in place in terms of re-integration into policing. It was their penalty for treating me like a guinea pig, but it didn't reflect what had gone on since: the lies, the deceit, the collusion and conspiracy. It had already been a real rollercoaster; it had badly affected my personality and my health, and without my wife's support and my own resolve, I could easily have gone under. Yet I was sure that it would have been much worse if I hadn't spoken out, and there was still more to come.

I told William that I was happy to go with his advice, and at this stage it wasn't about the money. I was more interested in my non-award of the QPM, and trying to find out why I had been discredited. Within a few weeks he came back to me; their defence team had agreed the counter-settlement figure of £8,000, which I would receive shortly. In effect, much of this went towards replacing the insurance policies I had had to cash in early when I went on half-pay. Also I meant what I said to William: at this stage it wasn't about the money, but we were absolutely brassic. So to be told, in the run-up to Christmas, that you are going to get £8,000 was fantastic. It was a huge relief and meant that our financial pressures were eased a bit, at least in the short term.

On 15 December 1998 I'd taken a day off work and my wife and I had spent the day in Chester completing some last-minute Christmas shopping. When we got home I opened the front door and the post was waiting in the porch. Among the Christmas cards and the usual junk mail, one envelope looked different to the rest. It had a postmark on it from London. I opened it, and inside was the following letter from the Police Policy Directorate at the Home Office, 50 Queen Anne's Gate:

> Dear Mr Rogers,
> Her Majesty the Queen has been pleased to award you the Queen's Police Medal for Distinguished Service.
> The Home Secretary wishes me to convey to you his warm congratulations on this award.
> The announcement will appear in the *London Gazette* to be published on Thursday 31st December 1998. It is customary to keep this information confidential until that date.
> Yours Sincerely
> Deborah Loudon.

I read this letter several times as initially I thought I was imagining it, and then I wondered if it was someone's idea of a sick joke. It took a while, but eventually I realized that it was for real. When the penny dropped, the sense of relief to know that I'd finally got the QPM was almost indescribable. I immediately felt euphoric, as the huge levels of stress I had been carrying around with me for years started to melt away. I told my wife and she was delighted, almost as excited as me.

The Queen's Police Medal had always meant a lot to me, long before I'd been told I had been nominated for one. I said before that I was in awe of the fact that Harry had been awarded one for his services to policing, and to undercover work in particular. I felt then that in some ways it was the pinnacle of policing, particularly if you earned it for what you had actually done rather than just hanging around long enough or getting promoted enough times to receive one. I guess that was one of the reasons I had felt so strongly about being treated unfairly, and so angry that I hadn't received this letter three years earlier.

To get it now went some way to redressing that, and also made me feel that I was justified in everything I had been doing. We had our own little family celebration at home – no big party or anything like that as I still couldn't tell anyone – but I knew it was a huge relief for my wife too. That Christmas was one of the best I had had for quite some time and, before I knew it, it was 1999 and I was back at work, this time with a bit of a spring in my step.

Almost immediately I started to receive letters[19] from all and sundry, congratulating me on my award. Some meant more than others. One of the first was from the Chief Constable David Wilmot, who said he was delighted to hear the news, which was lovely to receive. With hindsight I don't think he'd known what was going on, what I'd been up against, and once I'd got to meet him he tried to turn things around for me, which I really appreciated. Fred Broughton had certainly never done me any harm; in fact he'd tried to help me, so it was great to get one from him. There were several other letters too: one from Alison Halford congratulating me, and another from my GP, the late Dr Brian Sides, who had helped me a lot initially and to whom I am forever grateful.

By contrast, I thought that the letter from David McCrone was the biggest joke ever. It read like he was one of my best mates, had always supported me and been behind me, but the reality was that he'd done nothing for me. He didn't even want to discuss it when it came to the grievance procedure. I didn't want a letter from him at all.

One of my favourites was from an old colleague with whom I had worked several years earlier. He congratulated me on my 'fantastic news', and signed off with 'Game, set and match I believe!' Messages like that meant a lot.

Another one that was important to me was from John Tapley, Mr Stevens' staff officer, who had helped me immensely. He was one of the first people in authority who took notice of what I was saying and had helped me from behind the scenes. He sent me a congratulations card with a simple message:

Congratulations – You Must Be Over The Moon!
It took a long time coming, but no QPM was more deserved.

Best Wishes
John Tapley

* * *

222

A Christmas to Remember

All awards in the New Year's Honours are reported in the *London Gazette*, and my award was in the copy printed on 30 December 1998. However, you can't just go along to your nearest paper shop and buy a copy, you have to order it, and the only place you could get it was at Her Majesty's Stationary Office (HMSO), which was then situated in Albert Square in Manchester. While I was at work I phoned them and by chance they had one copy left, so I asked them to keep it to one side and I would call and collect it on my way home. This would mean taking a detour on my bike into the city centre.

I was still cycling to and from work at Bradford Park on Ashton New Road as money was still tight and it was also keeping me fit. I'd survived for quite some time on a pretty rickety old bike, but my aunt had recently passed away and left me a few hundred pounds, and with it I'd bought a decent Claude Butler bike. I'd started at 7.30 am and so finished at 3.30 pm, and duly set off with my £5.20 in my pocket. I arrived in Albert Square and I thought it would be a quick ask at the counter and the paper would be handed over, paid for and I would be on my way again. Sod's law being Sod's law, this was not to be.

When I got into the shop there was one other customer standing in front of me and only one assistant on the counter. I'd parked my much-loved bike in the entrance hall to the shop where I could clearly see it from inside, and I was standing in my cycling gear, sweating and getting more impatient as I listened to the exchange taking place in front of me. All I wanted was the paper, but this customer had a million and one questions and all the time in the world to ask them. I was keeping one eye on the rear wheel of my bike when all of a sudden I saw it move. I rushed to the door and by the time I got there I could see this man with my prized bike in his hands, trying to get on. He got in the saddle and tried to get the pedals going to get away.

By now I was inches away from grabbing his coat, but he suddenly got momentum going and the inches between us started to increase as he and my bike moved away from me. I was running after him now, backpack still bouncing around and cycle helmet on my head. There were plenty of people ahead of me and him, and I shouted to them to stop him and that he was nicking my bike. No one took any notice, he was getting further away from me and I then had to watch as he just disappeared into the distance. I never saw him or the bike again.

I still didn't have the *London Gazette*, which was the reason for me being there in the first place. I was now sweating profusely, having completed the 100-yard dash in all my gear. I went back to the shop in utter dismay and the customer who was there holding things up when I left was still at the counter. I won't tell you what I thought. I only had the £5.20 on me to pay for the paper, so the shop let me ring the police to report the theft so that they could put out the details and hopefully an officer might see him. I walked over to Bootle Street Police Station to report the theft in person, but now I had no money on me, so I started the long walk home, found a phone box and made a reverse-charge call to my wife to see if she could pick me up. I was back in that boxing ring again; the QPM gets you back up off the canvas, then bang, another punch – this time a bike thief – puts you back down!

*   *   *

In early April 1999 I had twenty-two years' service in the police, and having completed this I collected my Long Service and Good Conduct Medal. By now I had also received notification for the presentation of the QPM at Buckingham Palace. It was to be presented by Prince Charles on 20 May 1999 as the Queen was away presenting colours to the Guards.

I could take up to three guests, but as we had three children one of them would have had to stay at home and I didn't want to take two and leave one behind, so we made the decision that just my wife and I would attend. We were given train travel and booked in for one night's stay the evening before by GMP, which was essential as we needed to be there in plenty of time on the day. I was up early on the big day and went for an early-morning run around St James's Park opposite the Palace. It felt strange to be looking in through the large wrought-iron gates at the front, knowing that in a couple of hours we would be walking through them and into the Palace for the one and only time in our lives.

A Christmas to Remember

After a relaxing breakfast we both got ready and left in good time so as not to be late. At the main gate our paperwork was checked and we were allowed entry. At the same time the large gates were being opened and these big expensive cars, the Rolls-Royces and Bentleys, were driving through with faceless people inside, all obviously arriving to be presented with some award or other.

We walked into the quadrangle behind the Palace's front façade and at this point my wife and I were separated. She was directed towards the main ballroom where the ceremony would take place so that she could take her seat. As the recipient of an award, I was directed to a large room with a magnificent display of art hung on every wall. The room was full to bursting with people from all sectors of society, who probably only had one thing in common: they'd all received an award in the New Year's Honours for 1999. As I looked around, I noticed a 'celebrity' face, that of the British boxer Prince Naseem Hamed who has since fallen from grace. He was there to collect his MBE, of which he was later stripped after a serious road accident in his £300,000 silver Mercedes-McLaren. Hamed was jailed, and the driver of another vehicle involved broke every major bone in his body as a result of the crash.

After a while all the expectant recipients were carefully placed into groups of twelve and were then escorted in their groups to the main ballroom. As you approached the entrance, your name was checked for one last time, it having been checked several times en route to make sure they had the right people. As I stood at the entrance, I could see ahead of me Prince Charles standing on a dais to my left. To my right, seated on rows of chairs on the main floor of the ballroom, were everyone's guests, eagerly looking to the entrance for their family member or friend to appear. Up above in the minstrel gallery, music was being played by a band from one of the Queen's household regiments.

I heard my name announced and I walked forward towards the dais and towards Prince Charles. I don't mind admitting I was pretty nervous; not just at being in front of royalty, but also in front of so many other people. As I walked forward I noticed one of his uniformed staff whispering in his ear, probably prompting him as to who was coming next. I had been instructed to walk to the dais and, when I got alongside, to turn and face Prince Charles, bow my head and take a further step forward towards him. As I did this he was immediately in front of me, looking down from the dais, and it was a surreal moment as I became aware of all his facial mannerisms that impersonators copy.

He then smiled and spoke to me. He was obviously very well versed on whoever he meets at such occasions as he asked me questions about my past in the police, and some of the operations on which I'd worked. I was quite impressed really, considering how many people were receiving awards, that he'd obviously been given background on all of us and was able to talk to us about what we had received an award for. After a short conversation he pinned my QPM medal on my jacket. I'd been told that when he offered his hand to shake, that was my signal to move away; I had to take one step back, bow my head and then move off to my right. His hand came up, and I took one step back, but then forgot to bow my head and started to move off! A split second later I remembered, turned back, bowed and carried on. My mistake can be seen on the video we got on the day, although I'm sure I'm not the only one to have ever done this. As you walk out of the ballroom another member of the household staff meets you, takes the medal off and places it in its protective box, then hands it back. You're then free to go and meet your guests in the ballroom and watch the rest of the investiture. It was a fantastic day, one we enjoyed immensely and something we will probably never get to experience again.

As I reflected on the day though, it still felt like the icing had been taken off the cake. That may seem crazy to say, especially when you've been fighting all those years for something, but it just made me realize how I'd eventually come to get it and the lengths I'd had to go to. I still didn't feel like it had been given to me willingly; I'd only got it because I had backed GMP and the Home Office into a corner. I'd had to force the issue.

When people say well, that doesn't matter, you got it and you deserved to get it three years before, my answer is yes, that's when I should have got it, and it would have saved me three years of stress, torment and aggravation. I could still remember the way I felt when I'd phoned Reg before returning to work, and he told me that he'd got the QPM. I knew then that I hadn't got it and it was a horrible feeling. Collecting it now couldn't take that away, but deep in my heart I knew I deserved it; in the end, that was all that mattered.

Chapter Thirty

Back to College, and Justice in the Courts

So from the glory of Buckingham Palace back to the normality of Bradford Park and the Video Imaging Unit. In one sense I was on a bit of a high, what with my QPM and my successful legal action against the force. Yet still, sitting at the back of my mind, was the knowledge that I didn't have answers to many of the questions I'd asked. No one was willing or able to explain what had gone on, and in my mind it had all been a cover-up.

With my newly-acquired trainer's certificate I applied for a position as a trainer at Bruche in Warrington and was told that I would go on the list; it was then just a case of waiting for a vacancy to arise. I eventually heard that I was to transfer to Bruche in October. So after three and a half years feeling rather trapped in GMP and embroiled in an ongoing argument with the force, I was now escaping the organization. Bruche was in Cheshire, and was staffed by officers from several different forces – Cheshire itself, Cumbria, Lancashire and Merseyside, as well as GMP – and my secondment was for three years. I had to get measured up for a new uniform, which was strange after all these years, and I did the usual thing when I got it, dressing up at home for a private viewing.

As for the Video Imaging Unit, while I'd had some of the most difficult years of my life there and the work had been less than interesting, I'd got to know all the staff well, and (apart from the boss of the unit) I thought a lot of them. There were some really good people working there. When I left they all clubbed together and bought me some lovely gifts, including a Parker Pen set inscribed with my name for me to use in the next stage of my career. I was genuinely very grateful.

I started at Bruche as a Police Law Trainer on Monday, 4 October 1999. This sounded great, but there was an awful lot of law and legislation that I had to first learn myself before I could teach it to others. Since I'd been at the training school in 1977 the law had changed considerably, so I knew it was going to be a major task.

To be honest, when I first arrived at Bruche this time around I hated it. I felt like a fish out of water as I walked round the centre in my new uniform. I know it's a generalization, but I felt that some of the trainers were those who didn't want to be out on the street. They had a great knowledge of the law, which is obviously what you want from a trainer, but some of them had done very little real policing and they would have been lost trying to implement that law in a practical situation. I think you need a mix of both: of the law, and of dealing with people. I knew I was good on the practical side, but I would have to work really hard on learning all aspects of the law well enough to be able to train others.

I initially met with one of the uniformed inspectors who was from Cheshire Police, Derek Christmas. Yes, Christmas, and pretty soon it would be just that. He allocated me to a class with two experienced trainers so that I could sit in on their sessions and observe what took place. My evenings were spent burning the midnight oil, studying and studying. One thing I noticed while observing was that there were an awful lot of 'what if' type questions from students, sometimes with genuine queries but on other occasions just hoping to catch you out. If you didn't know – or at least didn't appear to know – the answer to the hypothetical scenarios, it could leave you in an embarrassing situation, so I knew I had to be prepared for them as well.

I knew I couldn't keep sitting at the back observing forever and soon enough the day came when I had to get up and perform. It wasn't quite how I'd planned though, and I didn't really get chance to prepare. I had gone to class as usual, but a sergeant arrived to tell me that one of the trainers had gone sick, so could I take the lesson on drug legislation? For the next couple of hours, I got through by the seat of my pants. I was fortunate that I had good knowledge of the different types of illegal drugs available and the relevant legislation as I had been buying them in my undercover role and had been on the Drugs Unit for two years. I had to keep to the lesson plan, but managed to survive it. I was eventually teamed up with a partner, and was then allocated a new class of my own, and the course was an intense one over the following twelve weeks. There was a lot of pressure on the recruits, but equally there was pressure on the trainers to get results and you were constantly under scrutiny to do so.

My knowledge of the law increased dramatically, and pretty soon there were certain lessons I could sail through as I enjoyed the subject matter, although there were others that I hated. You would work out with your co-trainer who was going to present which particular lesson throughout the course, so you knew well in advance and could prepare accordingly. I was able to bring my own experiences into the classroom too, including videos from operations in which I'd been involved, to help illustrate certain lessons or explain points of law. I even had the video of me having my cheekbone broken as part of a session on the use of force and what is reasonable. Things like that made sure that students sat up and took notice; it got them interested, because it was an example from real life.

There were a lot of internal politics at the centre and I preferred to keep well out of it. You were allocated your own room and could stay all week if you wanted to, which was obviously great for those members of staff from Cumbria who would invariably stay and go home at weekends. However, being there eight hours a day was enough for me and I went home most nights, only occasionally staying when I had to really prepare for a lesson the following day.

There was also a big social scene at the centre for the staff, and there were regular events organized. I can honestly say that in my twelve months at Bruche I never went to one of them. This might seem strange, but I never had any longing to socialize. I didn't really know why at the time, but with the benefit of hindsight it was largely down to the PTSD with which I had been diagnosed and for which I still wasn't being properly treated. It would affect my mood, and a red mist could come over me at the drop of a hat, sometimes catching me completely off guard. This could happen at work, and there were many times when I could have punched some of the senior officers that I came across and had to restrain myself from doing so, but it also happened away from work, which was still making life difficult for my wife and family.

One example around this time was when I took my son to Bolton for his driving test, which would have been nerve-racking enough for him without my current condition kicking in. We got there early and I parked at the centre in a bay that I thought was for those taking their driving tests. We had been there for about ten minutes when a driving school car pulled in and the guy in the passenger seat admonished us for being in these bays, which must have been for driving centre cars. The red mist came down and I gave him both barrels. I think he realized he was not dealing with a sane person and he backed off.

We got out and I went with my son into the centre office for his allotted time. I could see this had already affected him and I was feeling guilty, but what made it worse was when the examiners came out of their office: the guy I had ranted at outside was the same guy who was taking my son for his test. I was gutted.

Thankfully the examiner was professional and didn't let what had taken place affect his judgement of my son's driving ability; he duly passed, no thanks to me. This was an example of how I could just go off like a bottle of pop and I couldn't control it. I hadn't always had a temper like that, far from it. In fact, although I could be a bit moody or aggressive when I had been in the middle of an undercover operation, it was only over the last two or three years, with the stress that had built up, that I'd developed such a quick temper. There were many other instances, but I carried on regardless, and all the time this anger and frustration about what had happened slowly simmered within me.

Despite the fact that I enjoyed part of the job, felt that I had learned a lot and was performing well as a trainer, I realized that I didn't really fit in at Bruche. I was worried that if I stayed there I would either go mad or end up getting into trouble for something I did or said. Such was my anger that I took out a further grievance against the powers that be for something I perceived as the old pals act taking place. To extend my scope for training, I'd applied for a course as a public order trainer and was told my name was on the list. When the next available vacancy for a course came up, I would be notified. Weeks and months went by without anything being said. A female police trainer then arrived from Cheshire, and within a few weeks of starting she was shown as attending the next public order course ahead of me. I was a bit bemused by this and delved further into her situation. I soon discovered that she was the girlfriend of the head of the Physical Trainers' Department at Bruche who, funnily enough, had some say in who would attend the course.

Maybe it was a bit of the red mist coming down again, but I wasn't happy. I saw it as a form of nepotism and that I had, unfairly, been put at the back of the queue. I instigated the centre's grievance procedure and took it up to the Head of Centre, who obviously wouldn't confirm my suspicions. All I can say is that I was on the next course, which saw me away from Bruche for two weeks; I duly passed, and was then able to train the new recruits in public order techniques.

After twelve months I was ready to leave, and it was at this point that someone up above must have been looking down on me and offered me a lifeline. The number of recruits going through the system at that point was so high that Bruche couldn't house them all, so they developed a plan to have a satellite training school nearby but separate from the main training centre. It was eventually decided that it would be based at Padgate College in Warrington, about 4 miles from Bruche. It would consist of two separate classes of approximately eighteen students in each, with four police trainers, two per class. There would be student accommodation on site, with a separate block consisting of two classrooms, a trainers' office and a lecture theatre. The centre would also provide other locations and facilities to help with things like practicals.

Whether they realized I wasn't 100 per cent happy or they weren't happy with me and wanted to get rid of me, I was one of the chosen four to go to Padgate as a trainer. This was a completely new concept in police training, to have police courses within a public building where we and the students would be rubbing shoulders with other college students and staff on a daily basis. We knew we would be under public scrutiny. Because of that, it wasn't the sort of place or situation where you would send your worst staff members, so I was quite heartened that I had been asked. My other three colleagues were great to work with and I could not have asked for anyone better.

This was a win-win situation all round, as the police obtained the extra capacity to train more recruits and the college received much-needed funds. We were left largely to our own devices, trusted to get on with the job, and – as long as we delivered the results at the end of each course – nobody really bothered us. It was a lot less regimented at Padgate and we soon settled in and joined in with college life. For example, there were catering courses based at the college, and after they had cooked their delicacies they needed people to sample their wares. So as an entire group, students and instructors, we were invited at lunchtime once a week to have lunch in the restaurant where we were served by trainee waiters and waitresses and sampled a full three-course lunch created by the trainee chefs. We would then give feedback (no pun intended) on what we had feasted on. The students loved it (as did we), the only problem being that after such a big lunch we had to 'up the ante' in the afternoon to stop people falling asleep. It was well worth it though.

This new working environment, with its relaxed atmosphere and minimal contact with Bruche, reduced my anxiety levels and I felt comfortable continuing as a police trainer. I also decided to study for the Certificate in Education (Cert Ed) qualification through the University of Manchester which, if I was successful, would mean I was qualified to teach in an adult education centre. Padgate College ran this through their campus and I attended evening classes and then had to prepare lessons, on which their examiners would sit in to evaluate me. It was a long-drawn-out process and there were many times when I questioned whether it was worth it, especially during the winter. However, I stuck with it, and eventually the hard work paid off: I duly qualified, which was another string to my bow and a real bonus to have achieved it while at Padgate.

* * *

While I was enjoying life at Padgate, I heard through the grapevine that things weren't working out quite so well for Ken Seddon, who had been granted the rank of superintendent while on secondment in Australia. His contract with New South Wales (NSW) Police, which was integral to his much-publicized job introducing new, improved crime management techniques for a force previously beleaguered by allegations of corruption, had been terminated by the Australian force amid a number of controversies. Seddon had been handpicked by the then Police Commissioner of NSW Police, Peter Ryan, who was himself a former high-ranking British police officer. Ryan had been chief constable of Norfolk Police, and then the first National Director of Police Training at the Police Staff College before his appointment to the Australian force. Seddon was one of two British police officers selected by Ryan to try to turn the force around and tackle some of the corruption highlighted by a Royal Commission.

Picked supposedly because of his expertise in child protection and his wider experience of detective work, Seddon was eventually appointed to lead the Crime Management Support Unit, established to improve performance in criminal investigation. Things certainly hadn't gone to plan though, and Seddon's contract was terminated, along with those of some of the staff he had appointed. It was a high-profile controversy which led to a series of public hearings in front of the Police Integrity Commission (PIC), and a report to Parliament, known as the Malta Report.

While no formal action or prosecutions arose from the investigation or the report, no one involved came out of the process unscathed. Some of the allegations against Seddon would have been familiar to anyone who had worked with him before. There were questions over the private use of police cars, expenses claims, and what tax he had – or should have – paid. It was unclear whether Seddon's disciplinary issues while heading up the GMP Covert Operations Department (that ridiculously lenient slap on the wrist for the misuse of a covert property, car and caravanette) were ever declared to NSW Police before he took up his post. The report highlights various areas of concern, including a senior officer's conclusion that Seddon's claims about the success of his work in NSW amounted to 'distortions of truth, and, being less generous, outright lies'. Not to be outdone, Seddon told the

PIC hearing that his name was being 'openly bandied about' as the next commissioner of NSW Police, but that because of their success, he and his colleagues had become victims of a smear campaign by senior ranks to discredit them. How ironic…

Of course, I didn't know any of these details at the time. I've since had sight of an email from the Assistant Commissioner of NSW Police, Mal Brammer, to Detective Superintendent Peter Boylan at GMP shortly after Seddon was sacked, which stated: 'Peter, I do not know what his [Seddon's] history was with your service, but he was not a great ambassador for either of our services and certainly tested the waters close to criminality.'

So Seddon had big problems in Australia, which rumbled on through the various hearings and inquiries, but he had even bigger problems to face back in the UK. On 2 June 2002 it was reported that Seddon, the top cop imported from Manchester to help clean up NSW Police's corruption and poor performance, had been remanded by a Lancashire magistrates' court on twenty-six fraud charges. He and his co-accused, car dealer Colin Heaney, were charged with obtaining services through deception and attempting to obtain services by deception. The charges related to car loans in 1993 (the year he became boss of Covert Operations), 1995 and 1998, which were offered by Greater Manchester Police to serving officers at favourable rates; they related to documents that had allegedly been falsified.

Seddon and Heaney were both remanded on unconditional bail. Seddon had resigned from Greater Manchester Police on 1 February, just a few days after being interviewed by police. On 8 October 2003, the following report appeared in the *Manchester Evening News*:

TOP COP FACES JAIL
Detective who headed anti-corruption unit admits car loan fraud

The reputation of one of Britain's most respected detectives is in tatters today after he admitted defrauding police bosses. Detective Chief Inspector Ken Seddon is facing a jail sentence after he used forged documents to apply for car loans from Greater Manchester Police.

Ironically father of five Seddon was seconded from GMP to head an anti-corruption taskforce in Australia. He was dismissed after an alleged expenses scam and tax irregularities.

But Seddon's fraudulent conduct in Manchester was discovered two years ago when staff in GMP's finance department became suspicious of his repeated loan applications. Seddon was arrested and quit his £43,500 a year job in February 2002. Seddon pleaded guilty at Manchester Crown Court to obtaining services by deception, attempting to obtain services by deception, making a false instrument [document] and false accounting between 1993 and 2001.

Prosecutor Michael Harrison QC told how Seddon was entitled to low-cost car loans through the Greater Manchester Police Authority, but began applying for cash using bogus documents sometimes for vehicles he did not own. Seddon was arrested and a fabricated engineer's report for a bogus application was discovered on his Police computer.

Seddon's friend, car dealer Colin Heaney, also admitted obtaining services by deception, attempting to obtain services by deception, making a false instrument and false accounting.

Judge Bernard Lever adjourned sentence until October 28 for the preparation of pre-sentence reports but added he wanted 'chapter and verse' on Seddon's financial situation.

When he did appear for sentencing, Seddon escaped a jail term but was fined £5,000 with £35,000 costs – a total of £40,000 – at Minshull Street Crown Court.

These offences took place while he was in charge of the Covert Operations Department, together with his friend who was a car dealer from Oldham. It was the sort of behaviour I had highlighted in my concerns about his activities and may well have been mentioned in the anonymous letter sent to the force and the newspaper. So why had it taken a decade for Seddon's behaviour to be punished?

When I heard about the court case I wasn't surprised, and I would be lying if I said I was anything other than delighted to find out he had finally got at least a taste of what he deserved. This was the man who, along with his cronies inside the job and the Lodge, ruined my career in the police. On this occasion though, they couldn't save him and he was exposed for what he was: a liar and a cheat. For once, 'they' did not – or could not – side with him.

Chapter Thirty-One

A Revealing Report

The next two years of my secondment were spent at Padgate, which was brilliant. I really enjoyed the teaching set-up, I had three great colleagues to work with, and we were getting really good results. So I was more than happy when in December 2002 I was granted a twelve-month extension to my original three years.

Unfortunately, I could also feel that I was starting to get itchy feet again, although I knew I didn't want to go back into GMP. It was then that I saw an advert for a vacancy with the newly-formed National Crime Squad (NCS), which had taken the place of the old RCS. The vacancy was at the Chorley Office in Lancashire, well away from the GMP senior management. I applied, was granted an interview and word came through that I had been successful. I never got to use all of my twelve-month extension as in February 2003 I once again handed in my uniform and transferred to the NCS at Chorley.

The office was in another non-police building which, from the outside, was to all intents and purposes a business address. I was soon off on an advanced car and motorcycle refresher course, which got me back up to speed having been stuck inside for the past few years, and it was great to get out and about again. The Chorley office was staffed by officers from GMP and Lancashire; I didn't know any of them, but some knew of me from my days on the Covert Operations Department. It was general knowledge when I arrived that I'd been awarded the QPM, although no one knew the trials and tribulations I'd been through to get it. I wasn't prepared to go into any detail as I still didn't wholeheartedly trust anyone from GMP; you could never be sure who knew who.

I really thought that a move back to do something I'd enjoyed doing so much in the past would boost my interest in the job again, especially now that Seddon's conviction finally meant he had got some of what he deserved. However, I was wrong: I hated it, and every day it was a trauma to go to work. The job itself just wasn't right. When I was on the RCS we were out every day, we had specific targets and lots of surveillance to do, all of which I loved. With the NCS, we hardly seemed to do anything and the jobs we did have were poorly run. The next main job we were running was going to be office-based, and I was being earmarked to take on the role of exhibits officer, which really wasn't what I was looking for.

Yet a much bigger part of it was about my state of mind and the unresolved issues I was still experiencing. It was now eight years since I'd been diagnosed with PTSD, yet I'd still not had any treatment. Everything that had happened in the intervening years continued to eat away at me. I kept going in, thinking each day would be better and I would be okay, but I would come home even more depressed, and my low mood and anger were starting to return. I eventually realized I could not get away from the fact that I now hated the police for what 'they' had put me and my family through, and I knew I couldn't go on.

On one particular weekend in June 2003, I thought deeply about my situation, my continuing depression and my sudden bouts of anger. I was about as low as you could get: all my negative thoughts were back again, I could see my old demons returning, and it's fair to say that at times I was bordering on suicidal. I had virtually no sleep all weekend; I just lay awake thinking.

On the Monday morning I got up, got ready and left the house. To all intents and purposes my wife thought I was going to work, but instead I drove to Police HQ at Chester House and went directly to see Inspector Smith in the Police Personnel Department. I'd never met him before, but he did know a bit about my background and what I'd been through and he had a good 'bedside manner'. I told him that I couldn't go on any more, that I was close to having a complete breakdown, and that if I couldn't get a move or some sort of change, I was ready to resign. You can imagine how bad I was to say that I would walk away from the job; I'd stubbornly refused to do that through everything else that went on, and now here I was, supposedly with some sort of resolution and having received my QPM, yet ready to leave the job that I'd once loved.

Inspector Smith told me that I hadn't been dealt with properly in the past. He talked with sympathy and understanding, attributes that were sadly lacking in most of the senior officers I had encountered so far, and arranged for me to be moved immediately to a different post in Chester House while some form of re-entry programme was initiated, which he agreed should have been in place previously.

So on 30 June 2003, I moved to the Force Policy Unit. Again, it wasn't a vacant position. There was an inspector and a sergeant in the office who clearly didn't get on, and I was given a desk and chair in the same office and a load of paperwork to go through. They were menial tasks, and the officers would take it in turns to moan about each other whenever one of them left the office, but I was still relieved that I didn't have to go to Chorley every day.

* * *

People sometimes say that things happen for a reason. On that basis, I'm truly thankful that I went to see Inspector Smith at the end of my tether, as otherwise the following events may never have taken place. By the Wednesday of that first week, and having only been at the Force Policy Unit for a couple of days, I was already starting to climb the walls with boredom. Yes, it was better than Chorley, but I hated being surrounded by all the senior officer types with their shiny-arse trousers from sitting at their desks pushing paper around, thinking they had the worst job in the world, while officers were out on the streets working unsociable shifts with fewer resources, struggling with the daily demands placed on them and getting no thanks for their efforts.

You can probably tell that as well as growing bored, I was starting to get angry again. I was sitting in an office with nothing to do, listening to other officers moaning about each other. So just to get out for an hour, I decided to go and have a look at my personal file. I'd never asked to see it before and I didn't know what the system was, so I just went up to the Personnel Department and asked. I found out afterwards that the usual procedure was to ring them first and make an appointment; obviously not everyone worked at Chester House, so if you were out on division somewhere the idea was that you would ring in, book a time to come in and your record would be there ready for you to look at. The commonly-held belief was that this also gave the Personnel Department time to get anything out of your file that they didn't want you to see, which they would then return to the file after you had left.

However, not knowing any better, I went up to the Personnel Department and walked straight up to the counter. The lady on the counter, who apparently hadn't worked there long, asked what I wanted and I told her I'd like to see my personal file. She invited me into the office, sat me at a desk and then went and got my file, which she put on the desk in front of me. She actually said to me: 'If there's anything in there you want photocopying, just let me know.'

After twenty-eight years in policing up to that point, my file was pretty thick, but I didn't really have any idea what would be in it. What I found was a trip down memory lane, starting with my initial application to join the Police Cadets back in 1975, including everything that my dad had filled in, together with his signature, and two referees who had also now sadly passed away. I looked through all the forms and paperwork from 1975 onwards, including applications to join the various departments, training, commendations and so on.

As I worked my way through the file I came across an A4-sized brown envelope. Handwritten on the stick-down flap on the back of it were the words: '**ONLY TO BE OPENED BY A DIVISIONAL OR BRANCH COMMANDER**'. The flap had an old piece of Sellotape over it that had long since lost any adhesive qualities. Could that be due to the number of times the envelope had been opened and the contents read? My curiosity soon took over: just because it said that on the back of the envelope, I wasn't going to leave it closed and, after all, it was in my personal file. I opened the flap and took out the report. It was written by Superintendent Homan (the same Homan who, five years earlier, had written to my wife refusing to accept her letter of complaint about my situation), and was addressed to ACC McCrone. It was dated June 1995, which made it eight years old. I read it from start to finish, then I read it again, then again, and then once more as I was struggling to take in what it contained.

The report said that I was paranoid that the underworld was looking for me. It also stated that I was under investigation within the force as I was suspected of sending anonymous letters to the *Manchester Evening News* crime reporter, Steve Panter, as well as to GMP, about events in and out of the Omega Unit and the actions of senior officers.

To be honest, I didn't read anything else from there on. Each time I re-read the report, it was as if light bulbs were switching on in my head, one after the other. The reason I may have been concerned – not 'paranoid' – about the prospect of some of the Manchester underworld trying to track me down was due to the fact that I had, by chance, seen the secret memo from Seddon to Mr James, stating that private investigators had been hired by some of the violent criminals I had met, with the aim of trying to find out as much as they could about me. Wouldn't anyone be a little 'paranoid' after becoming aware of this?

It seemed to me that I had been tried and convicted by certain members of GMP's senior management as being the man responsible for Seddon's sudden fall from grace from the Covert Operations Department back in 1995. The anonymous letter or letters had been firmly placed on my shoulders. What also amazed me was that these letters were apparently pointing out to the force, and to the *Manchester Evening News*, the indiscretions that were taking place within this department by the man in charge. Yet the force's whole focus was on who had sent in the letters, not whether the allegations they contained were true! They effectively ignored those allegations; Seddon was given a reprimand for something totally obscure and unconnected, and was then sent out to Australia as an ambassador for GMP. They then chose to go after the person they mistakenly believed was responsible for the letters – me – and tried to ruin me. This was the behaviour of one of the largest police forces in the country.

The implications were such that if anyone read the report they would be left with a totally tainted and untrue view of me. They would have a perception that I was dangerous, untrustworthy, a loose cannon. I had no recourse to make them think differently, the damage had been done and I would be none the wiser. What gave GMP the right to act like this? All of this came from Superintendent Homan, a man who had never met me before (and who I haven't met to this day), but who I imagined was safely tucked away on a comfy chair every day in his office, working 8.00 am to 4.00 pm with Saturdays and Sundays off.

As I read it one last time, everything became clear, as if the report was the last piece of the jigsaw. It confirmed for me that the fact that I was being blamed for the anonymous letters had resulted in my recommendation for the QPM being shredded, and for commendations being 'lost' or ultimately being labelled worthy of nothing. So now there were even more questions than answers. If a police officer is placed under investigation, he or she should be made aware of it and the force is required to serve a written notice on them outlining the allegations. Superintendent Homan's report stated that I was under investigation. So too did the note, in ACC McCrone's handwriting, which was attached to DI Brown's report. Yet I'd never been served with any sort of written notice, nor had I ever been informed that I was under investigation or given the opportunity to respond accordingly. So what was the truth? Were Superintendent Homan and ACC McCrone both wrong, in which case their errors (giving them the benefit of the doubt) had seriously damaged my career? Or had I been the subject of an internal investigation, in which case, why was it a 'hushed up' unofficial investigation that had no legitimacy? What was the outcome, and why hadn't I been given the opportunity to respond?

After my experience with the NCS and now stuck in an office where I didn't want to be, reading this short report took me down even further, but I managed to keep my practical head on. I took the lady on the counter at her word, got a few things together – so it wouldn't look like I was just interested in that report – and asked her to photocopy them, including the envelope. I then returned everything and she took the file back, complete with the brown envelope and its contents.

I was incredibly angry about what this report inferred and the damage it had done to me over the last eight years, and I was still furious when I went home that night, but I deliberately didn't tell my wife as, given what we'd already been through, I didn't want to burden her further. It had an obvious effect on me and my mood though, which understandably caused another huge row but I was determined not to say anything until I'd worked out what to do.

* * *

I decided that the next step was to ask to see my discipline record at the Y Department; this would allow me to see all the investigations and complaints that had been recorded against me since I joined. I was asked why I wanted to see it and I told them simply that it was for personal reasons. The request was granted, but I was told that I would not be able to take any written information away and that I would have to be escorted by an inspector.

A week later I went to the Y Department offices in Chester House and was met by Inspector Hailey. My record was put on the screen, and he actually commented on just how good my discipline record was, especially considering the type of work in which I had been involved. It was quite clear that there was no record of any investigation against me in 1995. I confirmed that with Inspector Hailey, and then openly told him about the report I had found. He double-checked their records and came back with the same conclusion: no investigation in 1995.

Armed with this, I submitted a report to the senior management of Y Department, explaining about the report I had found and what it contained. I also asked the following questions:

- What were the circumstances of the investigation?
- Why was I not told of the investigation against me, in line with official procedures?
- What was the result of the investigation?

At this point I returned to the Personnel Department and spoke to the lady who had originally given me my file. I wanted to make sure that there was a record of me having been to see my file, as I feared that things might disappear. I asked the lady to get my file out again and I gave her permission to read the vindictive report from Superintendent

Homan so that she could later be a witness to its existence and where it was. The report was then replaced. I was later informed that the report had been removed from my file and taken up to the eleventh floor, the Command Suite!

At 10.30 am on Thursday, 24 July, I was summoned by phone to go to see Chief Superintendent Don Brown, Head of Y Department. I went to his office and he told me that he had made enquiries and that despite the contents of Superintendent Homan's report, there was no official investigation held. He apologized to me on behalf of the force. Chief Superintendent Brown also said that he had heard these brown envelopes existed, but he had never seen one before. He thought this investigation was an unofficial one held by the then senior management of CID, led by Detective Chief Superintendent James, and that he believed it was some kind of 'Masonic conspiracy'. Chief Superintendent Brown kindly reaffirmed his findings in a report to me, which also went on my personal file.

I could not believe that a superintendent, in this case Homan, would submit an official police report to an Assistant Chief Constable (Mr McCrone) if he didn't believe the content of that report to be true. If a police officer goes before a magistrate to obtain a warrant, the magistrate asks questions in relation to why the police want the warrant, what they expect to find and how reliable is their information. Only when they are satisfied is a warrant issued. In this case Mr McCrone must have asked questions and been aware of this so-called unofficial investigation, bearing in mind that this report was submitted to him in June 1995, the year before I commenced my grievance. So I was pretty sure that there was an investigation and people at Mr McCrone's level knew about it.

In hindsight, it would have been much better for me if there had been an official investigation; they could have investigated my supposed involvement until the cows came home as I had nothing to hide, and they would have had to clear me and my reputation. Instead, they chose to carry out an unofficial investigation, and then hang me out to dry without any evidence.

The report, and the apology on behalf of the force from Chief Superintendent Brown, could have been seen as some sort of closure, except in my mental health state, it only served to make things worse. Having thought that things had been partially resolved several years before, the whole question of who had known what and who had done what was now reopened in my mind. Now I also knew that this activity went across senior ranks, and involved officers at various levels and roles within the force. Far from bringing closure, it marked the start of another very difficult time.

* * *

As a footnote to these events, during my earlier work within the Video Imaging Unit I had become friendly with the Unit's Photographic Manager, John White. I came to trust John and kept in touch with him. I collect signed autobiographies, and it was something he was interested in too, so we used to meet up every now and then and go searching for them.

One day we were talking about some of my experiences with GMP, and I mentioned the report I'd found in my personal file. He talked to me about some unusual events that he remembered taking place in the Imaging Unit in the early part of 1995, which appeared to be associated with my story. When I contacted him to say I was writing this book, he provided me with the following statement:

15th November 2016

I am John Christopher White. I was employed by Greater Manchester Police as a senior photographer, later becoming photographic manager based at the Force Headquarters, Chester House, Boyer Street, Stretford, Manchester from 1990 to 2002.

I wish to recall certain events that took place of which I had personal and direct involvement and my recollections are based on fact, not speculation.

On or around February/March of 1995 I was working in the photographic studio of the Imaging Unit, Chester House when Detective Chief Inspector Geoff Keeling (Deputy Head, Scenes of Crime Unit) and Pat Davies (Head of Imaging Unit and my line manager) came into the studio and closed the door. I was instructed to photograph a series of fingerprints on a letter which were indicated by a small white label bearing an arrow and a single letter of the alphabet, i.e. – a.b.c.d. etc. There were no Divisional Scenes of Crime reference numbers or any other crime reference numbers.

When I queried the absence of any reference numbers I was told that it was 'officially, unofficial' and that all photographs, negatives and the original document were to be returned personally to DCI Keeling and no-one else. I was also instructed that the task should take priority over any other work, and that no record should be kept of the requested task. I was cautioned that no word of what had been discussed was to be mentioned to anyone other than DCI Keeling or Pat Davies.

During the course of the photography I noticed a reference to the *Manchester Evening News* newspaper and the name of a police officer whose name, unfortunately, I can't recall. On completion of the task I returned all the photographs, negatives and the original document personally to DCI Keeling in his office and took no further part in the investigation.

John C. White

It was something that really stuck in John's memory, because he was a stickler for doing things right and he knew this wasn't being done right. It was also the only time that he was asked to do something like this. Also as Chief Superintendent Don Brown later confirmed to me, they would never have been able to officially search for fingerprints on that letter, because no crime had been committed.

Chapter Thirty-Two

Can I Have That in Writing?

By now my illness, which had continued unchecked, was worsening. It was causing me problems at work, but more importantly at home. I didn't want things to go back to how they had been in 1995, but I felt like it was quickly heading that way.

Everything that I'd found opened up a lot of old wounds, and I could now see for certain the level that this cover-up, corruption – or Masonic conspiracy, as I was now being told by the head of the force's internal investigation department – had reached. I definitely didn't want to be in work, although that was the least of my problems. As the days and weeks went by, I waited to hear what was going to happen about my complaint. By November I knew that my mental health was getting worse and all my symptoms were returning with a vengeance.

The force had no idea how much this affected me. If I'd been a lazy, corrupt, pain-in-the-neck copper who'd sat on his arse doing nothing all day, then you could argue that I'd got what I deserved, but I'd given everything I had to the job, up till the point they had hung me out to dry. By contrast, those above me weren't taking the risks or the responsibility. Instead, when it came to it, they knifed me in the back. I didn't deserve that. I'm sure, for them, it would have been easier if I had just gone off and killed myself. It would have been a problem out of the way for them. I suppose one of the things that stopped me from doing that was not giving them the satisfaction.

Even now, sitting here with the QPM, it doesn't take away the effect that these things had on my life. I'll never quite get over what they did to me. My career was ruined for no reason. None of it had to happen. However, it started with Seddon and continued with James, Homan, Keeling, McCrone and a handful of others. They did what they did without any justification, they were happy to do it and then lie to my face about it, to the point that I felt there was something wrong with me; that I'd done something wrong. All for the sake of someone like Seddon, who eventually got shown up for what he was.

This was all brought about by Seddon's own mistakes, not just his corruption. You never normally tell police officers that they have been nominated for the QPM. I would never have gone around saying I'm the best thing since sliced bread, therefore I deserve an award. I would have been more than happy with the results and the recognition that we got. Yet Seddon could never do things properly. He wanted me out of the unit because I was a 'Harry clone', so as a sweetener to soften the blow, he told me that Reg and I would be getting the QPM. The fact that I didn't get it when I'd been told I would was the main reason I started the whole grievance process.

It was also bizarre to see the lengths they would go to to protect someone who was so crap at his job. He'd come in to run a high-profile unit, brought in other questionable people, taken advantage of his post and the department – with results that could have been extremely dangerous for those working in it – and had then been moved overnight. So why go to such lengths to protect someone like that: the investigation into who sent the letters, trying to pin that on me so that they could discredit the allegations, when they must have known them to be true? Unless, of course, there were other allegiances at play. Even then, they could have protected Seddon and protected GMP from the fallout (which I'm pretty sure, as things started to unravel, was part of the aim), without trying to ruin my life. More than anything else, that's what I can't forgive them for and what I certainly will never forget.

All of these thoughts were spinning around in my head at the time, and some of them still surface today. So in hindsight it was no surprise when, on 11 November, after visiting my GP, I reported sick with stress and depression. Once again I cut myself off from everyone, not wanting to speak to anyone and only really happy with my own company.

Things dragged on; the days turned into weeks, and the weeks into months. The nightmares returned and I could hardly sleep, going to bed feeling shattered, but waking two hours later and then being up for the rest of the night. The events of the last eight years were eating away at me. I was put back on anti-depressants, and my own GP once again arranged for me to see a counsellor through the surgery, but after several sessions he concluded what I already knew: I needed to see someone more specialized.

* * *

By now I had requested an audience with the new Chief Constable, Michael Todd. It was important for me and my recovery that the people at the top knew first-hand the events that had taken place and I couldn't rely on others to do it; as I've said before, the good news had a habit of getting to the top, but the bad news would never make it that far.

My request was supported by the Force Medical Officer, Dr Deighton, who I'd also been to see several times and who wrote to the chief constable. Dr Deighton had offered me the services of a Dr Andrew Peden in Eccles, one of two specialist counsellors that GMP retained on their books purely for officers with psychological problems. I accepted the offer because I knew that I needed help – although I wasn't too optimistic – and my first appointment was due to take place on 24 March.

I was informed that ACC Vincent Sweeney wanted to see me, as he was the only member of the present command team who had been there eight years ago and knew more of the background. This was put to me by his staff officer Sergeant Sheila Mohammed. I agreed to speak to him on the proviso that I could still request, if necessary, an audience with Mr Todd. So at 10.00 am on Tuesday, 9 March 2004, I went once again to the Command Suite on the eleventh floor of Chester House, together with Richard Eccles, my representative from the Police Federation. Richard was the chairman of the North Wales Federation Office and he gave me excellent advice and assistance. I still wasn't comfortable using the Manchester office of the Federation, as I had little confidence in their allegiances either.

We were eventually met by Sergeant Mohammed who escorted us through to Mr Sweeney's office. He greeted us and we all sat informally around a large coffee table. Sergeant Mohammed and

Richard took notes during the meeting, which was programmed for an hour but which in fact lasted two. Mr Sweeney started the discussion by informing me that he had in his hand the brown envelope with the report inside that I had found in my personal file. He said he was going to shred it in front of me before I left that day, so that I could be sure it no longer existed.

I couldn't believe what he was suggesting. Far from wanting it shredded, this was an important piece of evidence and as police we're trained to secure evidence. I wanted to get to the bottom of this damaging, vindictive report. I explained how I felt about it, and he then agreed that he would preserve it. It seemed strange to me that someone in his position, so shortly after the report was found, wanted to get rid of it. I wondered what their stance would have been if the report had been something that I had concocted, full of untruths about one of them. Would they still want to destroy it and cover it up?

Mr Sweeney went on to tell me that a lot of good had come out of me finding the report as he had now ordered that everyone's personal file should be checked for anything similar and any offending items removed. This, of course, was great news for everyone else but didn't really help me.

Knowing that time was at a premium, I had made a list of things that I wanted to get across to Mr Sweeney. I discussed Seddon's indiscretions, the events in and around Operation Bluebell, and how I had gone on sick leave and ended up on half-pay. I talked him through my grievance procedure regarding the non-award of the QPM and other commendations, my subsequent postings, and then the recent discovery of the report in my file. ACC Sweeney's main response was that the people responsible for all of this had now left the job, so were no longer subject to disciplinary procedures. When I talked about all of Seddon's indiscretions in the Covert Operations Department, his brother staying at the covert flat, and how after all of that he was only reprimanded, Mr Sweeney said simply that if Seddon had come before him he would have been dealt with severely. I pointed out that the people responsible had still been in their posts eight years ago when I had taken out my grievance, and that the only thing different between then and now was that I had found the report from Homan. So why hadn't they been spoken to and dealt with before now?

That seemed to fall on deaf ears and Mr Sweeney didn't really respond. Instead, he told me that he had been instrumental in bringing Seddon back to England from Australia, and that the first time he spoke to him on the phone, Seddon had lied to him. He added that Seddon had made several complaints of abuse of process by Mr Sweeney and others, and that he had been glad to hear the conclusion of Seddon's court case.

With regard to my QPM, Mr Sweeney confirmed that the original report disappeared and that after seeing me, Mr Wilmot (now Sir David Wilmot, having been knighted in 2002) had tried but failed to get to the bottom of it. The chief constable had been 'very angry' about it, according to Mr Sweeney, and didn't want anything like it to happen again, so as a result of my experience, the process of nominations for awards changed.

ACC Sweeney asked me what the way forward was. I told him that the report from Homan was untrue, and that I would like some form of report to be placed in my file to counter what had been inferred about me. I'd also been given the details of a Professor Gisli Gudjonsson, a specialist PTSD counsellor based at King's College Hospital in London, who had worked with undercover officers as well as members of the armed forces. I'd read up about him and he was acknowledged as the leading expert in the field. I'd enquired whether he would be able to take me on as a patient and knew he was willing to treat me. So I requested to be allowed to attend King's College Hospital to see Professor Gudjonsson. After two hours the meeting closed with Mr Sweeney promising to get in touch with me, adding that consideration would also be given to my wife receiving some more counselling.

*   *   *

I'd been advised to seek help again from the Police Federation and see what I could do legally about my situation. I contacted them, but because of Seddon's legal problems he was using the Federation solicitors, Russell, Jones and Walker. As my case involved him, they would have had a conflict of interest. Strange, really, isn't it? I was about to start legal action against the force, the underlying cause of which was the decision by some officers to try to protect their corrupt colleague, but the lawyers I should have been using as a member of the Police Federation couldn't help me because they were busy working on behalf of that same corrupt colleague. So I was farmed out to other solicitors, Whittles in Manchester. I went to see them on several occasions, but they didn't instil a great deal of confidence in me.

Out of the blue, a good friend recommended a solicitor advocate, Simon McKay, who had his practice in Leeds. I was told that, if necessary, he would work on a 'no win, no fee' basis. I didn't think that would be an issue because I knew that, as a member of the Federation, my monthly subs should cover legal representation if required.

On Tuesday, 16 March I travelled to Leeds and met Mr McKay at his busy offices. He listened intently to everything I had to say, examined certain documents I had brought and then told me: 'It's quite clear to me what's gone on here: it's a case of misfeasance in public office.' This is a civil claim where, basically, someone in a position of public authority has abused or misused the power that comes with their position. I thought that fitted the bill of what had happened to me, so I was keen to hear more.

Mr McKay said that if I went down this road, all the relevant documents would be exposed. By contrast, Whittles wanted to take an action for loss of earnings. Mr McKay said he knew the barrister that Whittles had appointed as he was Leeds-based and didn't think he was the right man for the job. He also said the Whittles' proposal wouldn't be a good idea because of the success of my previous claim for £8,000.

I made notes in my diary at the time, saying that I found Simon McKay relaxed and easy to talk to, which helped to win me over. He certainly appeared to know what he was talking about. I was also impressed by his previous record: he had represented the paratrooper Lee Clegg, who was convicted in 1993 of the murder of two joy-riders at an army checkpoint in Northern Ireland. He'd assisted in overturning that conviction and getting Clegg released from prison.

By the end of the meeting I was in no doubt about using his services. He said that he would take my case on, if necessary on that 'no win, no fee' basis, but that if I contacted the Federation I could find out whether they would transfer their fees from Whittles to him. He also confirmed that I had six years to commence my claim from the date I found the report in my personal file.

I contacted the Greater Manchester Police Federation with my request to transfer my case to Simon McKay. They refused point-blank. They viewed him as the devil incarnate because, as they explained, he had represented members of ACPO, the Association of Chief Police Officers. The Federation represents officers up to and including chief inspector, so he was persona non grata to them. To me, this was completely ridiculous. I would have thought that, within reason, they would just want the best man for the job for their members. They didn't want to use his services because he had acted for senior officers, yet the Federation was happily supporting a senior officer (albeit a chief inspector) who had screwed me over completely and put the safety of other officers at risk.

I told Simon McKay what the Federation response had been, but he said it didn't matter and he would carry on regardless. At the time it felt really reassuring to know that I had someone like him on my side, that he was willing to get on with it and that he could see what my case was about. I had every confidence in him, and I duly had all my files transferred from Whittles in Manchester to him in Leeds.

* * *

By the beginning of April I still hadn't heard anything from my meeting with Mr Sweeney, so I hand-delivered a letter to Chester House for his attention, requesting that I now be granted an audience with the chief constable. A couple of days later I received a telephone message asking me to contact Sergeant Mohammed. I called her back, and she explained that he was still putting the document together and that they were looking for someone closer than Professor Gudjonsson in London for me to see.

I confirmed to her again that I would still like to see the chief. A short while later I received a letter and the report[20] Mr Sweeney had produced that was to be placed in my file as I'd requested. I must admit that when I asked for it, I didn't think I would ever see it, but Mr Sweeney did as he had promised. My jaw dropped when I read it. I never thought they would allow him to write something like this but here it was in black and white, confirming so many of the things about which I'd raised concerns.

He made it clear that someone in V Department had halted my recommendation for the QPM, for which, in his words, 'there will never be a satisfactory explanation.' The situation had been recognized by Sir David Wilmot who held the awarding of such honours as 'a matter of the highest integrity' and who felt that I had been 'wholly deserving' of the QPM.

He also confirmed that he was exploring the counselling options available, including Professor Gisli Gudjonsson in London. I think, when he wrote the report, he was still under the impression that with the right counselling I would be back at work. He seemed to think that my aim 'above all else' was to recover my health 'and return to full police duties'. To be healthy would be fantastic, but I still couldn't see myself back in the job.

When it came to the 'brown envelope' internal investigation, he said that the lack of documentation meant it was 'impossible to know whether such an investigation ever took place', although on the balance of probabilities he believed some sort of allegation had been investigated. ACC Sweeney said that since all of those involved had now left GMP, we would never know what had happened for sure, but added: 'I was able to reassure Garry that he is regarded as an officer of the highest integrity and that there are no doubts whatsoever about his character.'

That was fine, but as I'd explained to him, I'd raised all of these issues when those people were in the force eight years ago and no one had wanted to talk about it. It wasn't until I got to see Mr Wilmot that something had been done, at least in relation to the QPM. Now, eight years down the line, it was only because I'd found the report in my file that things were coming to light. So really it was no good saying now that they had all gone. They certainly weren't willing to go after those people when they were there, as I had found out.

So, to sum up the report: my QPM nomination had been stopped by someone in the CID command structure which, for me, had to be Detective Chief Superintendent Dave James, the same man who told me to my face that he had submitted it; Chief Constable David Wilmot didn't know what had gone on at the time, but after I got to speak to him personally had taken steps to rectify it; if I hadn't taken the stance that I did, I wouldn't have the QPM today; and although all these people had left the job, I'd raised my concerns while they were all still there and nothing had really been done.

Looking at that again today, I suppose it was no surprise that I no longer wanted to be part of the organization. However, on reading the report at the time, I did have a small sense of achievement: if nothing else it proved that I wasn't going mad, and that these things had happened to me.

* * *

Dr Peden was based in a little back-street building in Eccles and I'd been granted six sessions with him. Yet it was pretty clear that he had no idea about the work that I'd been involved in or the state of mind that I'd now reached. I went along to the first three sessions because I knew I needed help and I hoped that this would do at least some good. I was really conscious that this was the second time I had sunk into depression, and I was desperate to make sure that I didn't get as low as before or that it didn't continue for as long as before. However, by the end of that third session I knew that I could have completed all six sessions and still felt the same way I did at the start. I was pinning all my hopes on getting to see Professor Gudjonsson, but I still hadn't heard any more, so on Wednesday, 21 April I was back at the Occupational Health Unit at Sedgeley Park to see Dr Deighton.

We discussed recent events and I vented my anger and frustration at all the delays. He apologized and said some of it was his fault, but that he now had news that Mr Sweeney had sanctioned my request to go to see Professor Gudjonsson in London. Dr Deighton said I no longer had to go to see Dr Peden and that if I spoke to the Occupational Health appointments team, my sessions with Professor Gudjonsson would be arranged.

With all this going on, my stress levels were through the roof, but again I didn't appreciate how this was affecting others. At 07.45 on Friday, 14 May I got a phone call telling me that my mum had had a heart attack and collapsed in her bathroom at home. She'd then been rushed into Victoria Hospital in Blackpool. Eventually Mum had to undergo heart bypass surgery.

I suppose what was happening to me must have affected her to a certain extent, although we never really spoke about it, but she would have seen how my appearance had altered, how rough I was looking and, more importantly, how my mental state had changed. Stupidly, even when she had the heart attack and I was on sick leave, I still had blinkers on, not wanting to talk about it too much with my wife or mum, and trying to figure a way out of it all on my own.

Only recently I was going through some of mum's belongings and I found a card with a long, handwritten message inside that she sent to me around this time, before she had her heart attack. It was telling me to hang on in there, not to let them grind me down. I'd forgotten all about that. Maybe I didn't even take it in properly at the time, but it's clear that it was on her mind too. I don't know – and obviously I'll never know now – how much what was going on with me affected her. Yet I do know that, as a parent, you never really stop worrying about what your kids are going through, so I'd been naïve to think I could deal with it all without her knowing what was going on.

Chapter Thirty-Three

The Doctor Will See You Now

With my health still in a poor state I remained on sick leave, effectively just treading water until I could begin my treatment with Professor Gudjonsson. I was usually spending my days shut up alone at home, not really speaking to anyone, apart from regular contact with Simon McKay.

At 2.00 pm on Tuesday, 1 June I had my first appointment with Professor Gudjonsson. I was up early as usual as I couldn't sleep, so I made my way to Piccadilly train station to get the 09.47 down to London. We arrived at St Pancras just after 1.00 pm, but there were delays on the underground and by the time I'd got to the Elephant and Castle I missed the connecting train to Denmark Hill by two minutes. By now it was 1.50 pm, so I tried to ring Professor Gudjonsson to explain but the number was constantly engaged. Eventually I got through and he said it was okay. When I finally arrived at the King's College Institute of Psychiatry on De Crespigny Park at after 2.30 pm I felt terrible for being late, but Professor Gudjonsson met me at reception and took me to his office.

I expected it to be quite plush, but it was a working office with papers everywhere. He had very piercing eyes that never seemed to leave you. He immediately put me at ease though, and he had a great manner; I took an instant liking to him. We discussed my whole situation from start to finish. He asked a lot of questions and delved into certain aspects of what I was saying, while making copious notes. I then completed six tests, which he evaluated.

I seemed to have a good rapport from the start with Professor Gudjonsson. That may have been because I knew he had no ties or allegiances to Greater Manchester Police, so I felt comfortable talking to him. I knew he was working with me for no other reason than to try to improve my situation, but I think it was also because I knew just how good he was, how experienced he was in this field, and I really believed he could help me. I'd read up about him and seen what he'd done, not just on PTSD but also on psychology more widely. He had a worldwide reputation, and he'd been involved in some really big cases: he had given expert testimony in the cases of the Birmingham Six and Guildford Four, helping to get their convictions overturned. So with Professor Gudjonsson, I was able to open up a lot more, talk honestly about what had gone on and what I felt about it.

He said I had suffered a trauma in 1995–96 that had affected me and left me with a lot of anger, which was eating away at me. If not treated it could kill me. He had seen this anger many times in undercover police officers who felt let down at the end of their undercover role by their relevant organization. FBI agent Joe Pistone (Donnie Brasco) was a good example, after what happened to him at the end of his six years undercover. The anger needed to be treated in a positive way.

It was a pleasure to meet and speak with Professor Gudjonsson, and it was obvious to me that this was who I should have seen from the start of my troubles instead of being passed from pillar to post with people who had no perception of what was wrong with me. Before I left, a second appointment was made for 14 June. It was 1.00 am the following day before I eventually got home, but it was worth the long day. GMP eventually sanctioned ten sessions with Professor Gudjonsson, initially one every fortnight, in an attempt to get me back to work.

* * *

I was finally granted a meeting with the new Chief Constable Michael Todd, so on Tuesday, 27 July I arrived at Chester House for my 9.00 am appointment up on the eleventh floor. An hour had been set aside again for the meeting, which began with Mr Todd telling me that ACC Sweeney had been keeping him up to date with my situation. He then said straight away that it appeared to him that I had been the victim of 'some kind of corrupt Masonic influence within the CID' and that this would never happen now he was in charge. He also said that I should feel proud to be the holder of the QPM, that all those officers who were involved had left under a cloud, but that I was still a member of the GMP family.

Part of me felt that he was just going through the motions. I appreciated that he was new to the force and had nothing to do with my earlier problems, but he was repeating messages I had already been told and that I wasn't sure I believed anyway. So everyone from those days had now left and it couldn't happen again. Really? As I pointed out to ACC Sweeney, I'd been banging on about what had gone on for eight years and they were all here when I started trying to tell the force what had gone on, but no one was interested then when they could have actually done something.

They certainly had plenty of opportunities. For example, forget for a minute about the grievance procedure, the concerns I raised about what had been done and what was going on. Why weren't alarm bells ringing when the HMI was refused access to my personal files? That sort of behaviour is pretty unprecedented, yet no one in the force, to this day, has ever commented on it. John Tapley knew it was wrong, Mr Stevens thought it was unusual – although didn't want to rock the boat formally – but no one else ever took a moment to think why the hell are they doing that? So it was easy to say now, when there wasn't anything they could do, that it would never have happened on their watch. The only message I was getting eight years ago was that I was paranoid, that everyone was doing their best to help me but I was just being 'difficult'.

I'm not sure how good Mr Todd's listening skills were either. Towards the end of our meeting I told him that I was getting great benefit from seeing Professor Gudjonsson and that I was going for my second appointment the following day. By then my hour was nearly up, so I thanked him for his time and as we stood up and shook hands, he said: 'When do you go and see the Professor again?'

Yet his unsolicited comment about 'some kind of corrupt Masonic influence within the CID' hit home with me. It wasn't particularly a moment of inspirational enlightenment. After all, I'd been told as much by Chief Superintendent Don Brown, head of Y Department, and it was something I had suspected for a long time. It was the fact that Mr Todd was coming into this situation new and he could see this for himself. He had been briefed by ACC Sweeney, but Mr Sweeney had made no mention of a Masonic conspiracy to me; this was all down to Mr Todd's own judgement. So if it was that obvious to someone relatively new to the force, why hadn't any concerns been raised years earlier? Unless of course, many of those in CID or senior ranks across the force were all part of the same organization...

I know for a fact that several of the key players in my fall from grace were and probably still are members of the Lodge or the Brotherhood, and my own personal view is that this Masonic influence played some part in the events that took place. I'm not sure when I first began to seriously think there was an element of conspiracy. I knew Seddon was a Mason early on, after we'd seen the daggers and apron in his desk drawer at Prestwich, as was his mate who he brought into the unit, and I knew Mr James was too.

There was some general chat among us about who was in and who wasn't. I suppose, when I got that offer from the RCS guy who I hadn't heard from for years but who I knew was a Mason over at Oldham, the same as Seddon...that really got me thinking, and things seemed to stack up from there. So although it was unexpected to actually hear Chief Superintendent Brown, and then Chief Constable Mike Todd, tell me that I'd been the victim of a Masonic conspiracy, I wasn't surprised by what they were saying, only the fact that they'd said it.

Even if I had thought that early on, it would have been a difficult thing to say because I had no proof. I've no proof now, even though that's what I believe and what I've been told by two of the most senior officers in the force. All I can do, as I've said before, is put the facts out there and then let people make up their own minds.

It's worth stating again, though, I never hated Masons then and I don't now. I just felt (and still feel) very strongly that Freemasonry has no place in policing, if for no other reason than it can cast doubt on the motives for someone's actions, and in an organization such as the police, those sorts of doubts can do immense damage. To illustrate that point, read p.183 of *Ronayne's Handbook of Freemasonry* written by Edmond Ronayne, the Past Master of Keystone Lodge and author of *Master's Lodge*, *Masonic Oaths* and *Chapter Masonry*:

Whenever you see any of our signs made by a brother Mason and especially the grand hailing sign of distress, you must always be sure to obey them, even at risk of your life. If you're on a jury and the defendant is a Mason and makes the grand hailing sign, you must obey it, you must disagree with your brother jurors, if necessary, but you must be sure not to bring the Mason guilty for that would bring disgrace on your order.

You must conceal all crimes of your brother Mason's except murder and treason, and these at your own option, and should you be summoned as a witness against a brother Mason, be always sure to shield him. Prevaricate, don't tell the truth in this case, keep his secrets, forget the important points, it may be perjury to do this true, but you are keeping your obligations.

Times may have changed since Ronayne wrote this, but do Freemasons still abide by this or a similar code? Only they know. Could such a code be applied to what happened to Seddon? Was he protected by such a code, by those brother Masons within GMP, where the CID was renowned for membership of Freemasonry? Again, only they know.

*　　*　　*

The day after my meeting with Mr Todd, I was up early again and on my way to London to see Professor Gudjonsson for one of my now regular sessions. To understand just what an impact he was having, below are my notes from my diary following that appointment:

We talked through events over the last two weeks since I last saw him and referred to my daily log. [This was something I had been directed to complete by him to record my thoughts and feelings each day.] Discussed my anger and the situations where it has suddenly flared up. Prof G highlighted that my only emotion is anger, and all others have shut down.

I spent two and a half hours with him, he is very knowledgeable and I can see that what he says makes sense, which makes me understand things better, which makes me feel better.

He was then going on holiday, so my next appointment was on 3 September, but he gave me a list of things to do while he was away and said he would telephone me to check that I was okay.

On 1 September I received a letter from GMP informing me that I was to go on half-pay. I was gradually becoming acclimatized to being on this rollercoaster. I spoke before about the boxing analogy: that every time you get up and start fighting, you get knocked down again, and this was another one of those punches. The way they did it was pretty unhelpful too; no conversation, no discussion about how it might affect you or your family, not even a phone call; just a letter to say your income is about to be cut in half.

I took this letter with me on 3 September and showed it to Professor Gudjonsson. He was amazed, and while I was there he tried to phone both ACC Sweeney at GMP headquarters and Dr Deighton. Neither was available, but he spoke with Mr Sweeney's staff officer and left a message for Dr Deighton. He described the decision as a major setback and felt that it had ruined his session with me.

Professor Gudjonsson later wrote[21] to Mr Sweeney, asking that I be put back on full pay. He explained that I was now 'very worried' about my financial position, which was going to put me under added stress and hinder the progress of my treatment. He also spoke about how much we had already achieved in our first three sessions, and described me as a 'highly motivated patient'.

Two weeks later I received written confirmation that I would, for the present, remain on full pay. This was a big stress reliever for me and something for which I will always be grateful to Professor Gudjonsson. I'm not sure they would have reacted the same way if a counsellor with a practice in a little street in Eccles had written to them with the same advice. All of these ups and downs meant that the GMP rollercoaster ride would continue, doing little to diminish my overriding anger towards them. In fact, it fuelled it.

In the meantime I continued to travel to London for my fortnightly sessions, and on and off received certain updates from Mr McKay in Leeds. I was happy at this time that he was doing what he had to in relation to my case against GMP, so I concentrated on my health.

On 19 October I arrived once again at King's College Hospital and made my way to Professor Gudjonsson's office. I didn't know at this point that by the time I was on my way home, a life-changing decision would have been made. We spoke in depth about my current situation, how I felt and whether I thought I could go back to work with GMP. It was Professor Gudjonsson's view that I had PTSD with clinical depression, all of which resulted from my dealings with the force, and that I would not get better until I was released from the environment that was causing my problems. He then said that he was going to write to Dr Deighton and advise that I be discharged from GMP on ill-health grounds. He also said that if and when this day came, I could continue to see him at no cost whatsoever apart from my travel expenses, which was an incredible offer.

I headed back to Manchester, deep in thought.

*　*　*

On Tuesday, 26 October I went to Sedgeley Park Training School to see Dr Deighton. He had by now received the Professor's letter, with his recommendation that I be retired from the force. He explained the new procedures that had been introduced by the Home Secretary, David Blunkett. The report had to go to ACC Sweeney, who would check to see if there was anywhere else I could be deployed or if there were any outstanding disciplinary matters. Then, if sanctioned, I would have to go and see an independent doctor to assess me again (someone who was occupational health-trained), who would then report to the Police Authority with a yes or no.

Dr Deighton said he would submit the report to get the process started, and as I got up to leave he shook my hand in case it was the last time he saw me. It had taken a while, but I think he had eventually realized that I was genuine, that I was struggling with depression and PTSD, and once the penny had dropped he had tried to help me as much as he could.

On Wednesday, 15 December I went to London for my last of the ten initially-agreed sessions with Professor Gudjonsson. He informed me that he had written to GMP requesting a further six sessions, starting in January. I took him a card and a bottle of ten-year-old port for Christmas as a thank you, for which he was really appreciative. I'd still heard nothing from the independent doctor for my assessment. The following day, a letter arrived telling me that my assessment was to take place at Wythenshawe Hospital on 25 January with a Dr McNamara.

Chapter Thirty-Four

All Good Things ...

Christmas and New Year came and went, but I had too much on my mind to really enjoy it so I was glad to get into 2005 and, as I saw it, a new start. However, I began to feel really rough, physically as much as mentally. The last few years seemed to have caught up with me – the medication for depression and the effect it had on my heart; the weight loss which had led to concerns that I may have cancer and a whole load of tests for that; and just the physical symptoms of the stress I was suffering – and were now taking their toll. By the end of the first week of January I was ill in bed with really bad headaches, aches in my neck and no appetite.

I was feeling pretty isolated again too. I knew I had my wife's support, and of course the sessions with Professor Gudjonsson had really helped, but almost all contact with the force (other than my visits to Dr Deighton) was by letter. I know that was partly my choice, what with the PTSD making me feel quite reclusive. Yet from a welfare perspective, no one from the force (or the Police Federation) ever wanted to talk to me to see what was happening, find out how I felt or what I was thinking. It was all paperwork: assessments, reports and letters.

By now I was also getting additional stress and anxiety from a different source: Simon McKay. I'd been phoning his office in Leeds and speaking to his secretary, Camilla, asking her to get him to ring me with updates, but either she was not giving him my messages or he was just ignoring me because I never got any response, and I was starting to worry that things weren't going as they should have been.

On the odd occasion I did get to speak to him, he would have some excuse or other as to why certain things had not been done, but that he was going to get on with it. My anxiety was made worse because I knew I no longer had the support of the Police Federation; I'd chosen to go with Mr McKay, even though they had said they wouldn't fund it or work with him. So when I did get the opportunity to speak to him, I had to temper the need to blow off a bit of steam at him with a belief that what he was telling me, as a solicitor advocate, was true.

Professor Gudjonsson called me to say that he had received a reply from Dr Deighton to the effect that GMP were not going to sanction any more sessions with him. The treatment had been put on hold until after my appointment with Dr McNamara. I wasn't too concerned as my appointment was only a couple of weeks away, and Professor Gudjonsson told me to ring him anytime and to keep in touch.

On Wednesday, 12 January, I finally managed to get through to Simon McKay on his mobile phone. He said he had heard about the withdrawal of sessions with Professor Gudjonsson and told me that ACC Sweeney thought he had been misled, as he had only just found out about my possible legal action. Mr McKay said he would write to Mr Sweeney about the withdrawal of my ongoing treatment. He sent me a copy of the letter,[22] which explained that the force had been aware of my legal action since August of the previous year.

Apparently Mr Sweeney was concerned that 'personal correspondence' he had sent me (I'm assuming he meant his report after our meeting) was being used as part of the litigation. Mr McKay pointed out that the basis of the litigation was the 'improper conduct of GMP officers' rather than anything that Mr Sweeney had sent to me, that I was still suffering because of the way those officers and the force had behaved, and that Professor Gudjonsson's treatment sessions were essential in alleviating some of that suffering. He added that, given the Professor had written and told Mr Sweeney that I needed another six sessions, he would be 'in breach of his duty of care' towards me if that treatment wasn't funded.

It would have been interesting to see what the response to this letter would have been, and whether the force would have ever recognized that 'duty of care' they had to me. As events unfolded, it became clear that I would never know the answer to that one.

*   *   *

At 12 noon on 25 January 2005, I was at Wythenshawe Hospital to see Dr McNamara for his assessment of me for GMP. I felt it was going to be hard to condense everything that had happened to me into an hour or so. Professor Gudjonsson had already said that as far as he was concerned, I would never be able to return to a career with the police. Now it was down to Dr McNamara to make his judgement, although he had Professor Gudjonsson's opinion – a man who was at the top of his profession – weighing down on him. I was assuming it would have been hard for him to disagree.

I still needed to go through everything again with him though. I'm not sure what his background was, but I got the feeling he didn't really understand the nature of my illness; how PTSD was affecting me. By the time I left the hospital at 1.30 pm, I was totally drained.

Three days later Professor Gudjonsson called me to say that he had received a joint letter from ACC Sweeney and Dr Deighton, stating that funding would not be continued for any future sessions with him as it was likely that I would be retiring from the police. He said that he would write to them again as he felt it was important that I continued with the treatment, and that he had spoken with Simon McKay who felt the same.

I then had several weeks to sit and wait, until I went back to Occupational Health to see Dr Deighton. He told me that Dr McNamara had supported my retirement, and that his report would now go to the deputy chief constable for the final decision. I received my own copy of Dr McNamara's ten-page report by recorded delivery on Tuesday, 1 March. Below is his conclusion:

Evidently there are three strands to Mr Rogers' case. First is his Post Traumatic Stress Disorder which was probably precipitated by problems that he had encountered as a result of his duties as an undercover Policeman and he still has symptoms of this condition such as sleep problems with distressing dreams, hypersensitivity and social withdrawal.

The second condition is that of clinical depression, which continues to affect him; thirdly he is extremely bitter and angry against Greater Manchester Police for the way they allegedly treated him.

Hopefully his clinical depression will improve with treatment from Professor Gudjonsson if further sessions can be arranged, but I doubt whether this PTSD will improve to the point of him being able to undertake ordinary police duties. Therefore I consider that this will be a permanent problem for him.

The anger and bitterness that he shows towards the Force is not, of course, a medical condition but it is acting as a barrier in respect of the treatment of his other conditions.

In conclusion, I feel that he would have great difficulty carrying out key capabilities such as the ability to make decisions and report situations to others. Also, the ability to understand, retain and explain facts and procedures. He therefore would have difficulty with ordinary police duties such as patrol and supervising public order, incident management and dealing with crime. Taking into account all his past medical problems, I do not see how he could rehabilitate successfully back to ordinary police work.

Dr J F McNamara, LLM, FRCP (Glasg) FRCP (Edin) FFOM,
DIH
Consultant Occupational Physician

I wasn't sure that Dr McNamara had really got to grips with everything I had been telling him, or realized the extent of how much it had affected me. That would have been no surprise, given that I only had ninety minutes with him, and I think that was evident in the result of his assessment. Professor Gudjonsson was pretty clear that my PTSD wasn't caused by my operational undercover work, but dated back to 1995 and the way I was both exposed by the department and then treated by the force. Dr McNamara seemed to have decided that it was brought on by my undercover work; something I have always known wasn't the case.

Professor Gudjonsson had also explained to me that the anger and frustration I felt was common in cases of PTSD; for example, he had often seen the same thing when working with soldiers. Dr McNamara thought that it wasn't a symptom, although he acknowledged it was affecting my treatment. So while I don't think he really understood the condition, his recommendation was the same: my time in the police was coming to an end.

On Sunday, 13 March 2005 I received a hand-delivered letter at home, deliverer unknown, from an Inspector Viv Loder, someone to whom I'd never spoken. It informed me that the deputy chief constable had decided that I was to be retired from GMP on ill-health grounds as of 31 March. So after twenty-eight years, I was told I was retiring by letter; very matter-of-fact. So much for being a caring organization. I didn't want a march past or a big brass band, but to be told personally, face-to-face, would have been a nice touch. It wasn't to be, though.

Because my service was longer than twenty-six years, it meant that I could claim my police pension; something into which I had been paying 12 per cent of my monthly income for the last twenty-eight years. I say this because some people believe police officers receive a free pension when they retire, but the truth is they pay a substantial amount of their income into it. After thirty years, for most, it is well-deserved.

As I understand it today, police officers now have to complete thirty-five years service, with a chance that it may become forty years. The thought of rolling around on the floor with drunken yobs or the ever-increasing violent criminal when in my late 50s is not something I would relish. I don't think those who are changing these pension rights would want to do it either.

* * *

Thursday, 31 March 2005 marked the end of my police career for good. It was a job, as I have said from the outset, that I more or less always wanted to do. For the first eighteen years, despite certain ups and downs, I loved it, and although I might be biased, I believe I was good at what I did. I was giving 100 per cent to a job that gave me great satisfaction, and I moved around and worked in departments that other police officers could only dream about. While in the Covert

Operations Department I'd travelled abroad extensively and got to visit places I would never otherwise have seen. I was going from strength to strength, and passed both the sergeants' and inspectors' exams at my first attempt.

As far as I'm concerned, I would have been in the police until I had completed my thirty years' pensionable service. Unfortunately, through events over which I had no control, this was taken away from me. I never had a problem with any of the work I did, especially as an undercover police officer; in fact, this time was one of the best times of my service. I need to keep reiterating that my PTSD and depression were not caused by police work but by the events I have described in these pages. Those events were orchestrated by corrupt and vindictive elements within Greater Manchester Police, who ruined my promising career and, more importantly, ruined my life, and for what? To save the career of a more senior officer who believed he was bigger than the 'club', that he could do whatever he wanted, whenever he wanted to do it? I still couldn't believe all this had happened to me.

I didn't spend the day celebrating as I had very little to celebrate. I was still only 46 and now had no career. The good thing was that I was now free of an organization that I had grown to hate, one that had fuelled my anger and my ill health, and I knew I was better off out of it.

Little did I know, but the effects of my experiences in the force and the rollercoaster ride that resulted from them still had a few more twists and turns left. This time it was my solicitor advocate, Simon McKay, who would be at the controls...

* * *

As I said, I was growing increasingly concerned about how my legal case was progressing, and I seemed to spend most of my time chasing Mr McKay for updates. Then I started to catch him out, as he would be telling me that something had been done or sorted and I would later find out that wasn't the case. It was an awkward situation as he was still taking my case on a 'pro bono' basis – no win, no fee – which meant that I didn't feel I was in a position to call the shots in the same way as a paying client. Whenever I did manage to talk to him, he was reassuring me all the time that we had a really strong case; that GMP didn't have a leg to stand on. Even my wife got to the point where she was saying what's happening with your case? If it's so strong, why isn't it going to court yet?

Perhaps the most embarrassing moment came when I was asked to travel down to London for a meeting with Mr McKay and barrister Heather Williams QC, who was going to be taking my case. We were due to meet in her chambers, but on the way down McKay rang me to say he couldn't make it and that he would send one of his staff. When I arrived there the guy he had sent along clearly had no idea at all about my case and couldn't answer any of the barrister's questions. To say she was furious was an understatement. She also believed that certain papers regarding my case had been served on the courts but, once again, this hadn't been done. To go down to London on the train only to hear that all this stuff hadn't been done while the guy supposedly standing in for McKay had no idea at all about my case was a complete waste of time.

I was struggling to get to the bottom of what was going on with the case, but every time I got to speak to Mr McKay, he had an answer. He informed me at one point that he had obtained advice on my case from his good friend and eminent QC Keir Starmer (before he became Director of Public Prosecutions and Labour MP for Holborn and St Pancras), who had supposedly told him that I had a good case against GMP. Obviously I wasn't convinced though, and I started to record everything, including conversations; again, with the benefit of hindsight, I'm glad I did.

I continued this combination of waiting and chasing and the months dragged by; eventually, by October 2006, I had had enough. I wrote once again to Simon McKay, explaining that since he hadn't responded to my earlier letters or the call to his office the previous day, I would be coming into his office on 17 October to collect all my files and transfer them to Whittles. A few days later I received two calls from one of his staff, Dawn Oxley, to say that they were going to send my files back by courier. I told her there was no need, that I was coming personally to collect them and that I would like to speak to Simon if he was there when I arrived. She said he had a meeting at 11.00 am so I set off from home at 9.30 am in order to catch him.

I got there for 10.35 am and headed for his new office in St Paul's Square, Leeds. As I made my way there I bumped into Simon on the street walking away from his office. He took me back to the office and there was no one there, no staff at all. The last time I'd been there a couple of years before, it had been a really bustling office, but now it was like the Marie Celeste. He showed me a letter from GMP's representatives. He said he still wanted to represent me, that my case was strong and that he could now get on with it without any interruption. He added that he had been going through a divorce and that his dad had been ill, all of which had been weighing on his mind and he had not been 100 per cent on my case. He was very convincing, so I relented and left my files with him.

Unfortunately the lies kept on coming. I would speak to him one day and he would say he was just walking across to the court now to serve some papers or that they would be lodged the next morning, and I would find out months down the line that it hadn't happened. I continued to chase him for updates, and when I did get to speak to him he would reassure me that everything was okay.

The following conversation illustrates the way things were going. It's taken from the recording of a telephone call between the two of us in February 2008, and discusses a forthcoming meeting he was due to be having with the barrister. It highlights not only how much I was still affected by all that had happened, but also how adamant Simon McKay was that we had a strong case that should be successful at court:

GR: 'And then what's the longest you think it will take to get the proceedings drawn up and issued, you know, get them on the go?'

SM: 'Garry, it's just a question of somebody sitting down for three to four hours and drafting them out. Now, if she comes back to me and says well, I want this evidence and I want that evidence, it may be a question of me coming back to her with that material. But I can tell you that on Wednesday.'

GR: 'Right, okay.'

SM: 'After the meeting on Wednesday, if she says to me she wants all that, when I speak to you on Wednesday I'll say right, she wants a witness statement from this person, she wants all of err...the officers concerned disciplinary records...stuff like that...if she's saying that's what is stopping her we will know what she wants and then I can demonstrate to you that I am getting it...'

GR: 'I fully appreciate everything you are doing and what you are saying, it's just...I'd like to know, you know, if it's not going to go anywhere. I'd rather know so that I can draw a line under it.'

SM: 'But Garry, if it wasn't going to go anywhere mate we wouldn't be having this conversation, because I would have told you from the outset that it wasn't a runner.'

GR: 'Well yes, and I appreciate that. Like I say, it's very difficult. Like with the meeting we had in August, when my wife came with me; she was then thinking right, another thirty days we will be off on the go with this, and because nothing has happened since she's like took a nosedive and she thinks the case is not worthy now.'

SM: 'I know; it's very disappointing, and erm...'

GR: 'I find it very hard to explain, because I don't know one half of the things that are happening you see.'

SM: 'I understand mate. It sounds like I am making excuses, I'm not really; I personally feel like I am letting you down, but I can't move it forward unless...'

GR: 'Yes, like you say, with the barristers...it's just it still simmers in me, it's just burning away, especially when I see the likes of Sweeney who got the QPM and he's retired. I just think, they are bloody going and, you know, nothing has happened on my side, it's like my case isn't very strong against them.'

SM: 'No, it's a strong case Garry.'

GR: 'I want to hit them with both barrels you see. I can't get myself right until I get this thing sorted out.'

SM: 'I understand that, I really do understand it Garry…I really do.'

GR: 'You know I am still suffering with it now, and when it all gets dug up again, if there's nothing positive it knocks me a hundred steps back, if you know what I am saying?'

SM: 'I do know what you are saying. Listen, I am doing everything I can, just bear with me until Wednesday and then I will phone you Wednesday evening.'

GR: 'Alright, and then we will see what the situation is.'

On 16 April 2009 – five years and one month after instructing Simon McKay to bring a claim for Misfeasance in Public Office against GMP and almost six years after finding the 'official, unofficial' report in my file – I received an email confirming that, having sought a third barrister's opinion, there was no reasonable prospect of a successful action against the force. It had taken more than five years just to establish whether there was merit in the claim. My previous legal action against GMP in 1998 had effectively ruled out any future claim. This was despite the fact that I had found and experienced things since I'd received my original payout that had seriously affected me, such as discovering the internal investigation report. In my eyes, that first settlement didn't cover the things that had taken place after it was agreed.

Those five years had been like running a marathon and by 2009 I was once again dejected as I realized that all that time spent meeting, chasing, waiting and hoping had been for nothing. Rather than holding on to the case for five years and spinning me a load of lies, I would have much rather Mr McKay had told me two or three years earlier that it wasn't going to go anywhere. I would have been disappointed, but I could have handled that. To be hanging on for much longer in the hope that it might come through, when actually nothing was being done… that was far worse.

* * *

All my files were returned to me from Mr McKay's office. I was advised to contact the Solicitors Regulatory Authority (SRA), which I did, and my case was overseen by their representative, Bridget Stark-Wills. I provided her with all my contact notes with Mr McKay over the last five years; after she had digested all this and researched everything to her satisfaction, she concluded that I had received an inadequate professional service, sufficiently grave as to amount to misconduct warranting a referral to the SRA.

This decision was sent to Mr McKay, and he was given the opportunity to respond and deny the allegations. A formal decision was reached in August 2010 by David King, an official adjudicator for the SRA. It ordered McKay Law Solicitor & Advocates to pay me £2,500 'in respect of distress and inconvenience' within seven days of the date of the letter, and for them to waive any rights to claim from me any costs and disbursements, such as barristers' fees to date.

Unsurprisingly, given their performance in my case to date, McKay Law didn't comply with the order within seven days; in fact it took until 15 November for McKay Law to send me the cheque. They said that the original cheque that they sent me was effectively lost in the system and this was the cause of the delay...same old Simon McKay.

Chapter Thirty-Five

Thanks for the Memory Loss

Writing this book has been both challenging and, in its own way, therapeutic. It's been tough to revisit some of the emotions I felt during the later years of my police career – the stress, the fear, the isolation, the anger, the frustration and the overwhelming sense of injustice – and to think again, with the benefit of hindsight of course, why events unfolded the way they did. Could I have done anything differently? Perhaps. Should I have just swallowed what happened and got on with life? Possibly. Would I have been any happier if I had? I really don't think so.

The sense of therapy comes from going through those events again, in close detail, and reminding myself that I wasn't being paranoid, that I didn't do anything wrong, and that (as I see it) I truly didn't deserve to be treated the way I was. Of course, there are some good memories too. I mean, I could have just sat on my backside in an office somewhere for a thirty-year police career, got the same money and been better thought of... but I wouldn't have missed being an undercover police officer. I loved every minute of it; it was the best part of my career, despite what came afterwards. I wouldn't have given up the sense of achievement we felt when we'd really made a difference, when we'd taken hardened criminals or football hooligans off the streets. Nor would I swap the sense of camaraderie we had on some of those covert operations or even back on shift in my early days in uniform, and friendships with officers like Tony Quinn.

So what could have been done differently? Well, apart from the obvious – not putting someone like Ken Seddon in charge of a covert operations unit, not trying to cover up his failings, and then not lying to my face about what had gone on – a bit of honesty and clear communications could have made a world of difference. No one was ever willing to get me into the office, sit me down and just say look, we've made a lot of mistakes, we've ballsed things up, but work with us and we can put things right. For a long time, that is all it would have taken, but they never did. Eventually, I got beyond that point.

Finding that 'confidential investigation' report in my personal file was the last straw. Up to that point I knew I'd been lied to, that senior officers had tried to cover up not only what their mate Seddon had done, but also the way they had wrongly treated me. I knew my health had suffered; that my family had suffered. Yet for a while it felt like I'd reached a turning-point. They had tried to rectify some of the mistakes: the QPM had been put through, and I'd got away from force HQ and was doing something I was good at, albeit not a career I would have chosen. Deep down, I knew I was still suffering mentally, but if I'd got the right help then and someone had sat me down and said, we know we've made mistakes, this is what went on, what can we do to put it right, even at that point, I think there was a chance that I could have got the treatment I needed, stayed in the job and worked things out.

However, that report made me realize that senior officers must have known what was going on all along. Saying that 'they have all gone now' is no answer. Knowing that this wasn't about mistakes, that this was a deliberate effort to discredit me, and yet I'd done nothing wrong – absolutely nothing – that was too much to take, I think. So when I was advised by the Federation that I had a case against them, I felt that it was my chance to make them understand what they had put me through. Yet even then, I couldn't use the Federation solicitors because they were defending the man who'd put me in this position in the first place.

That lack of communication, and the lack of a duty of care, was evident more than once. Things like finding out that one of the gangs were hiring private investigators to try to track down undercover officers freaked me out. So too did the fact that the force was willing to put me and my family in jeopardy. Knowing that I found all of that out by chance – through poking around by myself or because someone else in the office had thought I should know, unofficially – made me angry. Yet again, no one from the force has ever really discussed those things with me. To this day, they haven't asked about my family's safety. Other than suggesting we could stick an alarm in the house that went straight through to a police station where I knew there was at least one bent copper linked to operations in which I had been involved, they have done nothing. No one has ever been brought to book about the fact that criminals from two operations ended up being put on remand together in the same prison. It was avoidable, and previously they had made sure it didn't happen, but for some reason they just stopped caring. Even now, no one gives a damn about it.

* * *

As I've said before, I've only ever wanted to be a policeman, so I've never really wondered where I would be now if I hadn't joined the force, but I have often thought about where I would be now in the police if things had turned out differently.

I think one day I could have been running the undercover unit. I turned down the opportunity to go and do other things, because that was the role I loved. There were six or seven of us – out of a force of 7,500 officers – who were doing that job full-time, so such chances don't come up very often.

I came up against a number of middle-ranking and senior officers who were hunting for promotion, looking for the next rung up the ladder, and they weren't prepared to upset anyone above them or to rock the boat, even when they knew something was wrong. By then I wasn't interested in promotion; once the trouble had started in my career, I knew I wasn't going to go any higher. The question is, what rank could I have achieved? Where could I have ended up?

I'll never know that now, but to have got through the promotion exams first time, one after the other, was quite an achievement. Some officers – even those who work their way up the chain – take several years to get through their exams. I studied hard and passed them. The Regional Coordinator of the RCS had even recommended me for immediate promotion. So I obviously had potential. I'd like to think that I would have been promoted, and eventually maybe even moved on as Harry did. Knowing how far I could have gone was something else that the force, and those corrupt or lying officers I came up against, took away from me.

One of the reasons I got as far as I did, and survived the last ten years of my career, was the support of my wife and the rest of my family. She hasn't read this book; or at least, hasn't so far. She can't bring herself to read it. I don't think she wants to know the full extent of what I did at work, and also how I felt about the things the force did, and I can understand that. She still believes that the police ruined my life, and I can understand that too.

She never actually said to me: 'Just leave the job.' I think she knew I wouldn't, and I'm glad I didn't. It's had a big enough effect on my health anyway, but if I'd jacked the job in I think it would have rotted my brain.

It says a lot that we've managed to survive as a family though, considering everything we've been through. My two daughters have read the book, so they have more of an insight. One of them now works for Greater Manchester Police, and she has a better understanding of the situation I was in and the things I was coming up against. Yet as I say, I don't regret going into the police, and if I had my time over again I would still join up.

* * *

This book isn't all about looking back though. Some of my experiences are still relevant to policing today, maybe even more so. For example, those officers who tried their best to deceive and discredit me did so because they really thought that I had tried to shaft Seddon. They spent a lot of time trying to prove that, and they were completely wrong. Yet think about it for a moment: there's supposedly more support today for whistleblowers, for people who report or expose wrongdoing within their own organization. Yet when they wrongly suspected me of trying to expose Seddon, they went after me, and that was when they just *suspected* me of trying to expose him. What do you think they would have done if I'd actually put my head above the parapet, reported him or gone to the papers with what I knew? I can only hope the GMP force of today, and the service as a whole, has a very different attitude to anyone brave enough to blow the whistle on corruption within their own organization. If they haven't, I don't have any real confidence that anyone who did decide to speak out today would get much better treatment.

Also, what about the influence of Freemasonry on modern policing? Obviously, there will be those who to this day still argue that I wasn't faced with any Masonic conspiracy and that I'm imagining it. As I've made clear, the idea of a Masonic conspiracy wasn't my first thought when I came up against corruption and collusion. Yet it clearly was the belief of those who would be much better placed than I to know how the senior management team operated, and once you started viewing events from that perspective, things quickly fell into place.

What I do know is that, even at the time, it seemed highly strange and suspicious that someone like Seddon could get away with what he had done, be moved overnight and then shipped out to Australia as an 'ambassador' of the force without some sort of protection going on. What he had been doing was clearly an embarrassment to the force. To have someone running an undercover police department behaving in that way was extremely politically sensitive for GMP. The nature of the crime and the criminals we were dealing with in that unit meant that any suggestion of incompetence – or worse, fraud and corruption – would put all of the work of the department at risk. So there was a huge incentive for the force to deal with him as quickly and quietly as possible and just move him out of the spotlight, almost overnight. If it had been made official at the time (which, under today's regulations and focus on greater transparency and accountability, it would have had to be) the integrity of all of the previous jobs done by the department, and the safety of those convictions, would have been called into question.

This all took place at a time when Seddon, the head of the CID and most of the department were Masons. So what about the Masonic influence today? Well the issue certainly doesn't seem as prevalent as it was back in the 1970s, '80s and '90s, and it would appear that the organization as a whole, having launched several campaigns and initiatives to become more open and accessible to the public, is now seen to have less of an adverse impact on people's perceptions of those in senior positions. At least, that's what I thought.

However, as I was writing this book, a new story appeared in the media that seemed to bring the whole issue back into the spotlight. Days before he stepped down from office, the then Chair of the National Police Federation, Steve White, gave an interview to the *Guardian* newspaper (31 December 2017), stating that attempts to reform the Federation were being blocked by Freemasons and that their influence in the service was affecting the progress of women and people from black and minority ethnic communities. White told the *Guardian*:

What people do in their private lives is a matter for them. When it becomes an issue is when it affects their work. There have been occasions when colleagues of mine have suspected that Freemasons have been an obstacle to reform.

We need to make sure that people are making decisions for the right reasons and there is a need for future continuing cultural reform in the Fed, which should be reflective of the makeup of policing.

It's about trust and confidence. There are people who feel that being a Freemason and a police officer is not necessarily a good idea. I find it odd that there are pockets of the organization where a significant number of representatives are Freemasons.

A spokesman for the United Grand Lodge (the governing body for Freemasonry in England) said there was no clash of cultures and no reason for serving police officers not to be Masons. In fact, a Masonic Lodge, Sine Favore ('Without Favour') had been set up by Police Federation members in 2010.

Yet clearly that was not a view shared by White. More than thirty years after the publication of *The Brotherhood* and twenty years after my own experiences with the Masonic network in policing, it seems that the issue has far from disappeared.

* * *

Things at home have certainly been a bit different since I left the job. Professor Gudjonsson had said he would continue to see me, but asked me to speak to my GP to see if I could get a referral. Once this was in place, I had three more sessions with him in the April and May, which were free apart from the cost of my travel, which I funded myself. Professor Gudjonsson would have continued after these as he felt I still had unresolved PTSD, but he also knew that being away from the police generally, and GMP in particular, could be the start of my recovery. Only time would tell.

For my part I couldn't afford to fly to London as I had done for some of my earlier sessions and the train was pretty expensive too, so instead I went by coach. Given that my mental health was still quite fragile, the travelling started to become too much and the cost was a factor as well, so after those three sessions my formal treatment with Professor Gudjonsson ended. I still spoke with him by phone though; in fact, during those first twelve months after retirement, he was one of the only people outside my family that I did talk to.

I knew deep inside that I wasn't okay, but I was relieved to be away from the place and the people that had made me ill. For much of that first year, I kept myself to myself and was still pretty much a recluse. While there had been a sense of relief when everything came to an end and some of the pressure was now off, I was struggling. Finishing a career like that doesn't make you feel good and I was still a fairly young guy, so I couldn't just sit around for the rest of my life. I started looking for another job. I used to go and read in the library some days – another example of that reclusive trait, finding somewhere quiet where people won't talk to you – and I would check the job pages. I saw an advert working for the North West Ambulance Service, where they wanted care assistants for patient transport. I applied, had the interview, took the driving course and got the job. It was twenty-five hours a week, taking people to hospital for their appointments, and I loved it.

I got to meet so many great characters, most of them lovely people. This was the only job I'd had as an adult other than being in the police, but it made me realize that in the right situation, I had a lot of transferable skills. Surprisingly perhaps, considering what I'd been through and how it had affected me, I found it easy talking to people again. Those interpersonal skills you first learn as a copper back in uniform, they hadn't gone away. I had all my driving skills of course, and I was more than happy taking responsibility for things and sorting out any problems. I did that job for four and half years, and it taught me that there was much more out there than just policing. It got me out of the house, back out in the working world, and I earned enough to top up my police pension while still spending time at home with my wife and the family. So I owe that job a lot.

I still work for the NHS today, although as a technician rather than on the ambulance or patient transport side. I enjoy it, and I'm proud to say that, in the twelve and half years I've worked for the NHS, I've never had a day off sick. However, I'm still much more comfortable working on my own rather than in an office or as part of a larger team. I think that's a legacy of my experiences in GMP, and the effect of my PTSD. If you spoke to my wife now, she would tell you that I'm a different person to the one I was before all this happened. I don't suffer fools gladly, and occasionally I can still lose my temper really quickly, traits that I didn't use to have. I also don't socialize anywhere near as much as I used to, and I can be a bit of a recluse at times. So yes, it still affects me, but not as much as it did. Now I understand it, I know that I'm a different person, and I have ways of dealing with it.

I jokingly said to my wife not so long ago, I think I've only got about ten years left! My family history isn't one of long life, especially on the male side: Dad died at 42 and his brothers all died in their 60s, so if genetics are anything to go by, I'm not going to be getting a telegram from the Queen. Working in the NHS, I've also seen how trauma in people's lives can take its toll on their health and their bodies. I'm not being morbid; I don't plan on keeling over any time soon. Yet that's why writing this book has been so important to me. I wanted to put the final piece of the jigsaw in place and get the facts out there, so I can enjoy the rest of my life without feeling that I still had something to do.

* * *

What about the rest of the people who played such a big part in my experiences? Some have moved on to great things, others have just moved on and some are no longer with us. Harry took his considerable skills setting up his own company focusing on investigative work on a commercial level. As I understand it his replacement, Ken Seddon, has returned to Australia; they obviously enjoyed his contribution to the country so much last time around that they welcomed him back for more. His mate and sergeant, who came into the unit under a cloud and probably left the same way, has since passed away. I've chosen not to name him as it wouldn't make any difference now.

I've no idea where many of the other officers with whom I came into contact are now – people such as Dave James, Geoff Keeling and David McCrone – although I did try to contact some of the people I mention in this book to let them know what I was doing and ask for their comments, with varying degrees of success. Don Brown, the head of Y Department who I went to see about the 'officially, unofficial' investigation, was more than happy to talk (despite undergoing treatment for cancer at the time). Don joined GMP (then Manchester and Salford Police) in 1972, and received the Queen's commendation for bravery in 1975. When he took over the Y Department he said it had a 'Draconian reputation', which it found difficult to shake off. 'An investigation is a search for the truth, not a quasi-prosecution,' Don told me. 'That's an important distinction; investigate to prosecute and you become Draconian, investigate and search for the truth and you remain neutral.'

Don explained that while unofficial investigations were not unheard of, they were unlawful and breached regulations. If he found out they were taking place while he was head of the department he would always impose the regulations and make sure any officer under investigation was served with a notice, unless that would compromise an ongoing investigation. He continued:

As regards brown envelopes, yours was the only one I have ever seen. Having said that, we had no need in the Y to delve into personnel records. But in more than thirty years of policing, yours was the only brown envelope I ever saw.

GMP was for a while regarded as a Masonic force, particularly when the Stalker issue arose. All officers were asked formally if they were Masons, and there were three options on the form – Mason, Not a Mason, Don't want to say! The *Manchester Evening News* once superimposed the GMP HQ sign over the South Manchester Lodge, saying: 'The place where GMP does its promotions'. It was well known that David James ran a nest of Masons within his area of jurisdiction.

While Don could remember a lot of details from his policing career as well as my own issues with the force, not everyone else had such clear memories or, in fact, any memories at all. I emailed Andrew Marston, the former civilian head of police personnel at GMP, who told me at the time that he was 'embarrassed' about what he had been unable to find out, and that the brick wall he had come up against was an 'unusual set of circumstances'. I explained what I was doing and reminded him of the situation as I thought he may now be happy to speak, no longer being part of GMP. He replied that while he could 'broadly' remember seeing me, he couldn't recall any of the detail. I told him I was surprised as he had felt the circumstances at the time were pretty unique.

I contacted Les Owen via his business email. This is the man who was staff officer to David O'Dowd at the Home Office, and who had telephoned me in 1998 to tell me to basically keep quiet as I would come to notice for the wrong reasons. He also said that he knew exactly what had gone on and that when we both retired we could meet up and he would tell me all about it. Unfortunately he also had amnesia and couldn't remember anything about it. Nor could Vera Waters, who I was sent to by Dave James when I initially went sick in 1995.

By contrast, John Tapley, the staff officer to HMI John Stevens (who now sits in the House of Lords as Baron Stevens of Kirkwhelpington) has always been very supportive. He kindly agreed to write the foreword to this book. At the same time, he also filled in a lot of the detail of which I was unaware about what was going on behind the scenes while I was continuing my struggle for justice with the force. I couldn't include all of this information in the foreword – after all, no one wants to know how the story ends before they read it – but it's a fascinating insight, which is why I've included it in full here:

The following part of Garry's career cannot be fully told by him, so I shall do it on his behalf. Aside from the manner in which he had been treated, Garry's particular concern was that a subordinate undercover officer on the same operation had been awarded the QPM, but Garry's nomination had apparently been 'blocked' by Greater Manchester Police. Garry had been the lead officer responsible for the operation involved and had been at the greatest risk. This seemed to be grossly unfair to me and it could not be defended.

I asked the force to see Garry's personal file and all files relating to his situation. The Deputy Chief Constable refused my request. I was acting legitimately on behalf of an HM Inspector. HM Inspectors are granted a Royal Warrant to inspect police forces. For a force to refuse to release files upon legitimate request was not only unheard of, but a violation of the HM Inspector's Crown authority. It could also be considered as an affront to the Queen herself. I referred the issue to my HM Inspector immediately. He did nothing then or later. He thus undermined my position (and his own!). From this point the Deputy Chief Constable considered me to be an irritant, and he was to lodge a serious unjustified complaint about me to my HM Inspector. Again, I received no real support from my HM Inspector.

I did, however, arrange for Garry to meet personally with my HM Inspector. This was a former chief constable with a long and distinguished police career. He was a man with a reputation for action who had a high regard for police officers (especially constables) who would 'get stuck in'. I thought that Garry's career fitted into this category perfectly, and that my HM Inspector would clearly understand and support Garry's position. How wrong I was!

The meeting took place in my hotel room in the Old Rectory Hotel, Manchester, on 10 September 1997. I had arranged to use an empty meeting room but HM Inspector decided to use my hotel room. It was a bizarre meeting. After I had introduced Garry, HM Inspector picked up the packet of biscuits provided in my room and then laid full stretch on his back on my bed. Garry then proceeded to relay his position. Meanwhile, HM Inspector ate my biscuits whilst still lying on my bed. Garry became increasingly perplexed at this turn of events. I could not believe it.

HM Inspector didn't appear to be very interested, despite my written briefing notes and my prior verbal briefing. He did not appear to be listening fully to Garry. When Garry finished he was basically dismissed by the HM Inspector and I saw Garry out. On my return, the only comment from HM Inspector was that Garry would not be getting the QPM and that, as far as he was concerned, was the end of the matter.

I raised Garry's position whenever an opportunity arose during the inspection process. On one occasion the chief officer responsible for crime admitted, in an unguarded moment, that 'We didn't get it right with Garry Rogers.' There was no response to my consequent query as to what he was now going to do about it? It was clear that, for whatever reasons, Greater Manchester Police and some of its senior and chief officers were mistreating Garry. An independent observer might ask: 'Why were these people so keen to prevent Garry Rogers from being awarded the QPM when it was fully justified and had been awarded to a subordinate, subject to lesser risk on the same operation?' Garry addresses this question from his perspective in his book.

All police nominations for Crown awards must be sent from the force to HM Inspectorate for assessment. Consequently, the main problem with the process for Garry to receive the QPM was that his force had to submit a formal nomination. People within that force appeared to be acting to prevent that for one reason or another. The Inspectorate had been briefed on the justness of the nomination by me. However, without co-operation from

Greater Manchester Police, no progress could be made to further matters along the process. Then, out of the blue, on December 22, 1997, a formal nomination for Garry to be awarded the QPM was received, signed by the Chief Constable. I ensured that it was properly endorsed by the original HM Inspector. He signed the endorsement without comment. The nomination was then forwarded to the Home Office for the normal process of assessment and decision.

After this inspection, I transferred, at my request, to another HM Inspector, and Inspectorate responsibility for Greater Manchester Police later transferred to a newly appointed HM Inspector. I requested an interview with him about Garry. He ignored my request, so I submitted a written report to him outlining Garry's situation. Again, I received no response.

By an odd quirk, that newly appointed HM Inspector apparently decided that he was too inexperienced to inspect a force the size of Greater Manchester Police. So, the 1998 inspection then passed to my new HM Inspector and I found myself in Manchester talking to Garry again one year after our original meeting. Same Deputy Chief Constable – same 'irritant' – similar obstruction and another unjustified complaint! Garry didn't know that his nomination had been formally submitted, and I could not tell him that it had gone before the honours committee in London (I had tracked its progress). We agreed that he would not meet my new HM Inspector this time, but I would ensure that the HM Inspector was fully apprised of the situation. I had already done that regularly since Greater Manchester Police had been returned to us. This HM Inspector was much more amenable to Garry's situation. HM Inspectors met regularly, and always kept an eye on police nominations for honours. My HM Inspector needed to have Garry's nomination clearly in his mind through 1998 and to keep it there (his memory was not fully reliable).

My role in this part of Garry's life was very minor. Having read Garry's book I am convinced that the nomination only went forward from Greater Manchester Police because of the personal intervention of the Chief Constable, Sir David Wilmot. This was a chief constable who appeared to insulate himself somewhat from others (even his chief officers). My requests to Greater Manchester Police about Garry appear to have been shielded from Sir David by the Deputy Chief Constable. It seems clear to me that a critical factor was Garry's eventual one-to-one meeting with Sir David late in 1997. It was then that Sir David must have understood how badly Garry had been treated, and he then acted personally to support Garry's nomination for the QPM, thereby overriding all of the ranks below. I believe that was the first Sir David had heard of Garry, his situation and the nomination.

The award of the Queen's Police Medal to Constable Garry Rogers was duly announced in the New Year's Honours list of 1999 – much to his surprise and my relief.

On the subject of the Queen's Police Medal, it is necessary to explain that it is awarded to two distinctly different types of police officer. For the most part, it is awarded to chief officers (and occasionally senior officers) whose turn it is, who have no other medals or who might deserve it for some policing service. There are, however, a few police officers, nearly always at the bottom of the hierarchy, whose commendable police service is such that it deserves recognition by the Queen. Really there should be two official categories of QPM: 'Primary' for those few who really deserve recognition by the Queen, and 'Secondary' for all the rest. Garry Rogers' award of the QPM was in the Primary category. In my opinion, no other award of the QPM was more deserved at such cost for such meritorious police service. Garry and his wife were presented with the medal by HRH Prince Charles at Buckingham Palace. I believe that both he and Her Majesty would have reflected my views.

Reading John's words again today, it makes me realize that while my career – and to a certain extent, my life – was severely blighted by the actions of a few self-serving senior officers who lacked compassion or integrity, I was very fortunate to have a handful of honest, principled and professional people who were fighting my corner (sometimes without my knowledge).

John Tapley was certainly one of those. Maybe the last word should go to another, the late Sir David Wilmot, the former Chief Constable of Greater Manchester Police who, when he realized the extent of what certain senior officers under his command had been up to, fully supported my new nomination for the QPM in 1998, and to whom I am forever grateful. When Sir David retired from GMP he became Lord Lieutenant of Greater Manchester. I contacted him initially via email and then via letter to the Lord Lieutenant's Office in September 2013. The letter outlined my story again from start to finish (as briefly as possible), including my view that I had been the victim of a Masonic conspiracy. I was hoping we could meet.

Sir David replied a few weeks later, as he had been away. He didn't think there would be much benefit from meeting up, but did say: 'I cannot add anything to the conclusions that you already have.' He was in charge of a 12,000-strong organization, yet he didn't say he could not remember me. What he did say was that there was nothing more to add to the conclusions I had already reached. My conclusions were that this was a Masonic conspiracy within the then hierarchy of Greater Manchester Police.

As for those who turn round and say, as GMP did at the time, that it was all in my imagination… you might believe that this is the police and they tell the truth, the whole truth and nothing but the truth but I, John Stalker and quite a few others would beg to differ.

Notes

Transcriptions, letters, documents and reports

Chapter 22:

1. Transcript of meeting between DC Rogers and Mr McCrone, 10 July 1995

GR: 'That term's been used by Mr James to me about that…and nobody takes time out to even say come on in sit down let's have a chat about it, you know you have done too much work, now you can't work anywhere else, let's sit down and talk this through as to what you can do in the future, I mean I don't want to be in the position I am in now. I've been on the sick since February, I've lost all my allowances, I'm living on a real bog standard wage now, my wife's been off because we have had children, off on a career break, so it's no fun to be off on the sick at all and what annoys me is I needn't be on the sick had I been treated right in the first place and I didn't do anything wrong yet I have been treated like I have and then I hear whilst I have been on the sick that the policeman from Stockport on the last job, because they have not got enough to charge him, he's been sent off on a pension, on a full pension so the way I see that from my position is that he's laughing all the way to the bank and he is the culprit and I am not.'

Mc: 'Erm, now then we are obviously not going to resolve your situation today.'

GR: 'I could talk to you all day sir with this…there's so much in my head about it. It's untrue, I don't have to have notes to tell you, I can tell you from start to finish the whole thing, I mean since I've been off I've found out one of the flats we used at Salford, which I used on the last operation regarding the '…………' and this is when you are hoping people back you up at the end of the day, for your own safety, and whilst I've been off on the sick I've found out Mr Seddon, who has been moved, had allowed the place to be used by his brother who is a fireman and then he asks you to use the place afterwards on an undercover operation, you not knowing that the place has been compromised. You know it's attitudes like that that are putting my life and other people who are doing it at risk.'

Mc: 'What's the position when you saw Dr Deighton the other day?'

GR: 'I saw Dr Deighton and like I say I had to start at the beginning to tell him and he wanted to know what was medically wrong with me and I said I don't know what's medically wrong with me, I find myself in this position through no fault of my own and this is why the Dr seems to think there's something wrong with me, something's caused me to be the way I am now because of the worry I've got, so as I started to tell him he listened a bit more, it was at that point he said, this is an unusual step but I will write to the ACC of Personnel and get you an appointment to see him, so I said great because the way it was going no one's been to see me, no one seems interested.'

Chapter 23:

2. Grievance Procedure

With reference to the in force grievance procedure, I wish to invoke this in relation to the following:

On Friday, March 11 1994 I was attached to the Covert Operations Department and at that time was heavily involved in 'Operation Vixen' regarding a team of 'ram raiders' from the Leigh area. I was told by Detective Chief Inspector Seddon that I had been over-exposed as an undercover policeman and that it had been decided that I was to be moved within the next six months. He told me that both I and DC Reg had been nominated for the Queen's Police Medal for services to undercover work, but that I was not to ask any questions about it. I was told to return and see DCI Seddon one week later after he had returned from annual leave.

I was surprised, to say the least, at the manner in which this news was given and, being concerned for my future, I made an appointment to see Detective Chief Superintendent James at 9.30 am on Monday, March 14 1994 and made my way to Chester House. Whilst waiting outside Mr James's office I was met by Chief Superintendent Yates who asked me why I was there and then took me into his office. I outlined my concerns and what I had been told to him.

Mr Yates stated that what I had been told was not the case and that I was to remain in the office and that he was glad I had spoken to him first as Mr James would not have known about any proposed transfer from the office. Upon Mr Seddon's return, I was virtually 'sent to Coventry' for having been to Chester House and spoken to Mr Yates. Despite this, I continued with Operation Vixen, which came to a successful conclusion on April 5, 1994. I then spent one month at Prestwich Police Station in isolation transcribing the audio and video tapes for the operation.

The next time I was spoken to by DCI Seddon, after having been stopped from attending the annual undercover officers' seminar at West Yorkshire, was on May 19, 1994. On this occasion I was left in no doubt that the reason for my isolation was due to me attending Chester House on Monday, March 14.

I was told that he 'had considered mixing me a bottle' and 'sending me down the road' but that to 'act in haste, repent at leisure'. I was also told that he was a Chief Inspector and that 'rightly or wrongly, they would always back him, that's the way it is'. This one-sided conversation resulted in me being told that I was to remain in the office and that I would again be considered for future operations and overtime.

In February 1995, due to further internal problems at work, during which time my local MP Mr Terry Lewis became involved, I commenced a period of long-term sickness.

During 1993 Operation Crocodile commenced in the Middleton area, which very soon progressed into Salford and Manchester. This operation in my view was unique, as it was the first self-generated operation within the covert operations department as there was no informant involved, but many months of planning and infiltrating the community, including working on Middleton open-air market, resulting in the recovery of a stolen Porsche 911 motor vehicle from Staffordshire and two men being arrested, charged and convicted of conspiracy to rob a jeweller from the Eccles area of property in excess of £50,000.

Having been recruited into the team to commit this offence we were supplied with CS gas, imitation firearms and black balaclavas. We were also recruited to carry out a further robbery on a money-lender from the Irlam O'th Heights area of Salford. In September 1995, D/I Brown submitted a report recommending myself and DC Reg for a Chief Constable's commendation in relation to this operation in view of the dangers, long hours and successful conclusion of an operation made out of nothing.

I returned to work on January 22, 1996 and after making enquiries with D/I Brown and DCI Trevor in relation to Operation Crocodile, I was informed that the report was still with Mr James. In March 1996 I was informed, only after asking further questions, that a decision had been made to go against D/I Brown's recommendation and reduce the award to a Chief Superintendent's citation. The reasons given were that a Chief Constable's commendation cannot be given for every undercover operation and each one has to be taken on merit. I fully understand this statement, but I cannot understand why a report submitted in June takes until March for a decision to be made and then the decision, alarmingly, is to go against the officer in charge's recommendation. As I have already stated, if merit is to be part of the equation in this decision, Operation Crocodile was one of only two undercover operations (the other being Operation Vixen) that were purely self-generated, with no informant involved, each with a successful conclusion with persons arrested, charged and convicted.

Compare this to an operation run on the ALF (Animal Liberation Front) which was purely intelligence-gathering and this officer received a Chief Constable's commendation.

Operation Miracle was in relation to the infiltration of 'Vodaphone' drug dealers in the Moss Side area of Manchester which took place in 1992/93 and involved five undercover police officers. The result of the operation was that a large number of known drug dealers were arrested, charged and convicted of supplying Class A drugs on the evidence obtained by the undercover police officers. To this end, these officers put themselves at great risk and as a result, a report was submitted by C/I Harry for those officers concerned to be commended by the Chief Constable for their actions, as were the officers who had previously been involved in Operation China, all of whom were commended.

The end result of this, and the only explanation given, was that the report had been lying around too long and could not now go up to the Chief in view of the delay. These officers, of which I am one, received no award whatsoever for what was a highly dangerous and sensitive operation.

After outlining these few details, I wish to invoke the following grievances:

1) Having been told in March 1994 that I, together with DC Reg, had been nominated for the QPM for services to undercover work, why, with regard to the facts that I completed five years as a full-time undercover operative while DC Reg

did no more than two years before asking to become an overt officer, and when my operational experience and results exceed DC Reg's in this field, did he receive the QPM award and I did not?

2) Why, when a report was submitted in June 1995 for a Chief Constable's commendation in relation to Operation Crocodile, did it take until March 1996 for a decision to be made, when it is reduced to a Chief Superintendent's award despite the unique 'merits' of the operation. This is the only time this has happened in my five years in the covert operations department.

3) Why did undercover police officers, who had been engaged in a dangerous operation with a high-profile result for GMP, when on merit, an award was again deserved, not receive any award whatsoever, because of the fact that a report had been lying around too long to go before the Chief Constable?

I feel compelled to raise these grievances for what I hope are obvious reasons. I am not prone to complaining, as is highlighted by the fact that in July 1991 at the conclusion of 'Operation Forth' I was seriously assaulted by members of the drug squad during the arrest of the main targets which resulted in the fracture of my left cheekbone. Apart from the injury being recorded, I took no further action against those concerned.

I therefore submit this report for your information and attention.

Garry Rogers.

3. Transcript of Grievance Procedure Interview, 31 July 1996: Garry Rogers, Detective Chief Superintendent Dave James, Geoff Barber

DJ: 'I will respond to it verbally, then I will give you a written report to take away. If we go back to the meeting of June 6, my understanding of that meeting is there were three separate points for a grievance. The first one dealt with the fact that you were not awarded the QPM; I did not pursue that one, I told you we had no control, the force has no control over the award of the QPM. But I did undertake to pursue the second and third ones which related to Operation Crocodile and Operation Miracle. Well the issue was he recommended a commendation in relation to Operation Crocodile and I wrote on that at the time, I can remember the operation in detail and while the two officers performed their duties essentially well, it was not above what was expected from a trained undercover man. I have reviewed that again and I still think it didn't warrant a Chief Constable's commendation.'

GR: 'Why, bearing in mind that was put in in June 1995, did it take so long for a decision to be made?'

DJ: 'I have explained in this report here which you can read. I've said in retrospect there was obviously a delay and I am at a loss to explain why, from the conclusion of the original trial to you being informed of my original decision and for that I apologise. I don't know what happened to the paperwork, I deal with it when it gets on my desk; if for some reason it's not got here, and I can give you the date of Mr Brown's report which obviously I would suggest there is another report before this one somewhere, this one is February15.'

GR: 'February this year?'

DJ: 'This year…I mean I can only deal with the reports I get on my desk.'

GR: 'Well I was aware it went in last June, so there obviously was another one before.'

DJ: 'Well I would suggest there probably was because the conviction was in May 1995, but I don't know where the other report is. I've had to find this one, that's six months old, I had no difficulty finding this one but I haven't found the other one…

'As far as your personal file in terms of recognition, you know that whilst you were an undercover officer you received a Chief Constable's commendation on four occasions, three in this force and one from another force.'

GR: 'There's a few missing.'

DJ: 'Well I am talking about Chief Constables' commendations.'

GR: 'That's what they are.'

DJ: 'Well if there are others, that says it even more…'

GR: 'Yes, and like I said to you last time sir, that was the case up to a certain point, and then it seems beyond that point things have changed.'

We then moved on to discuss Operation Miracle and his explanation for this non-award.

GR: 'What I was made aware of was the fact that a report went in for Miracle and then it did not go anywhere and then it came to a point where it was picked up and said this can't go before the Chief now, it's been lying around too long, he's going to say, "Where's that been?", so it did not go anywhere.'

GB: 'What you are saying then; it was an administrative error'!

GR: 'It was because it had been left lying around too long to go before the Chief, because he would say, "Well where has that been all this time?", so the decision was made, let's not send it…that's what I was basing it on.'

DJ: 'Well, that would…'

GR: 'Like the report here for Crocodile that was submitted in February, I came back in January and asked about the report that was submitted in June and now the original report has gone missing and then another one appears in February.'

DJ: 'I don't think, I mean the issue is when did it arrive on my desk?'

GR: 'Well if it had done it would have gone through the system and that original report would be here for me to see.'

DJ: 'What I am saying is the first thing I know about Crocodile is when I get this.'

GR: 'In February?'

DJ: 'Yes.'

GR: 'Yet what I am saying is that I was told the original report was submitted in June whilst I was on sick leave, and when I did ask about it on a particular occasion I was told it had been held back with the other thing (QPM) to see what happened, as to whether I was coming back to work or not. That's something I was told by another officer. Then I came back to work in January.'

DJ: 'Is there anything you want to raise specifically?'

GR: 'No, because obviously you have made your mind up and you have explained to me verbally what's in there and that's your decision today, as I understand it is my prerogative to go to the next one up?'

DJ: 'Yes, oh I…'

GR: 'And as I said to you earlier on, that is what I intend to do.'

GB: 'It seems to me Garry what you are saying is this was submitted in June last year, after the conviction in May 95. In September somebody writes it up for this and it goes in, but when it goes in they know you are on the sick and what you are saying – I think, if I get it right – you are saying, we will hang fire with this because he is still on the sick; we don't know if he is coming back. You then come back in January 1996.'

GR: 'I had a discussion and said what is happening with the report for Crocodile because I was aware it had gone in; I was then told that it had been held on to with the other thing to see what happens.'

GB: 'Well I agree with Mr James that's not your problem is it...you deal with it when you get it...there is a five-month gap, I agree with you and someone is to answer for that.'

GR: 'No, the person told me that you, sir, had it and you held on to it.'

DJ: 'I mean I'm not going to have it, send it back and then ask for another report.'

GR: 'What I'm saying to you is that I am basing my belief on what I have been told.'

DJ: 'I know you tend to feel this is against Garry Rogers and no one is going to persuade you it is other than that.'

GR: 'So that one you got in February: did you ask for that, or is Mr Brown saying that he put that one in because the other one got lost? Why would he suddenly take it on board to put another one in?'

DJ: 'Well you may have started it.'

GR: 'That's got January 21 on it.'

DJ: 'Yeah.'

GR: 'Which is before I came back; I came back on January 22, 1996.'

DJ: 'I mean, that's another issue there, that's stamped January 21, 1996, and that's dated February 15, 1996. I can't give you an explanation for that.'

GR: 'So he has not put in that report further to my other report...that's the original?'

DJ: 'Yes. Now, whether you have stimulated that or not I don't know...I know I dealt with that as soon as it came on my desk.'

GR: 'Strange.'

DJ: 'I could have fucking altered that by now if I had done that!'

GR: 'That was obviously a Sunday because I came back on the 22nd, a Monday...that report...just the stamp...'

DJ: 'Clearly the stamp was wrong...you sometimes see things that are not there, there are a lot of people have done a lot for you!'

GR: 'Well I would like to speak to them, present company excepted.'

Chapter 24:

4. Transcript of Grievance Procedure Stage Four Meeting with Mr McCrone, 6 December

GR: 'Just a couple of points there Sir, about something you said. I appreciate you have looked into it and you agree with Mr James. Just a few things though. The report that I am saying was submitted in February, what was the result of that, when I was saying the original report was submitted in June last year yet there has been another report that I am saying has been falsified?'

McCrone: 'I've seen the original report and the wording in that report and the wording is not exactly...'

GR:	'Is this the report from June?'
McCrone:	'This is a report from, I am trying to think…the report you are suggesting recommended you for the commendation.'
GR:	'It's a report from Mr Brown from June. I've spoken to Mr Brown, it was put in with a note from himself recommending a Chief Constable's commendation. That report went missing and a further report was submitted in February with February's date on, which has been made out as if it was put in by Mr Brown in February. I've spoken to Mr Brown who says he did not put that in.'
McCrone:	'I've seen that report. There is a confusion really, one part of the report is dated February and the later part is dated January, it's clear that one part…something is wrong…'
GR:	'The main thing is that none of it was submitted in February.'
McCrone:	'No, well I…however the wording in that doesn't actually…'
GR:	'I fully appreciate what you are saying there Sir. That the wording doesn't say Chief Constable's commendation, but the point I am making is…what is the bottom line on that report, how was that report…'
McCrone:	'Well I, I can't find any more than that I, I, I don't know the answer… from that sense…I can't believe that anyone…er…if there was anything so untoward on that report which is quite glaring…one part in February, one part in January, as opposed to a deliberate cover up, well I mean it is incredibly inept…I understand what you are saying and I will further explore that part…'
GR:	'Because if it's the one from June that is missing, there should not be any other report.'
McCrone:	'No, there shouldn't be.'
GR:	'But someone has put that together?'
McCrone:	'Unless of course it's a copy that has been changed, I will look at that aspect and respond to you…but I want to try and concentrate on…I won't sweep that aside, don't worry…'
GR:	'I fully appreciate what you say Sir, but I have come through this grievance procedure since April and it's took what, 'til December? I was hoping certainly at this stage that something would have come to light as a result of some of the things I am saying. It's quite clear today that nothing's changed in that event and it's still as it was in April when I instigated it, despite certain things, like the report, that's obviously not true and isn't the original and somebody has took the time to do that. Well there is no other explanation for it, and it seems strange that those things are there to be seen, yet I am being told this is the case against you – that it was quite proper to make those decisions and the way they have been made, yet there is no question as to why has that been put in when it shouldn't even be here. There is something strange about it.'
McCrone:	'Erm…it is not unusual for papers to go missing, it is not unusual for copies of reports to be produced.'
GR:	'I fully appreciate it isn't unusual, but it's certainly unusual for another report to be produced which purports to be the original when it isn't.'
McCrone:	'Well I don't think it is that unusual…especially if the original report has gone missing, it's not unusual for a further report to be created.'

GR: 'Well as I say Sir, I expected certain things to come of it which haven't, and to tell you I am down is an understatement again. That is all I can think of at the moment, I just don't know, I need time to think about it.'

McCrone: 'Well I don't want to go into the reasons why I think the awards are not justified; would that be any help?'

GR: 'Well I thought the arguments I gave for that to be the case were pretty strong, and obviously I don't know what's been said subsequent to that. But whatever was said I would have liked to have been in a position to argue against it, but obviously I will never know that.'

McCrone: 'Well I don't think it will help.'

GR: 'No, well, all I can say Sir is thanks very much for your time having looked into it for me.'

McCrone: 'Well I've still got one aspect to look into.'

GR: 'What – to do with me?'

McCrone: 'No, the report with Mr Brown.'

GR: 'I know we are still under the old system in relation to the grievance procedure, and I have to ask knowing full well he won't want to see me, but is the option to see the Chief Constable closed?'

McCrone: 'Well, anyone can ask.'

Chapter 25:

5. Letter from Alison Halford to GMP Chief Constable David Wilmot

Grievance by Constable G. Rogers which needs resolution

Dear David,

I was contacted discreetly in September 1997 by one of your officers you command, Constable Garry Rogers who was employed within your Forces Omega Department from February 1990 until his spectacular fall from grace in January 1995.

Having experienced many appeals from disenchanted officers over the years and not having the time or capacity to take a personal interest in most of them, it seems to me that Garry Rogers has a serious grievance and I am worried by the treatment afforded this officer, hence my approach to you.

I met DC Rogers at a discreet location and he gave me certain information that I have no way of corroborating as to its accuracy but frankly, knowing how police management frequently leaves much to be desired his story had a depressing ring of truth about it. Briefly he feels dreadfully let down over the brutal manner of his departure from your prestigious, elite operational unit and the mundane type of duty he is currently performing which fails to recognise his enormous value to the service. His deepest hurt stems from the fact his supervisor promised that he would be honoured by the Queen's Police Medal and it has never materialised despite the fact that another squad colleague was subsequently honoured in the December 1995 Honours list.

Frustrated by the seeming hollow promises of his supervisors together with the pain and frustration of being given no help to re-enter the normal world of policing, having lived a dangerous double life for years in order to deter major criminal activities, the officer filed a grievance procedure in April 1996.

He contends that embarking upon this course of action only exacerbated the situation which deteriorated into making life difficult for him and brought him into conflict with his pay department which apparently reduced his salary to half pay, thus necessitating a claim to the benefits agency.

Constable Rogers has been discreet in all his allegations but he is very aggrieved that a DCI was moved overnight under a disciplinary cloud, was subsequently reprimanded by the Chief Constable and yet this same officer played a major part in the withholding of the promised QPM.

From my own experience, the most unworthy and occasionally, even corrupt officer has been honoured by receipt of a Knighthood. If Constable Rogers is to be believed, his squad efforts should be recognised in the most prestigious manner and that the Queen's medal should be a fitting endorsement for a difficult and challenging role performed by the officer.

I have a clear recollection of that interview room in March 1983 when fate cruelly decreed that the Merseyside ACC's promotion should be mine. In my short acquaintance with you then, I rather rated you and felt you were a cut above the rest.

It seems a great wrong has been perpetrated against Garry Rogers and that you as his Chief Officer are the only one capable of finding a solution. It is a sad fact of life that despite extensive training and seeming commitment to change for the better, the sensitive and compassionate management of many junior officers by the service's senior echelons leave much room for improvement.

I very much hope that you will be able to intercede and restore Constable Rogers' faith in his bosses and in the service he has diligently served for many years.

Yours Sincerely
Alison Halford.

Chapter 26:

6. Transcript of meeting with Chief Constable David Wilmot, 24 September 1997

Persons present:
DC Garry Rogers, Norman Briggs (Lancashire Police Federation), Chief Constable Mr David Wilmot, Head of Personnel Mr Andrew Marston.

NB: 'Hello Mr Wilmot, I am Norman Briggs from Lancashire Police Federation.'
CC: 'I want to tape record the session.'
NB: 'No problem.'
CC: 'What I want to say at the outset is that my acquiescence to seeing you is on the basis of one of my officers wanting a personal interview with the Chief Constable, so, I have to make it absolutely clear to you and for the sake of other people in the force that this is not an extension of the grievance procedure which is an agreed process between the force and the Federation and the trade union, Unison, and extends to the Assistant Chief Constable.'
NB: 'Yes, I appreciate that. The issues surrounding this are not solely to do with the grievance procedures, but clearly arise out of what seems is a failure to resolve the issue. It's not so much an appeal, but drawing your attention to one or two failures we feel in the system to take account of Mr Rogers' situation.'

'As you are well aware, he has been before you himself on numerous occasions, for commendations of various descriptions. This is a delicate matter and it's connected directly with commendations and the way they are dealt with, but in particular, concerns expressed over the way the withdrawal of Garry's name from a recommendation for QPM came about.

'I understand his name was confirmed as being put forward by senior officers and was in fact going through. The brief circumstances which has prompted this visit today is that in January 1995 Garry's name was in that list and together with another officer, Reg, was put forward in March 1994. After what can only be described as an unusual procedure, Garry attended work to find a memo in his desk dated January 9, 1995 telling him he was finishing on the branch and all appointments were to be returned. No previous discussions on this issue, no mention of the intervention or reintroduction procedures or re-enter procedures had been discussed with him.

'Shortly after appearing at court on a major issue, his undercover identity was jeopardised and this he felt put him in danger, he went to see his Doctor and went off sick. It was not long after that he was visited in February by Superintendent Fernside from the Y Department who was conducting an investigation into a Chief Inspector (Seddon) who has been before you I understand on disciplinary matters.

'Garry had it put to him that together with some other officers he may have been responsible for writing an anonymous letter into the Y Department that started off this investigation. He was never revisited for the purpose of a statement; he was never revisited for the purpose of an interview in connection with that suggestion. He understood that you actually forwarded the recommendation for the QPM in respect of Reg in March 1995.

'Garry's name was left out of the actual nomination list for some inexplicable reason and even Reg himself would confirm that he was not the leading light in the cases that he believed led up to his nomination for that award and in fact Garry was the person who was leading the situation. The reason why his name somehow came to be left out of the list is a question we would really like to ask Mr Wilmot. As I said before, it is a delicate issue and these procedures are generally not talked about in this sort of frame, but you will no doubt understand that it's caused him great concern. It's not so much an individual concern; strictly speaking, it's more a grievance in terms that his family feel that his contribution and his efforts have not been appropriately recognised. The strains and stresses of the family have felt in supporting him, during these operations, would have been more acceptable had the appropriate consideration gone forward.

'There was a further incident involving awards and commendations involving Operation Crocodile, when a command recommendation was sent forward intended for yourself and after the intervention of one of your senior officers this was repudiated and it appeared that documents in support of the recommendation had been altered, and the award, albeit recommended as a Divisional Commander's Award, had not been followed through. Therefore with some significant grounds of concern Garry feels that he has been discriminated against in terms of recognition of his services and his health has suffered adversely and that of his family. Our request today basically falls into two forms; one that you reconsider his position with regard to the facts in support of his QPM recommendation and B you consider investigation of the procedures for awards within the Force.'

GR: 'Mr Briggs has given an overall picture in relation to why I'm here today and obviously I will restrict it to those awards, although there are other areas which I would like to pursue, however time-wise I'm restricted today.

'In relation to the QPM, March 94, I was told by Chief Inspector Seddon that I had been nominated together with Reg. We were both told on the same day, we were told not to discuss it with anybody; I never did. I didn't believe it at the time to be the case; the nomination was for services to undercover work. Reg did three years full-time in covert operations, I did five years. The operations he was nominated for were operations we did jointly. If we had to stand shoulder to shoulder looking at the workload in relation to both of us, my working record far exceeds his. This culminated in Operation Bluebell in relation to the '.........' family in Manchester; you may recall that it was I that briefed you on this at that time.

'It was those types of operations I continued on over and above, if you like, those that Reg had been involved in. He specifically asked to come off after three years onto the welfare side because of the pressures in relation to his home life, with having a young son who suffers with arthritis. So in relation to events that took place which led up to me going off sick, I was off sick for eleven months. I then find out that Reg is to receive a QPM. I found out by chance; to say that knocked me sideways is an understatement.

'Bearing in mind I don't say these things without failing to see my workload on the Covert Operations. It exceeds anybody else's. So much so, that Mr James had said to me on my grievance interviews with him that I had received more awards/commendations than anybody else in this type of work. So then to find out that Reg had received the QPM for operations that we did together, bearing in mind that my work far exceeds his, and to date, nobody has given me an answer as to why my name was withdrawn.

'As a result of recently speaking to the HMI, Mr Stevens, I became aware that his nomination came up to yourself in March 1995. There is no record of my nomination at the Home Office; it would appear now that it never even reached you. I have had this corroborated from four different sources. Mr James openly admitted on my grievance interview that he personally had put it in. He also told me that day that it was still in and that I could still receive it, perhaps in twelve months or two years' time. This is a total contradiction to what Mr Marston was saying to me. He told me that as far as the force was concerned, the issue was dead and unless somebody else put in for it I wouldn't get it. So I was told two different stories, yet these people are supposed to be investigating the same matters I have raised. The strange thing is, that because of Mr Seddon, I fell foul of certain events that led to the position I found myself in. None of which I might say, I had anything to do with. In my opinion I am being held responsible for those events.

'This is a copy of a report that Mr Brown submitted in June 1995. Mr James told me it was a second report that had been put in because the original had gone missing. At the grievance interview with him I spotted that the original date had been "tippexed" out and a new date of February 15, 1996 typed over it. DCI Trevor had date-stamped it February 16 and finally Mr James stamped it January 21. This obviously meant that Mr James had received it before it had even been supposedly created due to the apparent loss of the original. I immediately asked Mr James about this and he told me his date stamp must have been wrong. When I held the report up to the light you can clearly see the original date of June 1995 so someone has altered that date and submitted it later whilst insinuating that the original was lost.

'This is Mr McCrone's handwritten notes attached to this original report which he states quite clearly that the report had been held back because of the investigation with the Y Department. I can only think it's in relation to Mr Seddon and that the report was held back amongst other things because I was being held responsible by certain elements within the force and this was their way of getting back at me.

'In my years in the service if a report had been lost a new one could quite rightly be submitted but you would never alter the original and then purport that it was a new one. If the original was found it should then have been attached to the new one with some kind of explanation as to what had happened. I immediately asked for a copy of that report from Mr James and he told me I could not have it. I took the grievance procedure as far as it goes in the force up to Mr McCrone, because I felt so strongly at the time. I pointed out to him that the report had been altered. I was then sent away for ten weeks. When I returned to see him he had not looked at that report and I had to point out to him again that it had been altered to my detriment and I was then sent away again for a fortnight whilst he looked into it again. The grievance procedure ended for me on December 19, 1996 and I was no further on with more unanswered questions than when I started.

'That aside, all I want to know is because of my commitment, hard work and achievements in relation to covert operations, why has someone with far less experience than me received the QPM whilst I, who did most of the work, did not? No one can tell me why; I have my own beliefs as to why and I think as this goes on and more things are uncovered it adds credence to what I believe.'

CC: 'Okay, at the end of the day I cannot comment apart from what was initially said by asking me to agree to look into the procedures within the force and to possibly investigate the procedure that led to this meeting today. It raises some significant concerns.'

GR: 'I apologise for any inconvenience it has caused you and I am grateful for you seeing me this morning. But I would like to stress that if I didn't feel so strongly about it and my family hadn't had faith in me so far, certainly my wife and kids. You know I am not making up what I am saying because I would not be sat here if I was; it's because of those circumstances that I am sat here and at the end of the day if nothing ever materialises out of it, it would have made me ill not to be sat here today. I just want to stress that point: I am not trying to waste anybody's time, I am not making things up, I am telling you as it is.'

CC: 'Okay.'

NB: 'I don't think I have anything further to add, Mr Wilmot. I think I stated it quite clearly about the review of procedures, awards and our concern was that problems appear to be some form of malpractice in the system has occurred and we have brought it here today for you to deal with as you see appropriate.'

CC: 'Okay.'

The meeting then closed.

Chapter 27:

7. Letter from DC Rogers to John Tapley, October 1997

Dear Mr Tapley,

Further to our telephone conversation today and my request to you for a letter confirming that as far as the HMI, Mr Stevens is concerned, his involvement in my case is now at an end, may I also respectfully request that you confirm in the letter, the following points:

1) That at our meeting on Wednesday, September 10 1997 at the Rectory Hotel in Denton, I informed both yourself and Mr Stevens of all the relevant facts surrounding my case, including the fact that a report submitted by Detective Inspector Brown in June 1995 had been deliberately altered to give the impression that it had been submitted in February 1996.
2) That Reg's nomination for the QPM was submitted to the Home Office on March 25, 1995 duly signed by Mr Wilmot.
3) That I also informed the HMI of the disciplinary matters involving DCI Seddon, former head of the covert operations department, and the resultant reprimand from the Chief Constable.

Thank you for your assistance in this matter.

8. Letter from Norman Briggs to Chief Constable David Wilmot, 23 October 1997

Dear Mr Wilmot
Interview-Det Con Rogers
You may recall a meeting we had in your office on Wednesday, September 24 1997, concerning Mr Rogers' disillusionment over the awards procedure and his personal circumstances, which gave him cause for concern when he learnt that whilst he had contributed significantly to various operations and had been nominated for a particular award, he had been overlooked, whilst a colleague under identical circumstances had received full recognition.

There were two sides to his problem. One relating to the Greater Manchester Police Service procedure and you will recall I asked you if you would revisit the circumstances concerning Mr Rogers' particular case.

Secondly you will recall that Mr Rogers wished to register a complaint which I asked if you could initiate an investigation into, the alteration of a document during the course of an award recommendation through your senior officers.

A month has now elapsed since our meeting and I therefore wonder if you are now in a position to respond, as I understand Mr Rogers has not been updated on these issues.

Yours Sincerely
N Briggs
Treasurer/Deputy JBB Secretary.

9. Letter from DC Rogers to *Manchat* magazine, 8 November 1997

Dear David,

I note in the October edition of *Manchat* that the December issue is to be your last as editor. I also note the comments you make that your feelings as editor have always been that if a subject needed to be broached and something had to be said then it was said. I read this with interest as these have always been my feelings entirely.

At this point may I first of all take time to applaud Barbara Ann Taylor's letter in the October edition 'Old-Fashioned Values' for being another from the minority who are willing to stand up and be counted at the way this organisation we call 'our force' disgracefully treats the majority of its staff, unless of course you are 'Lodged' with the right friends?

My thoughts and condolences go out to the family of the late PC Fiona Tait.

Having said that and in the hope that you publish my letter, I am writing to inform you about my own experience at the hands of 'Our Force'.

At this stage may I point out that the name David Burton at the foot of this letter is indeed an alias but is used, as it was in the article featured in *Police Review* (May 1997) 'Identity Crisis', to prevent the wrong people reading the letter and therefore discovering my real name, and can I thank ACC McCrone for informing the entire readership of *Police Review* that I had in fact used a false name (letters *Police Review* June 1997).

I have supplied my real name to the editor and I use the alias for no other reason. In an attempt to keep matters as brief as possible:

I am a serving GMP officer with 21 years' service, five of which were spent as a full-time undercover police officer on covert operations both at home and abroad. That is to say I was one of five full-time undercover operatives out of a police force of 7,500.

When you become involved in this type of police work, their aim is to de-police you and, if you are to be successful, but more importantly safeguard the wellbeing of you and your family then there are certain conditions that must apply which may affect you for the rest of your life.

As a result of the success of operations within the department, I, together with another undercover officer were informed in March 1994 that we had been nominated for the QPM for services to undercover work, operations we had completed together. We were told not to openly discuss this. I continued on operations up until February 1995 when, as a result of being informed that I had been over-exposed, I challenged the clear non-existence of GMP's re-entry programme as it stood at that time. I discovered from an internal memo that I should not have seen that a certain target's family had engaged the services of a private investigation agency to identify the undercover officer concerned in the arrest of certain members of their family.

As a result of these and many other unusual events which made me fear for my safety and ask that longstanding question 'WHY', I sustained a period of long-term sickness (11 months) during which time I was placed on half-pay which resulted in me getting into debt.

I was diagnosed with depression, lost four and a half stone in weight for which I went into hospital to have tests for cancer (negative) and for the last two years have been prescribed Prozac. When placed on half-pay I was not told until a month later which resulted in me being unable to claim income support for a three-week period of my sickness. The other officer received the QPM and I did not.

Whilst on sick leave my MP became involved and on one interview with ACC McCrone, I was informed that I had been a 'guinea pig' for the system and that they had learned a lot. Through financial problems and although my health was still suffering, I returned to work in 1996 to a purely administrative role where I have been ever since.

In April that year I instigated the in force grievance procedure (for what it's worth) in relation to certain awards I had been nominated for but which had suddenly, since speaking out against the organisation, been withdrawn.

I took the grievance procedure to its conclusion and found out certain things along the way:

1) It's one-sided.
2) Senior officers are allowed to alter other officers' reports to their benefit and your detriment.
3) When you discover this and make other officials aware, nothing is done about it.
4) Paperwork goes missing.

Compare this to being a certain senior officer involved in numerous acts of serious abuse of authority who was later simply reprimanded for offences that would have got other less well connected officers demoted or dismissed??

You may think I am on a kamikaze mission but I stand by and can prove what I say but I will understand if on this occasion this is one of them subjects that you do not want to broach. I apologise for the length of this letter but I can assure you it could have been longer?

10. Letter from HMI John Stevens to Garry Rogers, 19 November 1997

Dear Mr Rogers

I refer to our meeting on September 10, 1997 and to your letter dated October 10, 1997. I apologise for the delay in responding but, as advised to you by my staff officer, this was due to his, and then my, annual leave.

My role in respect of the issues raised at our meeting is restricted to an advisory capacity. On the one hand, I listened to your account and advised you to approach the Chief Constable, Mr Wilmot, directly to discuss your concerns. On the other, I also informed Mr Wilmot of the issues you raised to allow him to consider the situation further.

I have no direct powers in respect of the management and decision-making processes within Greater Manchester Police. However, Mr Wilmot is now fully informed of your concerns and I am aware that you have met with him subsequently. I also understand that the Police Federation and a solicitor are involved in support of your case. You may therefore, wish to consider their advice as to possible further action should the response from Mr Wilmot fail to meet your expectations.

As regards my further involvement, I have pursued my advisory role to its limits as things currently stand. That does not necessarily end my involvement because I encourage you to contact me, or my staff officer, again at any time, if there are further developments you wish to bring to my attention for consideration or advice.

As regards the other points in your letter, I respond as follows:-

1. At our meeting on September 10, 1997, you showed me a copy of a report signed by Detective Inspector T Brown which was dated 'February 15, 1996'. You informed me that the date on the original copy had been June '1995', but this had been covered over with 'TIPP-EX' and the February date added. The report copy also possessed two date stamps:-
   - 'February 16, 1996' signed apparently by several senior officers.
   - 'January 21, 1996, Head of Crime Operations', signed apparently, 'D JAMES'.
2. I can confirm from documentation in HMIC possession, that Reg's nomination for the Queen's Police Medal was dated March 24, 1995 and signed by Mr Wilmot.
3. I can also confirm that you informed me at our meeting of an internal Force investigation concerning a D/CH Inspector K Seddon and that this officer had subsequently been reprimanded by the Chief Constable.

As a matter of courtesy, I have sent a copy of this letter to Mr Wilmot for his information.

Yours sincerely
J A Stevens.
HM Inspector of Constabulary

11. Letter from Chief Constable David Wilmot to Norman Briggs, Police Federation, 28 November 1997

Dear Mr Briggs,

Thank you for your letter of October 23, 1997, I am now in a position to respond.

Firstly I now have a report regarding Constable Rogers' achievements and as per my policy with any other officer I do not intend to say how I have dealt with that report. I can, however, assure you that it is comprehensive.

Without wishing to be pedantic in respect of the wording of your penultimate paragraph, I do not recall agreeing to 'initiate an investigation 'regarding the date change on another award recommendation. I have, however, looked into the matter and a report is with the Awards Committee of the Force.

I have not written to Constable Rogers

Thank you for your patience.
Yours Sincerely
D Wilmot
Chief Constable.

12. Letter from Mrs Rogers to the Police Complaints Authority, 9 January 1998

Dear Sir,

I am the wife of a serving police officer with Greater Manchester Police, but I am writing to you to register my complaint in my capacity as a member of the public. As stated, my husband is a police officer with 21 years' service, five of which were spent as a full-time undercover officer within the force's 'covert operations' department. He was involved in undercover operations both at home and abroad, for which he was awarded numerous commendations from both his own force and other agencies.

Let me say at this point that we have three young children, and that the stresses and strains of being the family of an officer involved in this type of sensitive policing is unquantifiable. My husband was one of five officers out of a force of 7,500 who were full-time covert officers, which meant a commitment of 24 hours a day, seven days a week, 365 days a year. Because of this our family life took a back seat and he was always restricted, as he is today, as to where he could and could not go.

After a highly successful period of five years, my husband was informed that he had been over-exposed as a covert officer and that these duties should cease. He was fully aware that an officer could not carry out these duties indefinitely, but what he was not prepared for was the non-existence of the force's so-called 're-entry programme'.

His last operation left him and us with an associate of a main 'target' (now serving eight years) living three miles away from where we live. This associate knew my husband by his alias, but is now aware that he was in fact a police officer. This is one of many people whom, I have no need to tell you, would like to find out his true identity and whereabouts, but what is more frightening is what they are capable of if they obtained this information.

Because of this, he questioned the way GMP were dealing with his situation which resulted, mainly due to his fears for the safety of us, in him undergoing a period of long-term sickness. During this period he was diagnosed with depression, his health suffered resulting in the loss of four and a half stone in weight, and had to enter hospital for exploratory tests. For the last two years he has been prescribed the anti-depressant 'Prozac'.

He was placed on half-pay which crippled us financially and because the force were late in informing him, we were unable to claim income support for a period of three weeks.

After a period of 11 months' sickness, he returned to work but with limited options open to him, he was placed in a purely administrative role, where he remains to this day. That is a very basic background to my husband's recent history and I now wish to enlarge on certain matters.

In March 1994, he was informed that he was to be nominated for the QPM, together with another officer, for the work they completed together in highly successful undercover operations. My husband completed five years as a covert officer, and the other officer completed only three years. The other officer received the QPM and my husband did not.

This accolade was given while he was on sick leave but, more importantly, after he had questioned the re-entry programme and spoke out against the organisation.

Before sustaining the 11-month period of sickness, he was aware that he had been recommended for certain chief constable's commendations for operational successes, reports which should have gone through the system as normal. On returning to work, he discovered that these reports had gone nowhere and, after invoking the force grievance procedure (which allows them to be judge and jury on themselves) he was shown a report which was, apparently, the second one to be submitted as the original had been lost...

When he examined the report at the grievance interview with Ch Supt James, he realised that it was in fact the original, but that it had been deliberately altered to give the impression that it was a different report? He was then informed that this operation was no longer worthy of any recognition.

In February 1995, the Chief Inspector, head of Covert Operations, was moved from his post overnight for a number of serious abuses of his position, after which, an 18-month investigation resulted in a reprimand for abuses that would have resulted in any less well-connected officer losing his job.

In my capacity as a member of the public I am writing to you to bring these matters out of the internal domain of GMP. My husband has spoken to the HMI, Mr John Stevens on his last Inspection of the force when he advised him that he should seek the services of the Federation from another force and also seek a personal interview with the Chief Constable (the grievance procedure in GMP stops at the ACC of personnel). My husband acted on both these recommendations and was granted an audience with the Chief Constable who chose not to comment on the matters my husband spoke of.

He has been told lie after lie as he progressed through the grievance procedure by senior management of the second largest provincial police force, i.e. he was informed by Mr James that he had been nominated for the QPM and that he was still in the system and that he could get it next time or the time after that. Because of the lies he had uncovered, he continued to ask questions and discovered via his conversations with Mr Stevens (HMI) that this was untrue as all paperwork concerning this award had disappeared.

I apologise if my letter is disjointed and hard to follow in parts but we have suffered so much and I have so much that I want to say that I find it hard to put it into words. As a result my husband and myself have both received counselling.

The main points I want to bring to your attention are as follows:

My husband completed five years as a full-time undercover police officer for which, despite the awards which were stopped, he received the most commendations in this field of unique policing. Because, at the end of this successful five years, he quite rightly questioned the inadequacies of the force's then re-entry programme which after all was to affect both him and us, and the head of department was discovered to be involved in wrongdoings, it is my contention that he has been discriminated against by the force, so much so that they were willing to tell lies, alter official documents and suppress evidence to stop embarrassment to the force, and at the same time cause my husband's health and our family to suffer, despite having given 200% commitment.

The HMI was very supportive, but made it clear that his role is purely advisory and that he has no authority as such.

It is to you, therefore that I am writing without, may I add my husband's knowledge as I feel enough is enough and these matters must be investigated by an entirely separate unbiased body who will investigate these matters correctly.

My husband has tape recordings of all conversations and can prove the alteration of the official report.

I have tried to condense what is a long and involved situation and I therefore register these matters with you in the hope that you will initiate an investigation.

My husband has more recently obtained the support of Miss Alison Halford, ex-ACC of Merseyside Police and the once highest-ranking female officer in the country.

I look forward to hearing from you.

Yours faithfully

Rogers (Mrs)

13. Letter from Superintendent K.S. Homan to Mrs Rogers, 9 February 1998

Dear Mrs Rogers.
Complaint Against Police
Your letter of January 9, 1998 to the Police Complaints Authority has been passed to me for attention.

In respect of the matters you raise your husband has had discussions with both the HMI and the Chief Constable.

In addition the complaints have also been fully investigated and aired under the provisions of the Force Grievance Procedure.

Whilst I fully accept that you remain dissatisfied with the results, I must point out that the legislation surrounding complaints against police does not provide for you, as a member of the public, to make a complaint on behalf of a police officer.

Accordingly I will be taking no further action other than to write to the Police Authority informing them of the content of this letter.

Yours sincerely
K.S. Homan
Senior Superintendent.

14. Letter to GMP from DC Garry Rogers, 2 March 1998

GRIEVANCE PROCEDURE
Sir,
With reference to the above, I report that I instigated the in Force Grievance Procedure on April 24 1996 in relation to several matters that are self-explanatory and contained in my current Grievance file held in the Equal Opportunities Office.

These matters were 'investigated' via the procedure up to and including the ACC of Personnel and Training. I also had an audience with the Chief Constable, although this was not deemed to be part of the process.

Throughout this procedure, I was told and shown several misleading and inaccurate facts which were later proven to be so.

The reason for this report therefore, is to respectfully request a copy of this report be placed on both my Personal and Grievance File, to make clear that I totally disagree that these matters were, as per Senior Superintendents Homan's comment in his correspondence of 3rd February 1998, 'In addition the complaints have also been fully investigated and aired under the provisions of the Force Grievance Procedure.'

It is my intention in the near future to instigate a further grievance in relation to these matters as a result of further information I am now aware of.

DC Rogers

15. Letter from DC Garry Rogers to Home Secretary Jack Straw, 2 March 1998

I am writing to you with a feeling of utter dismay, due to what I am about to explain to you.

You will not recall, but I wrote to you on June 23, 1997 and again on August 12, 1997 when you directed them to the Chief HMI, Mr O'Dowd. I will not re-iterate these details again, safe to say that Mr O'Dowd's reference emg/lo/honours/rogers.

doc refers. As for my current situation, I continue to raise my issues despite the great many brick walls I come up against.

May I say at this stage that I always considered my correspondence to the Home Office, and in particular you, to be treated as confidential. Imagine my amazement when I recently obtained access to my grievance file, only to find the attached fax from Les Owen at the Home Office to Chief Superintendent Chris Cross which reads as follows: 'Chris I cannot send the letters he has sent to Home Secretary, apparently this would breach protocol. If you need any detail from them please give me a ring and I can paraphrase. Les.'

This fax was sent on September 19, as I was to see the Chief Constable on September 24. This fax implies to me that information I felt was confidential was passed by phone to assist senior management at GMP to be armed with certain information at the time of my audience with the Chief Constable. If I were to ring the Home Office and ask for information to be given to me over the phone, I wonder what the reply would be.

This type of back-door attempt to keep one step ahead turns justice into injustice. This is one further example of not what you know but who you know and raises a lot of questions over the system.

I return the copy of the fax to you.

Yours Sincerely

G.W. Rogers

16. Letter from Ian Smith at the Home Office to DC Rogers, 31 March 1998

Dear Mr Rogers,

Thank you for your letter of 2nd March to the Home Secretary, to which he has asked me to reply.

I do not understand the basis of your complaint. You allege 'back door' collusion between a member of HMIC and the Greater Manchester Police, but attempt to demonstrate it by producing a typed note which had been placed on the official record, to which you have access.

What did occur was a fair amount of work by people solely concerned with dealing fairly and properly with your grievance. To that end, HMIC contacted GMP to discuss some of the issues. This was done entirely professionally and properly with the sole objective of facilitating a meeting between you and your Chief Constable with a view to resolving your grievances.

I hope that this explanation re-assures you that nothing improper whatsoever took place and, in particular, the actions were designed to serve the interests of justice not, as your letter might be read to imply, to promote an injustice.

Because your comments relate to actions by GMP as well as by the Home Office, I am copying this correspondence to the Chief Constable.

Yours Sincerely

Ian F Smith.

17. Letter from DC Rogers to Ian Smith, Home Office, 1 April 1998

Dear Mr Smith,

Thank you for your letter of March 30, in which you state the Home Secretary asked you to reply. May I say first of all, with respect, that I did not expect anything better than the explanations you gave thus far, I have come up against one brick wall after another.

If, as you state, there was nothing improper in what took place, then why was it not possible for copies of my letters to the Home Secretary to be faxed through to GMP as requested? The information was, however, passed by telephone. If this was in order, surely my letters could have been faxed?

I stated previously that I considered those letters to be confidential correspondence between myself and the Home Secretary, yet you fail to answer that point in your reply. When I telephoned the Home Office postal room on March 27 I was informed that my letter had, upon being received, been sent directly to Room 12, which I was told was a police department. And so when did Mr Straw see my correspondence?

As to my grievance, I find it hard to understand that after 3 years of grievance procedures, discussions with two HMIs and an audience with the Chief Constable, I am still in a position where many of my questions remain unanswered for one reason or another.

I shall add your letter to that list.

Yours Sincerely

G.W. Rogers

Chapter 29:

18. DC Rogers to HMI David O'Dowd, 10 July 1998

Dear Mr O'Dowd

Thank you for your letter of July 2. I have read your letter with great interest and I thank you for the in-depth information you give in relation to the awards system.

However, that having been said I am once again saddened that after having informed you, the Chief HMI, of the irregularities and deceit that have taken place within GMP and that I have the evidence to substantiate these claims, your letter makes no reference to this?

My grievance is not with the Home Office as I am fully aware that all the underhanded actions took place in force as a result of me speaking out about certain inadequacies. It would appear though that the Home Office are not interested in this type of discrimination and one would assume that it is in order and acceptable as this is not my first enquiry with you.

I shall, therefore, take these matters elsewhere.

Yours Sincerely

G.W. Rogers.

19. Congratulatory messages following the award of the QPM:

Dear Garry,

I was delighted to hear that Her Majesty the Queen has awarded you the Queen's Police Medal for Distinguished Service and on behalf of all members of the Greater Manchester Police, might I send sincere congratulations.

I am sure that you and your family will be very proud and rightly so.

Sincerely

D. Wilmot, Chief Constable.

312

Dear Garry,

Many congratulations on receiving the Queen's Police Medal in the New Year Honours. Without doubt this is the professional medal of the Police Service and while I am sure that both yourself and your family will thoroughly enjoy it, I am sure your family are immensely proud of you for receiving it.

Well done, it is a well-earned award and I feel sure you will have a wonderful day at the Palace when you eventually have it presented by the Queen.

All the very best for the future

David O'Dowd, HM Chief Inspector of Constabulary.

Dear Mr Rogers,

May I on behalf of the Police Federation of England and Wales congratulate you on receiving the Queen's Police Medal for distinguished service in the New Years Honours list.

I know this will be treasured for the rest of your life.

Yours Sincerely

F.H.J. Broughton, Chairman.

Dear Garry

I was delighted to hear that you had been awarded the Queen's Police Medal in the New Year's Honours list and I think this is more than deserved after all you have been through.

Congratulations

Yours Sincerely

Brian Sides

Dear Garry,

It gives me very great personal pleasure to be able to write to you today. On behalf of the chairman and members of the No 1 (North West) Region Conference, I send sincere congratulations to you on your award of the Queen's Police Medal announced in the New Year's Honours list.

We are all delighted that your considerable contribution to the Police Service has been acknowledged in this way.

Yours Sincerely

David McCrone, Assistant Chief Constable.

Chapter 32:

20. ACC Sweeney report, following meeting on 9 March 2004

Constable 2642 Garry Rogers

I today had a two-hour meeting with the above officer, who is currently on sick leave with a stress-related condition, together with his Federation representative, Richard Eccles, JBB Secretary of North Wales Police. The purpose of the meeting was to give Garry an opportunity to discuss a number of issues that continue to be a source of anxiety to him and to seek to offer support to Garry and explore means of bringing closure to his concerns.

Undercover Policing and the Corrupt Secret Society Within

Three key areas were discussed. Firstly he remains unhappy over the circumstances whereby a recommendation for him to receive a QPM for his exemplary service on the then Omega Covert Operations Unit were not submitted to the then Chief Constable, Sir David Wilmot. In the absence of any documentation and given that all those involved have since left GMP, there will never be a satisfactory explanation of what occurred but I accepted and find no other explanation than that someone in the then 'V' command structure effectively halted the progress of that recommendation. This was accepted by Sir David who subsequently sought to remedy this wrong by personally supporting Garry's nomination for the QPM, which he subsequently received in the New Year's Honours in 1999.

One of Garry's concerns is that he may have been given this award to effectively pacify him because of the representations he made. I was able to reassure him that, to my personal knowledge, this was unequivocally not the case. I was privy to discussions with Sir David who was entirely satisfied that Garry was a most worthy recipient of this honour due to his exemplary police service. Sir David held the award of such Honours as a matter of the highest integrity and under no circumstances would he have supported Garry had he not been wholly deserving of the Honour and the award reflected the esteem with which Garry was held.

The second issue related to the contents of a sealed brown envelope present on Garry's file when he had exercised his right to examine it. The existence of the envelope and the nature of its contents were of further concern to him. Reference was made to a discipline enquiry of which Garry had not been notified and of which, on enquiry, GMP Complaints and Discipline Department had no record. In the absence of any documentary record, it is impossible to know whether such an investigation ever took place but one is forced to conclude that, on the balance of probabilities some allegations or suspicions, the nature of which are not known, had been made by an unidentified person and, whether recorded or investigated or not, some reference was subsequently made in Superintendent Homan's memo.

Again, all relevant parties have since left GMP, including DCI Seddon, who headed the Omega Squad. Mr Seddon was subsequently convicted of multiple offences of dishonesty, adding weight to his belief that there may have been a lack of integrity in the handling or recording of these matters. I was able to reassure Garry that he is regarded as an officer of the highest integrity and that there are no doubts whatsoever about his character. Unfortunately no evidence exists to explain what may or may not have been behind the reference to discipline and we can only offer reassurances that his exemplary conduct is not in any doubt.

I offered to shred the envelope in his presence but he asked me to retain it for the present.

Finally we discussed the support Garry was receiving and he expressed his frustration that the counsellors he had seen were not competent to deal with his case as they had no understanding of the unique policing environment in which he had worked. Garry identified a national expert in providing support to officers who had worked in covert operations and I undertook to explore whether this, or another expert in this field, could be engaged to offer support.

In conclusion, I have a great deal of sympathy with Garry. He is an officer who has given exemplary service and has been subject to what, on the face of it, is some pretty shoddy treatment at various times of his service. The absence of documentation and

Notes

the fact that those involved in his supervision and line management at the material times have all long since left GMP means that we will never know exactly what occurred or why. However, Garry has made it clear that he wishes above all else to recover his health and return to full police duties. We will continue to seek to offer appropriate support and make every effort to assist him in this goal. I was massively impressed by Garry's frankness and openness and hope that he will come to accept that he remains a valued member of GMP and is able to draw a line under the past and look forward positively to the rest of his career and beyond.

V.A. Sweeney.
Assistant Chief Constable.
9th March 2004.

Chapter 33:

21. Letter from Professor Gudjonsson to ACC Vincent Sweeney

Dear Sir,
Ref. Mr Garry Rogers
Further to my telephone call to your office earlier today, I would be most grateful if you could assist with ensuring, if at all possible, that Mr Rogers' salary is brought back to full pay. When Mr Rogers came to see me today he was very distressed by the fact that he had just received his pay slip, which showed that his salary had been reduced to half-pay. He had not anticipated a reduction in his salary and is now very worried about his financial position.

As you know, Mr Rogers is suffering from unresolved Post Traumatic Stress Disorder (PTSD), which is work-related and dates back to 1995. After an initial assessment, Dr Deighton referred him to me for treatment. Mr Rogers has completed three out of his ten agreed treatment sessions. He is a highly motivated patient, who has conscientiously completed all his prescribed homework. There has been good therapeutic progress, which will no doubt continue.

Mr Rogers recently met with the Chief Constable and this was of great help to him and has made my work with him easier.

I am concerned that if Mr Rogers' pay is reduced this will place him under considerable stress, which will aggravate his condition and hinder his therapeutic progress. Of course, I do not know about your policies and what discretion you have in this matter, but it is very important that everything that can be done is done to ensure that Mr Rogers has the maximum chance of recovery.

Yours Faithfully
Professor Gisli H Gudjonsson.

Chapter 34:

22. Letter from Simon McKay to ACC Sweeney, January 2005

Dear Mr Sweeney,
Garry Rogers.
I am instructed by the above-named.

As long ago as August 16, I wrote to the Chief Constable and the Force solicitor setting out details of a claim the above named proposed making for misfeasance in public office. This correspondence was acknowledged by Sandra Pope and passed onto Gallagher Bassett, the Force's claims handling agents, although we still await a substantive reply.

In the meantime, Greater Manchester Police had agreed to pay for our client's treatment with Professor Gisli Gudjonsson. This has now been suspended, I understand on the grounds that you felt let down that personal correspondence from you to Mr Rogers was being used for the purposes of litigation.

The purpose of this letter is to record a number of concerns:

1. Your correspondence is not being used as the basis for litigation, it is the improper conduct of GMP officers which forms the basis of Mr Rogers' claim;
2. Even if it was the case that your correspondence formed the basis of the claim, this is irrelevant to the issue of Mr Rogers' treatment;
3. Mr Rogers is suffering a great deal as a result of his treatment at the Force's hands and needs to attend the sessions with Professor Gudjonsson in order to assist him in alleviating this;
4. If Mr Rogers has to pay for the sessions himself, the costs of this can be and would be an item of claim within any subsequent proceedings;
5. If GMP insist on depriving Mr Rogers of this very necessary treatment, this will be referred to as part of the evidence in his case;
6. You have correspondence from Professor Gudjonsson to the effect that Mr Rogers needs six further sessions with him and possessed of this you are in breach of your duty of care towards an officer who you yourself described as having given 'exemplary service' to your Force.

In view of the above I would invite you to revisit your decision to revoke your agreement to pay for Mr Rogers' treatment.

I look forward to hearing from you as a matter of urgency

Yours Sincerely

Simon McKay

Solicitor Advocate.